SPORTS CRAZY

HOW SPORTS ARE SABOTAGING AMERICAN SCHOOLS

STEVEN J. OVERMAN

UNIVERSITY PRESS OF MISSISSIPPI / JACKSON

The University Press of Mississippi is the scholarly publishing agency of the Mississippi Institutions of Higher Learning: Alcorn State University, Delta State University, Jackson State University, Mississippi State University, Mississippi University for Women, Mississippi Valley State University, University of Mississippi, and University of Southern Mississippi.

www.upress.state.ms.us

The University Press of Mississippi is a member of the Association of University Presses.

Copyright © 2019 by University Press of Mississippi
All rights reserved

First printing 2019

∞

Library of Congress Cataloging-in-Publication Data

Names: Overman, Steven J., author.
Title: Sports crazy : how sports are sabotaging American schools / Steven J. Overman.
Description: Jackson : University Press of Mississippi, [2019] | Includes bibliographical references and index. |
Identifiers: LCCN 2018040486 (print) | LCCN 2018042691 (ebook) | ISBN 9781496821324 (epub single) | ISBN 9781496821331 (epub institutional) | ISBN 9781496821348 (pdf single) | ISBN 9781496821355 (pdf institutional) | ISBN 9781496821300 (hardcover : alk. paper) | ISBN 9781496821317 (pbk. : alk. paper)
Subjects: LCSH: School sports—United States—History. | School sports—Social aspects—United States.
Classification: LCC GV346 (ebook) | LCC GV346 .O84 2019 (print) | DDC 796.04/2—dc23
LC record available at https://lccn.loc.gov/2018040486

British Library Cataloging-in-Publication Data available

CONTENTS

3	CHAPTER 1	Interscholastic Sports in Context
23	CHAPTER 2	Understanding School Sports: Looking Back, Exploring Abroad
37	CHAPTER 3	The Problems with Governance, Funding, and Professional Coaches
65	CHAPTER 4	How Parents, Boosters, and Sports Fans Drive the Agenda
89	CHAPTER 5	Sports Culture Rules in the American High School
117	CHAPTER 6	The Troubled Relationship between Interscholastic Sports and Academics
135	CHAPTER 7	Physical Fitness—or Not?—of the Student-Athlete
151	CHAPTER 8	Character versus Bad Behavior
179	CHAPTER 9	The Corrupting Influence of Outside Interests
199	CHAPTER 10	The Case against Tackle Football
217	CHAPTER 11	The Tail That Wags the Dog
225	References	
245	Index	

SPORTS CRAZY

1

INTERSCHOLASTIC SPORTS IN CONTEXT

American education's experiment with elite athletics has been a failure.
—John Gerdy

Peruse the pages of your local newspaper (or access it online); tune in to the local TV news. Both news sources frequently cover what's going in the community's schools. But what gets the most attention? Which student activities garner the headlines? Every newspaper has a sports section; fewer have an education section. The last several minutes of local news programs are devoted to sports. More broadly, what school activities are being discussed at the local barbershop and café? I'll conjecture that the patrons know the name of the star quarterback. What about the class valedictorian? Are parents more likely to attend a PTA meeting or a junior varsity basketball game? We all know the answers to these questions. Extracurricular activities—notably sports—trump academics. Football upstages the forensic tournament and the science fair. In short, interscholastic sports have become the tail that wags the dog.

Four out of five middle schools and 98 percent of high schools in the United States sponsor interscholastic sports programs. Athletics is the largest nonacademic school program in which students participate. Thus, it is crucial that school administrators keep sports in perspective and assure that students' participation in sports constitutes positive learning experiences and promotes personal development. Schools must advocate sports programs that support rather than undermine academic integrity and student achievement. The purpose of interscholastic sports should be to enhance the whole school experience for all students (NASBE 2004).

Professor John Gerdy (2006, 12–13), a former college all-American basketball player, observes, "Incorporating athletics programs into our educational system represents one of the most significant experiments in the history of American education.... While the justifications used were certainly plausible and, indeed, desirable, they were guesses, with no research or track record to substantiate them." He continues, "It was assumed that the benefits of elite athletics could be achieved in a way that would supplement rather than undermine the academic values and educational mission of institutions."

With Gerdy's observation in mind, this book examines the current status and consequences of elite interscholastic sports programs in American schools. As journalist Amanda Ripley (2013b, 229) notes, "The unparalleled importance of athletic achievement at US high schools should be the subject of serious debate. Sports, for all the value they offer . . . siphon money and attention from classroom learning." The problems reach beyond compromising schools' academic mission, as this book makes clear. It's the unrestrained emphasis on sports that's causing the problems.

To assess the role of sports, we begin with a question: What is the purpose of secondary schools? What should be their primary goals vis-à-vis the students? The Cardinal Principles of Secondary Education were formulated in 1918 by a National Education Association commission. The commission set seven major teaching objectives for high schools: health, command of fundamental processes (i.e., the three *R*s), worthy home membership, vocational education, citizenship, worthy use of leisure, and ethical character. These principles are just as germane to today's curriculum as they were a century ago. Two of these principles, health and worthy use of leisure, have particular relevance to sports—and some would argue that ethical character does, as well. As for vocation, a very small minority of high school athletes will pursue a career in sports.

Over the course of the twentieth century, comprehensive high schools expanded their curriculum and instituted a range of programs and activities to serve their students. Sports became a major part of the extracurriculum. A connection ostensibly exists between the curriculum and the extracurriculum. Just as debate teams derive from speech classes, science fairs from science courses, and school orchestras from the music program, interscholastic and intramural sports can be viewed as evolving from physical education classes. In truth, however, interscholastic sports developed as a force in itself. Despite this historical anomaly, a brief review of the status of physical education allows us to put school sports in perspective.

Physical Education

Physical education became an established part of the secondary school curriculum during the early twentieth century as the emphasis shifted from gymnastics and formal exercise to a broader sports-based program. Following the invention of basketball and volleyball, indoor games increasingly permeated the PE curriculum (Pruter 2013, 47–48). Many public high schools began building gymnasiums and providing athletic fields during the prosperous post–World War I era. Physical education was reemphasized during the national fitness campaign in the 1950s. PE classes were gender-segregated through most of the nation's history but currently provide a shared experience for male and female students.

Educators are concerned with institutional policies that impact the physical activity of adolescents given that they spend a great deal of time in school. An important part of the school environment that shapes students' level of activity is physical education class. PE is the only subject in the curriculum with the primary aim of engaging students in rigorous whole-body activities, improving movement skills, and developing a positive disposition to participate in healthy physical recreation (N. Smith, Lounsbery, and McKenzie 2014, 127).

Schools vary in their support of physical activity. Suburban schools are more likely than urban schools to have a climate that supports such activity. Public schools are more than twice as likely as private schools to have supportive climates. Currently, several states are considering options for school choice such as voucher systems to offset tuition costs at private and/or charter schools. This development highlights the need to address the physical activity environment in all schools, public and private. The School Health Policies and Programs Study (SHPPS) conducted in 2000 and 2006 confirmed that private schools have fewer physical education policies and practices in place than do public schools (Samuelson et al. 2010). Public school offerings also vary from state to state.

Ideally, secondary schools would offer regular physical education classes that focus on physical fitness and lifetime sports skills. The American Heart Association recommends that middle school students participate in a minimum of forty-five minutes of daily physical education and that physical education be a requirement for high school graduation. The typical school PE class meets for forty-five or fifty minutes, of which about two-thirds at best is devoted to physical activity (N. Smith Lounsbery, and McKenzie 2014, 132). A 2007 survey found that middle schools provided approximately 110 hours per year of physical education instruction. California requires a minimum of four hundred minutes each ten days for grades 7–12 (Young et al. 2007, 41, 46).

States and school districts set policies for physical education classes. Surveys conducted during the first decade of the twenty-first century reported that no more than one-third of middle schools provided daily physical education for students and that only 2 percent of high schools did so. Some districts require only one semester of physical education during a high school year, and in Minnesota, students take only one physical education class during their four years of high school (Young et al. 2007, 46; Samuelson et al. 2010; Lowry et al. 2013, 5).

The Centers for Disease Control and Prevention reported that as of 2012, 86 percent of school districts had adopted policies stating that schools must adhere to national, state, or district physical education standards, a nearly 20 percentage-point increase from 2000, when only two-thirds of districts had such policies. Roughly three-fourths of school districts had specified time requirements for elementary, middle, and high school classes. Although the percentage of schools offering regular physical education classes declined from 2000 to 2006, school sports opportunities appeared to be increasing nationwide according to a report released by the Government Accountability Office (Toporek 2012c).

Many schools clearly are shortchanging physical education programs. A 2009 survey reported that only half of those teaching physical education in high school rated their principals as "very supportive." Most physical education program budgets have remained level or shrunk in recent years. In 2009, almost half of PE teachers reported that their budgets remained about the same over the last three years; more than a third said that budgets had decreased. High school physical education budgets pale in comparison to interscholastic sports budgets; this often holds true for other academic budgets as well. The problem with emphasizing interscholastic sports at the expense of adequate support for PE classes is that sports accommodate a select group of students (Kralovec 2003, 78–79; Stanec and Ley 2008, 112–15; Roslow 2007, 7, 22).

Lack of support for physical education is reflected in exemption policies. Some 30 percent of high schools allowed student exemptions from physical education classes, according to a 2006 School Health Policies and Programs Study (SHPPS) (N. Smith, Lounsbery, and McKenzie 2014, 127). Private high schools, in particular, have allowed students to substitute participation in interscholastic sports for physical education. A SHPPS spokesperson commented, "We believe that it's a mistake to continue to equate athletics with quality physical education—especially considering what we know today about quality P.E. and health programs" (Stanec and Ley 2008, 112–15). In addition, students can be excused from physical education class, and classes are shortened or canceled in favor of other instructional or school-related activities, including picture taking (Young et al. 2007, 46). At the high school level, last-period PE often serves as the warm-up period for varsity team members. Some schools offer physical education credit for cheerleading (N. Adams and Bettis 2003, 61).

Staffing conflicts are a further concern. Teaching physical education and coaching sports do not require the same tasks and skills. Realistically, the primary goal in coaching a major sport—beyond teaching and conditioning players—is orchestrating a public display for sports fans and promoting a positive institutional image deriving from this display. The goals of teaching physical education are developing physical fitness and movement skills and forming healthy exercise habits in students. Teachers may experience cognitive dissonance and tension when attempting to effectively fulfill the expressed expectations of both roles. In many cases, the teacher/coach either falls short of the expectations of these roles or devotes time and energy to one role and neglecting the other (Figone 1994).

Physical education majors learn that schools should promote a progressive hierarchy, with physical education classes forming the base, intramural sports providing an arena for students to utilize skills learned in the classroom setting, and interscholastic athletics offering a more rigorous experience for the highly skilled students whose needs are best served by competing against athletes from other schools. In short, athletics should arise out of and complement intraschool sports and fitness programs. Interscholastic sports aren't supposed to be a surrogate for PE classes or preempt them. To better appreciate this model, it is instructive to examine the role of the extracurriculum in secondary schools.

The Extracurriculum

The *extracurriculum* refers to activities that are meant to complement the academic curriculum but are separated from formal courses. They are ungraded and don't convey academic credit. Such activities usually take place beyond regular school hours, except when an activity period is scheduled during the school day. (Some Texas schools schedule an "athletics period.") Extracurricular programs may be held on or off campus and occasionally are sponsored jointly with community organizations. While extracurricular offerings are less directly linked to the school's academic mission than the core curriculum is, these activities can contribute to students' educational and personal development (Gerdy 2014, 49).

Virtually all middle schools and high schools sponsor extracurricular activities, which fall into several categories, among them student government, communications, performing arts, business, community service, athletics, and academic-oriented programs. Some large high schools may offer more than fifty extracurricular activities, including student clubs and sports teams.

Specific examples of activities include jazz band, 4-H club, and pep squad (Quiroz, Flores González, and Frank 1996). Interscholastic athletics tend to be the most visible extracurricular activity, and their influence reaches beyond the student population. School administrators are persuaded that sports create school spirit and bring the community together. This is not to say that student musical performances and theater productions don't offer similar benefits to the school and community (Gerdy 2000, 135).

The traditional distinction between curricular and extracurricular has eroded in theory if not in practice. This development has spawned the label *co-curricular*, implying that such activities should be viewed as an extension of learning experiences within the classroom setting. Interscholastic athletics are more likely to be labeled *extracurricular*, while science fairs are tagged *co-curricular*, given that students are applying concepts and techniques learned in science classes and they may be graded on their entries. The distinction is fuzzy, and the two terms are often used interchangeably. Ardent advocates of interscholastic sports frame these activities as co-curricular and thus semantically on par with science fairs and debate teams (Conn 2012).

Ideally, high schools would offer a wide variety of extracurricular activities. For example, the music department might sponsor programs such as choir, jazz band, marching band, and orchestra. There would be a drama club, a school newspaper, a yearbook, and maybe even a literary magazine. Despite the popularity of extracurricular activities among students, diminished financial resources have led schools to reduce the number and range of programs (Bocarro et al. 2014, S66). There are reports of the extracurriculum being dismantled by well-meaning but myopic school boards and by the actions of county commissioners and state legislators. In some school districts, extracurricular activities are viewed as an expendable luxury. Interscholastic sports have fared somewhat better during these purges (Gioia 2008).

Indeed, interscholastic athletics are the elephant in the extracurricular classroom. In a 2002 survey in New Jersey, of the twenty-nine high schools where spending was calculated, the percentage of extracurricular activity funds devoted to athletics ranged from 62 to 95 percent (Gerdy 2006, 32). There is every reason to believe that spending inequities occur in most states. The imbalance in favor of interscholastic sports over other extracurricular programs is reflected in the disparate staffing costs. While interscholastic coaches generally receive generous supplementary pay (see chapter 3), sponsorship of other extracurricular activities by teachers may be nominally voluntary. School principals may pressure teachers—especially those new to the profession—to sponsor activities with no stipend (Quiroz, Flores González, and Frank 1996). There are exceptions. In some states, including Florida, school districts often provide academic supplements to teachers who sponsor activities such as yearbook club, school newspaper, or National Honor Society (Jordan 2009).

Progressive educators remain convinced that extra/co-curricular programs play an important role in the education of youth and continue to support these activities. That said, it is imperative that schools examine, evaluate, and reconsider whether the types of programs they sponsor are appropriate to prepare students for the world they face after graduation (Gerdy 2014, 52). It is reasonable to assume that participation in most extracurricular activities has some effect on student behavior. It should be possible to compare the developmental benefits of various programs. Several empirical studies support sponsorship of extracurricular activities. According to the North Carolina High School Athletic Association ("Case" 2001), making diverse clubs and activities available to a range of students is quite beneficial. The opportunity for students to embed their identity in various extracurricular contexts and to experience multiple competencies facilitates attachment to school and enhances personal adjustment. Activity participation is also linked to affiliation with peers who are academically focused.

A study conducted in the 1990s found that total extracurricular activity participation is associated with an improved grade point average, higher educational aspirations, and reduced absenteeism (Broh 2002, 70). Broh concluded that participation in interscholastic sports, music programs, and student council helped students improve their grades but that participation in other extracurricular activities didn't have significant effects on academic achievement (84). Participation in the drama club and the yearbook/journalism club resulted in limited academic benefits. Cheerleading was unremarkable in this regard, and intramural sports and vocational clubs seemed to impair achievement. However, this study didn't control for self-selection of students into these various activities. (Self-selection bias arises in situations in which individuals select themselves into groups, resulting in a nonrandom distribution.)

When systematically comparing students involved in extracurricular activities with their counterparts who are not involved in such activities, researchers have found that participation in athletics transforms at-risk students and that other extracurricular activities appear to have similar effects (Gerdy 2000, 133). Participation in extracurricular activities in high school appears to be one of the few interventions that benefit low-status, disadvantaged students ("Case" 2001). Students who spend no time in extracurricular activities are more likely to use drugs and more likely to become teen parents. Arguably, the most significant influence of any extracurricular activity on the personal development and character of participants may not be the specific activity but rather the environment in which the activity occurs (Gerdy 2014, 89, 99).

Interscholastic sports, especially team sports, tend to be the most popular extracurricular activity. The National Center for Education Statistics (NCES) reports that students participate in interscholastic athletics more than any other school-sponsored program (Bocarro et al. 2014, S66). According to NCES figures, some 39 percent of high school seniors participated in interscholastic sports, followed by academic clubs, vocational clubs, and band, each of which had participation rates at around 21 percent (Sabo 2011). In many secondary schools with prominent athletics programs, intramural programs are slighted.

School yearbooks reflect the relative popularity of various extracurricular activities. Most yearbooks feature head shots of the students along with casual photos in a variety of settings. The distribution of these photos makes a statement about what the yearbook staff consider important. For example, a 1990s yearbook from Glen Ridge High School in New Jersey devoted twenty-three pages to athletes and four pages to the cheerleading squad; all other school clubs were allotted four pages total. The award-winning band received only two pages. The typical nonsport organization was allotted a quarter of a page (Lefkowitz 1998, 201).

Professor of education Etta Kralovec (2003, 2, 4, 9) argues that schools try to do too much. The often-chaotic schedule and the myriad activities and rituals of schooling—what many educators label the "sideshows of education"—consume a large portion of the school day and can interfere with teaching and learning. However, proponents of a comprehensive extracurricular program maintain that such programs help to prepare adolescents for the real world. They argue that schools should expand after-school academic-based clubs along with recreational sports through intramural offerings. Adolescents have a much greater chance of becoming doctors, executives, accountants, or lawyers than of becoming professional athletes. Students should be encouraged to participate in recreation and fitness activities that don't necessarily entail intense competition and specialization (Glover 1999). Intramural programs are designed specifically to meet this objective.

Intramural Sports

A number of health professionals including a former US surgeon general have advocated the promotion of school intramural sports programs, suggesting that these activities have a great potential for improving rates of leisure time physical activity in adolescents (Edwards et al. 2011, 158). The National Association of Sport and Physical Education (NASPE) recommends intramurals, along with other noncompetitive activities, as more developmentally appropriate for middle-school-aged adolescents and argues in favor of prioritizing these activities over sports that mimic high school programs (Edwards, Kanters, and Bocarro 2011, 603). High schools also need to seek a balance in sports offerings. Intramurals provide a healthy complement to the academic aspects of students' education; as with interscholastic sports at their best, participation in intramurals can enhance students' feelings of belonging to the school community (Campbell 2004, 16).

Intramurals are all-inclusive, not restricted to elite athletes, and don't have limited rosters. There are no cuts. Everyone who signs up makes the team, and all are assured of significant and meaningful playing time. This approach differs from interscholastic sports, which are structured in a way that excludes many students from participating (Campbell 2004, 16). Moreover, intramurals have the potential to provide more activity than interscholastic sports. Typically, there is less formal instruction and coaching, enabling more continuous activity.

Intramurals are less expensive than interscholastic sports, which require significant travel, team uniforms, and equipment (costs borne by both schools and parents) as well as paid officials. Schools emphasizing the intramural model should be able to divert some funds to provide a wider array of sports to attract more students, including those from low-income households. Intramurals can offer a wider variety of activities than interscholastic programs, which limit schools to sponsoring sports that match those offered at competing schools and sanctioned by state associations. Students may or may not have a good idea what a chosen intramural sport entails, but they aren't locked into a single activity and are free to try something different (although they are committed to an intramural team for the duration of the schedule) (Campbell 2004, 16; Edwards et al. 2011, 160; Bocarro et al. 2014, 68–69).

Additional benefits accrue from participation in intramurals. Students can be involved planning and organizing activities. Intramural directors often develop a cadre of students who help run the program. Not only do these students learn leadership skills, but this model reduces the workload of program directors. This interactive process can lead to increased buy-in from students and increase participation. In short, intramurals can be more student-centered, as participants have input in the structure and design of the program, in contrast to coach-dominated interscholastic sports. In addition, intramural sports provide opportunities for all skill levels to participate, and the reduced time commitment offers more students (e.g., those who work part time) the opportunity to take part. One of the main attractions is that participating in intramural sports doesn't require the protracted training time required by a varsity sport. Most intramural sports have few, if any, scheduled practice sessions and only one game a week, leaving plenty of time for studies. And intramural activities place the focus on enjoyment and socialization rather than intense competition. Finally, exposure to several different sports nurtures a sense of competence and enjoyment that can last beyond the school years and set adult lifestyle patterns (Byl 2004, 22–23; Campbell 2004, 12; Edwards et al. 2011, 60; Kanters et al. 2013, 114).

School resources should be employed to increase physical activity among students of both sexes, but gender equity remains problematic. One study found that intramural sports generated higher physical activity levels than interscholastic sports among boys but not girls (Bocarro et al. 2014, S68–69). Some middle school girls were discouraged from participating in intramurals by male dominance, pressure to adhere to social norms, threats of embarrassment, and possible injury. But norms are changing, and intramural programs have options. Coeducational teams are appropriate for most sports, although educators recommend that gender-specific activities also be made available within Title IX guidelines.

Intramural programs do require money: schools must provide financial support for staffing, schedules, facilities, and equipment. Schools should appoint an intramural director and compensate this person in accordance with other student activity sponsors and directors. Directors have to be creative in fund-raising and frugal in spending, although parent councils may be willing to sponsor some aspects of the program. School intramural programs may have to compete with interscholastic athletics for use of facilities and seek out alternative facilities in the community. Most schools have physical education equipment that can be accessed for intramural programs (Byl 2004, 22–23).

According to one study, intramural sports involved only about 3 percent of middle, junior, and senior high school students in the mid-1990s. By 2006, about half of US middle schools offered intramural sports. A study of middle schools in one state found that rural schools were falling short in efforts to provide extracurricular physical activity programming recommended by policy groups. Students in high socioeconomic status middle schools were more likely to participate in intramural sports than students in low socioeconomic status schools, with a participation gap of between 6 and 12 percent (Malina, Shields, and Gilbert 2015; Colabianchi, Johnston, and O'Malley 2012, 3; Edwards et al. 2011, 160; Edwards, Kanters, and Bocarro 2011, 597).

A 2012 survey of North Carolina middle schools found that some 39 percent of sampled schools offered intramural sports activities, while nearly all the schools offered interscholastic sports (Colabianchi, Johnston, and O'Malley 2012, 1). The number of intramural sports offered ranged from one to fourteen. Basketball and volleyball were most likely to be offered. The majority of activities were coeducational, although some activities were limited to a single gender. About a third of middle schools provided open gym or free play to students during extracurricular periods outside the formal school day. In a number of schools, community-based agencies organized some of the activities. Programs were expanded to include physical activity clubs to increase participation. More than 40 percent of middle schools in one survey offered late activity buses for students who participated in after-school activities. In Minnesota, almost half of the schools had both a policy and a practice of providing an activity bus for intramurals to take students home after school (Edwards et al. 2011, 600–601).

Progressive educators suggest that middle and high schools implement intramural programs that include a variety of individual and team sports and lifetime fitness activities. Schools could sponsor student-initiated sports clubs in activities like hiking and cycling. Intramural programs encompass both competitive and noncompetitive activities: the emphasis should be on participation, skill development, and enjoyment. If awards are given for championships, they should be of relatively low importance and in no way approach those bestowed in varsity sports. Emphasizing winning over participation and enjoyment would defeat the purpose of intramural sports (Reed 2015, 17).

Recommended practices for intramural programs include encouraging all students to participate and offering them assistance in overcoming barriers to participation such as lack of transportation or low skill levels. Noncompetitive clubs—for example, jogging, aerobics, yoga—should be part of school sports programs. These types of activities can encourage parents to volunteer or participate with their children. Also, local fitness/recreation centers can be invited to sponsor instruction in recreational sports such as tennis, racquetball, and golf. Students should choose their level of competitiveness and be matched by skill level when possible. If tournaments are organized, they should be designed to allow all students/teams an equal number of games or matches, such as round-robin tournaments. Elimination tournaments should be deemphasized. Students should be encouraged to self-officiate games and matches and learn to appreciate how honesty and fair play contribute to the experience (Glover 1999).

Reviewing physical activity programs in the school curriculum and extracurriculum provides a perspective for evaluating the status of interscholastic sports in the nation's schools—that is, for comparing the role that these programs should play in the education of adolescents with the role that they actually play. Regardless of perspective, one must acknowledge that interscholastic athletics are often the most prominent—and contentious—facet of the secondary school extracurriculum.

Interscholastic Sports

Sports in the context of the school setting most prominently take the form of interschool competition in the nation's middle/junior high and high schools. Organized sports receive less emphasis in elementary schools, though programs vary among local school districts. Secondary schools are the nation's largest institutional setting for sports participation during the teen and preteen years, and the overwhelming majority of American middle schools and high schools sponsor interscholastic sports programs (Hartmann and Massoglia 2007, 485).

Schools invest more heavily in sports than in any other extracurricular activity. Many secondary schools have teams at the freshman, junior varsity, and varsity levels in a variety of sports. Football is the most visible, if not most popular, sport; although more high schools offer basketball, track and field, and baseball than eleven-player football (Winfrey 2010, 46). The National Federation of State High School Associations (NFHS) sponsors baseball, basketball, field hockey, football, golf, gymnastics, ice hockey, lacrosse, softball, soccer, swimming and diving, tennis, track and field/cross country, volleyball, water polo, and wrestling. (The federation also sponsors music, speech, debate, and theater.)

The NFHS reports that between 55 and 60 percent of students enrolled in middle and high schools participate in athletics. The numbers vary by grade level. Based on data for the 2009–10 school year, the state of Texas (ranked second in population to California) had the most high school students participating in interscholastic sports. Nationally, football had the most male participants of all interscholastic sports, followed by outdoor track and field, basketball, baseball, and soccer (Winfrey 2010, 46). Gender inequality continues. Currently, more than a million more boys than girls participate in school sports. (In 1972, prior to the implementation of Title IX, for every ten boys participating in high school sports, one girl was participating.) A recent survey reported some seventeen hundred girls were participating in eleven-person football, and around fifteen hundred girls were involved in wrestling, both traditionally male sports. Track and field was the number 1 sport for girls, followed by basketball, volleyball, and soccer (National Women's Law Center 2012). According to the National Women's Law Center, the six states reporting the highest gender participation gaps (percentage of girls enrolled in school versus girls participating in sports) in 2012 were Texas, South Carolina, Alabama, Louisiana, Tennessee, and Georgia. In these states, more than half of the high schools reported a participation gap of 10 percent or higher.

Participation also varies along racial lines. African Americans are overrepresented in sports at urban schools that have lower participation rates, and they tend to play primarily basketball and football, perhaps because of socioeconomic status or neighborhood differences. White students have higher participation rates in swimming, soccer, baseball, and softball. School sports programs have been criticized for perpetuating a form of racial separation, although football and basketball squads tend to be more integrated (Glennie and Stearns 2012, 533, 535; Edwards et al. 2011, 158; Kanters et al. 2013, 114).

African American girls are more likely to participate in sports than are their white counterparts. A 2012 study of girls in the tween and teen years found that frequency of physical activity declined significantly for both ethnic groups, with the decline was greater for black girls (Glennie and Stearns 2012, 551; Kanters et al. 2013, 114).

Participation rates also differ significantly between large and small high schools (Roan 2006). Across sports, the proportion of students participating decreases as school size increases. Larger schools usually can support more sports teams, but if teams limit the number of participants, many students are denied the opportunity to compete (Glennie and Stearns 2012, 536). In the late 1990s, for example, New York's relatively wealthy Bethlehem Central School District supported football, ice hockey, gymnastics, golf, wrestling, field hockey, and boys and girls' lacrosse, swimming, cross country, volleyball, soccer, basketball, indoor and outdoor track and field, tennis, bowling, and baseball. The school fielded both junior varsity and varsity teams in some of these sports. Although Bethlehem had about 1,800 students from grades 7 through 12 and the team rosters included 1,072 athletes, the fact that students played multiple sports meant that only 20–30 percent of students participated (Svare 2004, 101).

Participation inequities are exacerbated by urban/rural/suburban distinctions. While nonschool sports and recreation programs have increased in the suburbs, such programs have decreased dramatically in urban areas. Students living in more rural communities with fewer commercial entertainment opportunities are more likely to play school sports than those in urban settings. But because rural communities tend to support more traditional notions of femininity for girls, those in rural areas tend to participate disproportionately in cheerleading and pep squads (Gatz, Messner, and Ball-Rokeach 2002, 41–42; Glennie and Stearns 2012, 535).

Some high schools sponsor freshman-sophomore teams, B teams, and intramural sports teams in addition to varsity and junior varsity squads, thus increasing opportunities for students of various levels of skill and dedication. In the late 1990s, Illinois's Glenbrook South High School offered an astounding seventy extracurricular clubs and twenty-three sports (Adler 1999). In contrast, other high schools have dropped their junior varsity teams and disbanded recreational sports programs, shifting the entire focus to highly competitive teams (Gerdy 2000, 143–44).

Elitist sports programs discriminate against certain groups of students. Those pursuing vocational education often do not participate in varsity sports as a result of either lower academic performance or apprenticeship obligations that hinder access to traditional after-school sports. Likewise, students with physical disabilities or even of average body size may have distinct disadvantages in the two most popular school sports, football and basketball. The average NCAA Division II point guard stands at 5'10". Half of American males are shorter. Centers and forwards on basketball teams average more than 6'1" tall. The average nineteen-year-old male weighs around 165 pounds, while the average high school linebacker weighs 225 pounds, and offensive and defensive linemen may be significantly heavier. These two sports receive much greater emphasis than wrestling, which has weight classes, or individual sports such as golf or swimming where body size is less critical.

Participation rates have also been reduced by homeschooling and the advent of club sports. But competing on a private team can cost several thousand dollars in fees, equipment, and travel expenses, beyond the means of many students' families (Roan 2006; Van Milligan 2014, 41). Some school sports also transfer expenses to families. Accordingly, sports participation by adolescents remains unequal across socioeconomic classes. Contrary to the myth of social mobility, youth from the lower classes have fewer opportunities to utilize the social good of school sports to better their educational attainment and cultural adjustment. In fact, students from higher socioeconomic levels, including those attending private schools or playing on private sports clubs, are most engaged in sports at the high school level (Fejgin 1994, 211–12, 225; Kanters et al. 2013, 113–14).

The economic bias has become institutionalized. The percentage of students participating in interscholastic sports increases with the school's socioeconomic standing. Schools with smaller budgets offer fewer sports and may limit the number of players on a team to further reduce costs (Seifried 2012, 79). Some smaller high schools have shifted to playing eight-man or six-man football, for example. The President's Council on Physical Fitness has estimated that restrictions on high school team membership reduce the total number of participants by 50 percent from the pre-high-school level (Roan 2006).

Nevertheless, in 2013–14, the number of participants in high school sports increased for the twenty-fifth consecutive year, reaching an all-time high of just under eight million. Baseball registered the greatest gain, followed by football and soccer. The 2013–14 school year saw the first increase in football numbers in five years, although several states reported a decline in participants according to the NFHS (NFHS.org). Sports participation figures are subject to double counting, as high school students often participate in multiple sports (although this practice is declining as a consequence of longer sports seasons). One high school reported that 300 out of 450 students participated in interscholastic sports. An examination of the names on team rosters revealed that 95 students were playing three sports during the school year, inflating the participation numbers (Kralovec 2003, 73). Despite fluctuations, sports participation is increasing in most schools. And schools offer an array of interscholastic sports. Shawnee High School, a public institution in southern New Jersey, for example, fielded teams in eighteen sports in 2013 (Ripley 2013a).

Sports culture is embedded in American schools in a way that is unique in the developed world (see chapter 2). Secondary schools spend an inordinate amount of time and money on athletics. Critics charge that this "sideshow" systematically undermines learning. The charge isn't baseless: American students excel at sports yet rank twenty-seventh among developed nations on a recent international math test (see chapter 6). What are we to make of this glaring reality? What signal does it send to students, parents, and teachers about the purpose of school? The challenges are real: how do we balance interscholastic sports and academics? Our schools must prepare students to succeed in a changing and increasingly competitive world. We must make choices regarding the most effective way to invest our limited educational resources. It is time to reevaluate the role of sports in the nation's schools (Kralovec 2003, 2,9; Gerdy 2014, x–xi).

We are asking our high schools to do more and more: training students in math and science as well as teaching computer skills. Supplemental services are provided by special education teachers, counselors, and school nurses. All this places an increasing workload on administrators and a strain on resources. We need to pause and ask what schools should be expected to do. Some things are more important than others (Svare 2004, 88). Rarely do we conduct a systematic analysis of how teachers and students spend the school day. Instead, we continually tinker with the agenda. The daily schedule often is chaotic, truncated, and not conducive to learning. Athletics routinely impinge on academics (Kralovec 2003, 4, 8).

The consequences of promoting interscholastic sports extend beyond academics. Edwards, Kanters, and Bocarro (2011, 603) comment, "Rather than considering extracurricular physical activity as a means of improving the health of students ... schools may emphasize popular spectator sports as a means of generating revenue and ... by promoting interscholastic sport's perceived cultural importance in connecting communities and building school spirit." Sports not only play an outsize role in American schools but have permeated the fabric of our communities (see chapter 4). Sports engage millions of families in the drama of their sons and daughters playing for their high school teams, take up a sizable chunk of the sports pages of local newspapers, and are accorded considerable airtime on radio and television (Pruter 2013, ix).

H. G. Bissinger's *Friday Night Lights* (1990) describes how the autumnal madness of high school football can engulf an entire community. What occurs in the West Texas town of Odessa is replicated in local communities across the nation—if not for football then for basketball or girls' soccer. Sports have become an element of American life so pervasive that virtually no individual is untouched by sports in one way or another. Americans arguably place more emphasis on sports than perhaps any civilization since ancient Rome. The Roman philosopher Cicero commented on competitive games oriented to the spectator and impoverished of ethical overtones: what would he think of present-day high school basketball in Indiana or football in Texas?

There's the sport, and then there's the public spectacle with all the ballyhoo that surrounds the staged contest. The relevant question is whether schools should be allocating precious resources toward activities whose essential function in the community is not education but entertainment (Almond 2014b) In spectator sports settings, the ceremony often overshadows the event. Pruter (2013, 327) asserts, "The very term interscholastic sports inherently poses a contradiction in an educational institution sponsoring sports for high school students, having them play before spectators, charging admission, and financing expensive programs with seemingly no educational purpose." Individual sports like golf and tennis have avoided most of the ceremony and regalia. It is primarily team sports like football and basketball that accumulate the glitzy trappings: cheerleaders, marching bands, banners, simulated smoke, blaring voices over public address systems, glitzy scoreboards, etc. School principals offer few objections to these sideshows—indeed, seem to embrace them. Today's high school sporting events are three parts show business and one part on-field competition (Isaacs 1978, 101).

Apart from the hoopla of spectator sports, school administrators maintain that athletics participation plays a critical role in the educational process. "As proof of the intensity of this belief, one needs only to consider the tremendous amount of money, time, and emotions invested in high school ... programs nationwide" (Gerdy 2000, 115) The stated purpose of interscholastic sports is the enrichment of the high school experience of students within the context of the educational mission. If so, school sports should contribute to the overall development of students, both athletes and nonathletes. These activities should enhance the health and welfare of students not only during the school years but continuing into adulthood (Malina, Shields, and Gilbert 2015).

In assessing interscholastic athletics' contribution to student development, it is important to distinguish between the nature of the sport and the culture of the sport. For example, the basic nature of team sports is distinct from individual sports, as are contact sports from noncontact sports. The culture of sports can be egalitarian or elitist, democratic or authoritarian. Whether football builds character depends on the individual athlete's interactions with coaches and teammates. The sports culture promoted by schools should be in the best interests of the individual student—whether an athlete, cheerleader, or member of the marching band. Students shouldn't be used to prop up a coach's ego, to sell tickets, as public relations props, or even to promote community spirit among the subset of rabid sports fans. Student development—intellectual, physical, social, emotional—is an end in itself, not a means to other ends.

Educators didn't create student sports programs by design. The array of competitive sports sponsored by secondary schools reflects tradition and popularity. The current offerings aren't based on a systematic assessment of their suitability or consideration of their appropriateness for adolescents. For the most part, school sports are replicas of professional and college sports with a few modifications. There is no reason these sports cannot be further modified for reasons such as improved safety. Indeed, the nation's major spectator sports have been transformed several times. However, educators act as if hand-me-down adult sports like tackle football contribute to the education and welfare of adolescents while downplaying the safety issues.

Sports are emotionally intense and socially rich experiences that often have profound effects, both positive and negative, on the participants. Proponents of school sports see them as a microcosm of the larger world, a vehicle for social mobility and preparation for adult life. They point to the benefits of participation, including development of physical skills, improved fitness, promotion of lifetime physical activity, and the learning of social skills. Tufte (2012, xiii) expounds, "In a world that provides every excuse to text instead of talk, watch instead of perform, and tune out instead of participate, high school sports brings young people together in ways that Facebook cannot." At their best, school sports can provide a form of much-needed physical exercise for a generation of students who are becoming more sedentary. Sports can reduce stress and increase self-esteem. Playing sports provides a social bond with others and valuable social connections. The argument is made that participating in sports helps students become better people (Tufte 2012, xii–xiii). If all this is true, then why don't schools provide athletics programs that serve all students? Interscholastic sports in their present incarnation benefit only a distinct minority.

Under ideal circumstances, interscholastic sports should be viewed as the crowning point of the overall physical education experience, providing opportunities to physically gifted students—activities that surpass the limits of the intramural program by providing more competitive, demanding, and concentrated experiences. Interscholastic sports should be considered an integral part of the total education process that has as its aim the development of physically, mentally, socially, and morally fit individuals (Stillwell and Willgoose 1997, 266–67).

Athletic competition can serve as a vital educational medium by incorporating worthy goals such as winning by fair and honest means, developing pride in accomplishments, building team spirit, and teaching self-discipline and control. Sports often play an important role in school culture and affect students whether or not they participate. More broadly, school sports can encourage spectators and nonparticipants to take an interest in and appreciate the values of competitive physical activities and can stimulate institutional interest and loyalty among students, alumni, and the public (Jensen and Overman 2003, 327–28).

But not everyone agrees about the educational and developmental values of interscholastic sports. Gatz, Messner, and Ball-Rokeach (2002, 5) charge that interscholastic athletics offers a pedagogy of exclusion, violence, and destructively competitive values in an increasingly commercialized climate. The negative experiences reported by students playing high school sports include the pressures of intense competition and the ramifications of major injuries. Balancing academic and other responsibilities with sports participation can be a challenge. One student commented, "During football my grades weren't that good but after I stopped playing my grades improved immensely.... [I]t took up a lot of free time that I could of done school work in" (Garcia 2015, 130, 133)

Gerdy (2002, 109) takes a broad view of school sports. He notes that the values, attitudes, and behaviors demonstrated by those who play, coach, and administer organized sports greatly influence societal values, attitudes, and behavior. Sports have prompted a profound change in our value system as it relates to the types of talents and skills we value. Gerdy believes that "organized sport in America has become too pervasive an influence to be considered merely a reflection of cultural values" (37). The relationship between the values of sports and the values of our culture is symbiotic, and "what occurs on the fields of play influences cultural values and norms" (37). The increasing expression of such reservations is why it is important to address the current excesses of interscholastic sports. The implications extend beyond our system of education.

◆ ◆ ◆

This book takes a critical look at interscholastic sports, first assessing their problematic influence on academics, student-athletes, school culture, and community and then proposing reforms to address these issues. History reminds us that the sporadic attempts at reforming school sports haven't accomplished much, just as reform of collegiate athletics has a mixed record. It is not worth incorporating additional reform measures that cannot be enforced. In this regard, the struggle to enforce "no pass, no play" rules is instructive (see chapter 6). Reform cannot be accomplished by a short flurry of corrective measures or piecemeal efforts but requires a constant, coordinated campaign to rein in the excesses of school sports (Svare 2004, 254).

Gerdy (2006, 25) remains skeptical of meaningful reform: "There are powerful cultural forces and structural limitations inherent in high school and community-based athletic systems that prevent ... sweeping change. Resistance to change at the high school and community level will be enormous because these institutions of sports are so ingrained in the fabric of local communities." Gerdy, a former associate commissioner of the Southeastern Conference, questions whether the administrative and governance structure necessary to drive reform of interscholastic athletics actually exists.

Yet some notable state-level efforts to reform interscholastic sports have occurred. At a 2004 Maine Sports Summit, three hundred student-athletes from eighty-seven high schools and twenty-four middle schools discussed what was good and bad about their interscholastic sports experiences. The following year, the Center for Sport and Coaching at the University of Maine unveiled a program, Sports Done Right, that was piloted in twelve districts around the state. The specific goals of the initiative included helping coaches respond to the pressures and demands of coaching and helping communities and parents create an environment that fosters positive experiences for student-athletes. This effort sought to provide clear frameworks that defined how interscholastic sports should be conducted and monitored. The report, sent to every school district in the state, listed out-of-bounds issues that coaches, parents, and school administrators should avoid, including requiring students to pay participation fees and coercing student-athletes to specialize in one sport (Beem 2006; Gehring 2005a, 1–16).

Missouri addressed the issue of escalating travel distances and costs. High school varsity teams were prohibited from participating in competitions outside a 250-mile radius of the school. This meant that teams could not travel to New York or Hawaii for national tournaments or cheerleading competitions and that high school bands couldn't march in the Macy's Thanksgiving Day Parade. In 2005, members of the Missouri State High School Activities Association voted to allow schools to compete in one distant tournament or competition annually per sport as long as the travel didn't interfere with class time. For most school districts, this translated to the possibility of competing in an out-of-state tournament over winter break or spring break (Beem 2006).

Implementing reforms through local initiatives remains problematic for reasons that are addressed in chapter 4. This book suggests a radical restructuring of school sports. Chapter 2 chronicles an early attempt at reform, when schools assumed control of student-organized sports (with mixed results) and then explores the European model of sports clubs. Subsequent chapters discuss specific issues related to interscholastic sports and frame reforms in the context of a more appropriate intramural/sports club model.

UNDERSTANDING SCHOOL SPORTS: LOOKING BACK, EXPLORING ABROAD

> I believe that the truth of any subject only comes when all sides of the story are put together.
> —**Alice Walker**, author, activist

Brief History of School Sports in the United States

Legendary pitcher Satchel Paige cautioned, "Don't look back. Someone might be gaining on you." With due deference to one of baseball's premiere epigrammatists, this chapter takes a brief look at the origins and early history of school-sponsored sports. When sports fans look back, they usually do so from a perspective of nostalgia: mythologized sports heroes, legendary feats, and broken records. Less often do we analyze the major events that have shaped contemporary sports. How did we arrive at the present system? Have we made any progress in improving our sporting institutions? By the same token, sports aficionados in the United States rarely look abroad beyond the Olympic Games for a sense of comparison. We count medals but discount any lessons we might learn from examining the sports systems of other developed nations. The chapter addresses this omission as well.

The nation's first public high schools were established in the 1830s and 1840s. By the early twentieth century, public education had evolved into a system of twelve years of instruction—eight years of elementary education followed by four years of secondary education. The final four years of formal education were housed in a high school or split between a junior high—which also included grades 7 and 8—and high school. (Middle schools began appearing in the 1960s.) In the World War I era, only about one in six children between the ages of fourteen and seventeen were enrolled in high school, but laws in most states eventually mandated school attendance until graduation or a set age—typically eighteen (Pruter 2013, 8).

Between 1910 and 1940, the "high school movement" resulted in the founding of schools in many larger cities and subsequently in suburban neighborhoods, small communities, and ultimately in rural areas. Both enrollment and graduation rates increased as schools were constructed and a practical curriculum was developed that focused on providing life skills as well as preparing elite students for college. This trend was promoted by a policy of local decision making by school districts and open enrollment. By the mid-twentieth century, comprehensive high schools were common in both urban and rural areas, and a large number of students were earning high school diplomas.

School sports first emerged in the boarding schools in the East outside the formal curriculum as unsupervised activities during nonschool hours. Prep school students imitated the American college model, which had followed the British public school model. In the mid-nineteenth century, students began organizing interclass competitions and then interschool competitions. By the 1860s, prep students were directing their own sports clubs, and athletic associations were formed to facilitate competition (Pruter 2013, 3–6). During this era, baseball, football, and track and field began to establish their place in American popular culture, influenced by the British sports ethos, which emphasizes competition to compare ability and set records. The basic principle is that two individuals or teams begin competition defined as equals and end competition unequal as a consequence of victory or defeat. In contrast, the German *Turnen* system emphasizes health, toughness, strength and skill, presence of mind, and courage in the face of adversity rather than comparison of achievement (Heinemann 1999, 21).

The United States was beginning to educate its youth for more years than most other countries even while admitting a surge of immigrants. The ruling elite feared that schooling would make Anglo-Saxon boys soft and weak, in contrast to their brawny, newly arrived peers. Oliver Wendell Holmes Sr. warned that cities were being overrun by "stiff-jointed, soft-muscled, paste-complexioned youth." Sports, the thinking went, would both protect boys' masculinity and distract them from vices like gambling and prostitution. "Muscular Christianity," fashionable during the Victorian era, prescribed sports as a sort of moral vaccine against the tumult of rapid economic growth (Pruter 2013, 47–48; Ripley 2013a).

Progressive educators came to appreciate that extracurricular activities could serve as a bonding institution for a diverse body of students. By the 1880s, Chicago's high schools hosted a variety of extracurricular clubs such as debate teams and literary societies. Schools in the city also sponsored intramural field days that attracted hundreds of participants and many spectators. For their part, students generally preferred sports to the boring, repetitive exercises in the physical education classes centered on formal gymnastics. Student-organized sports teams supplemented extracurricular offerings and were tolerated by school authorities. School sports clubs competed against teams from other private and public high schools, college teams, and sandlot teams (Gutowski 1988, 62; Pruter 2013, 16–23).

From early on, American youth had played sports in relatively haphazard way, appropriating vacant fields, sidewalks, streets, and alleys for pickup games and challenging other loosely affiliated groups of young athletes to matches. Many high-school-aged students belonged to community-organized teams in baseball and other sports. In the late nineteenth century, boys in public high schools began organizing teams made up of classmates. There are three distinct eras in the development of high school sports: (1) student initiatives with adult alliances, 1880–1900; (2) institutional control, 1900–1920; and (3) the first state and national governing agencies, 1920–1930 (Pruter 2013, xiii, 13).

As the number of public high schools increased, more students began forming sports clubs. These student-sponsored teams were informal and small-scale and operated largely without adult oversight. Student athletic associations raised money, secured playing fields, and scheduled matches between teams. Team members soon began wearing uniforms and adopting the other trappings that have come to define school sports. By the end of the century, a number of cities had student-organized teams. High school sports were gaining a foothold in the American system of education (Pruter 2013, 2–6, 13, 21, 23). An early instance of interschool competition took place in October 1900, when St. Matthew's Grammar School of Dallas, Texas, played a football game against the Wall School in neighboring Honey Grove, winning by a score of 5–0. The event was a milestone in Texas school history: the first recorded football game between two high school teams. By the 1920s, Texas had implemented a state football championship tournament (Ripley 2013a).

Chicago and Illinois played a significant role in the development of high school sports. Organized sports took hold in Chicago's public high schools when the students, like their prep school counterparts, formed football, baseball, and track and field teams and organized athletic associations to support them. A school baseball league had formed in Chicago by the early 1890s. The sports clubs collected dues, took donations, and organized fund drives or sold tickets to fans. Athletic associations began charging entry fees. (The self-financing model proved shaky, however; a number of clubs ended up in debt, and some dissolved.) The student managers for each sport would arrange the scheduling. Team captains often served as coaches. While most teams were managed and coached by students, some were coached by recent alumni; few teams had adult coaches. Faculty members occasionally would assist students behind the scenes. This pattern continued into the early twentieth century (Gutowski 1988, 61–65; Pruter 2013, xvi, 15, 23–25, 29, 53).

Most of the early student teams competed in outdoor sports—mainly football, baseball, and track and field. Chicago's student baseball and football teams practiced in vacant lots; track teams ran on the streets or on the cinders between railroad tracks. Concurrently, the Amateur Athletic Union was organizing track meets in which high school students competed. Golf, cross country, lacrosse, and other outdoor sports were incorporated into high school sports programs over the twentieth century. Following the invention of basketball in 1891, students at one Chicago high school set up a basketball gymnasium in an attic. Other student clubs used the gym at the local YMCA. More schools began building gymnasiums to accommodate the growing popularity of basketball, volleyball, and other indoor sports. In the late 1890s, indoor track meets were held where facilities were available. High schools soon were offering other indoor sports, including swimming, often utilizing YMCA pools. These activities filled a hole in the sports calendar. Educators generally looked favorably on student sports, but the incursion of outside agencies proved troubling, as it eroded the schools' control over these activities (Gutowski 1988, 65; Pruter 2013, 6, 125, 143).

Leagues and tournaments were organized at the local and state levels to support competition. The Chicago High School Football League was organized in 1885. Illinois organized state track and field meets for high school students in the 1890s, coordinated with the state's universities. Within a decade, there was a baseball league. Similar leagues formed for basketball and tennis. Facilities and equipment were often in short supply, as many early leagues were funded by students or by private charities. School districts eventually stepped in to provide money. Student-organized clubs often had to reach out to adults in the schools and communities for access to facilities and other resources. Track meets in particular required a coordination of resources, and student-adult disagreements occasionally occurred (Gutowski 1988, 62; Pruter 2013, 22–23, 26, 38–43, 72).

Sports clubs were plagued by problems. Students had difficulty keeping teams together and managing competitive events. Obtaining officials often proved challenging, and teams at times failed to show up for games. There were growing concerns about professionalism, particularly in baseball. Clubs and leagues experienced problems with "ringers"—that is, people who were not really students playing on teams. A number of "student" football players would drop out of school when the season ended. Conflicts emerged over athletes' enrollment and eligibility to play. Clubs frequently were poorly managed, and dissension among team members was common. Disputes over contests were frequent and not easily resolved. Fighting and occasionally even riots took place at high school football and basketball games. And injuries mounted, especially among football players (Gutowski 1988, 63, 65–68; Pruter 2013, 16, 75, 98–100).

School administrators increasingly turned a critical eye toward student-run activities, worrying about legal liability and consequently increasing control of extracurricular activities in the late 1890s. High schools began governing sports with athletic councils made up of faculty, alumni, and students. Teachers were put in charge of administering club funds and determining who could participate. Some schools banned advertising and ticket taking and required student-athletes to get physicians' checkups. Educators were concerned about the excesses. Students were devoting too much time to sports and were overtraining. Sports clubs began scheduling football games out of state, over the increasing objections of school officials. Schools continued to be concerned about external interests co-opting the sports clubs, as teams often were tied to fraternities or other private societies. Educators invoked antifrat rules and banned high school fraternities in some school districts (Gutowski 1988, 66–69; Pruter 2013, 55–56, 66, 88–93).

Illinois's Cook County High School Athletic League was reorganized and placed under control of faculty representatives in 1898. Student-athletes in Chicago schools were allowed to carry out some administrative functions but came under increasing faculty supervision. High schools began implementing grade standards for participation in sports. For the most part, disillusioned students welcomed faculty control, which brought about stability and more reliable funding. From early on, interscholastic baseball and football contests drew adult spectators. The reorganized sports leagues began charging admission to contests. Newly built high schools were furnished with athletic facilities, and paid coaches became common (Gutowski 1988, 69–71; Miracle and Rees 1994, 60–61).

While schools proposed measures that allowed students to collaborate in managing sports teams, students' role in the governing bodies gradually diminished. The students generally conceded or welcomed the emerging faculty control of interscholastic sports, which not only reduced the abuses and cheating but also provided assistance in raising funds and procuring facilities and expertise from teachers who served as coaches. But in some instances, students rebelled against school administrators' takeover of sports. Student coaches competed with faculty coaches. Some student teams objected to paid coaches (Pruter 2013, 65–66, 73–79, 84–85).

The managerial coach began to dominate the popular sport of football as the game developed a rich narrative structure that appealed to journalists and fans on both the high school and college levels. College football crowds swelled, with as many as forty thousand fans at games. But the sport was suffering from an epidemic of serious injuries. There was little protective gear. An 1894 photo shows football players at Chicago's Englewood High School lined up in a wedge formation in uniforms but without helmets or pads. In 1904, eighteen football players—most of them prep players—died. Scores more suffered serious injuries, including fractured skulls. Editorialists decried football as an abomination unworthy of a civil society. Teddy Roosevelt's son broke his nose playing the game, leading the president to convene a 1905 summit of football authorities tasked with reforming the game. Mass formations were prohibited and a neutral zone was established, but reservations about the safety of football persisted. Only in a few historical instances have specific sports been eliminated from the extracurriculum as a consequence of unreasonable risks, but one of those occurred in New York City in 1909, when tackle football was abolished in response to continuing unease about injuries and the misappropriation of school funds. Local officials reversed course the next year, allowing football with revised rules (Gutowski 1988, 64; Ripley 2013a; Almond 2014a, 10–13). Despite periodic reforms over the following century, serious injuries, including concussions, have continued to plague tackle football (see chapter 10).

Safety issues along with other concerns precipitated the 1906 formation of what became the National Collegiate Athletic Association to govern the college game. The public education establishment, for its part, had been forming conferences and associations to govern interscholastic athletics. Establishment of state high school associations cemented control of interscholastic sports by school authorities. Wisconsin claims to have formed the first state high school athletic association in 1895. The Indiana High School Athletic Association was founded in 1903 and conducted its first state high school basketball tournament eight years later. Other states followed. In the early 1920s, the National Federation of State High School Associations (NFHS) was established to coordinate state efforts (Pruter 2013, 81, 195; Humphrey 2002, 1) (see chapter 3).

By the 1920s, athletics were institutionalized in school districts across the country. During this prosperous decade, high schools began offering more sports and facilitating more expansive competition, including state championships. Some universities sponsored tournaments for high school students, and the number of participants grew. Most high schools sponsored the popular team sports plus a number of "minor sports"—golf, wrestling, gymnastics, swimming, and tennis. Seasons expanded; some high school football teams were playing nine or ten games during the school year. Newspapers reported on high school games. Professional (paid) coaches became the norm, although some had no official connection to the schools where they coached and not all were college graduates (Miracle and Rees 1994, 60–61; Humphrey 2002, 2; Pruter 2013, 173–76, 178, 190, 312).

Military academies, prep schools, and parochial Catholic schools began to model their sports programs on those of the public high schools, sponsoring leagues, meets, and tournaments. These schools had no district boundaries and could recruit top athletes. Rowing was a popular sport in the private prep schools, as was golf. Schools for African Americans in both the North and South created their own system of interscholastic sports based on the majority model. The system was separate but seldom equal, and American sports remained racially segregated until after World War II (Pruter 2013, 218–19, 290–91).

The main focus of interscholastic athletics was boys' programs. In the 1920s, opposition to sports for girls came largely from women physical educators, who had concerns about elitism and commercialization. Many of these teachers felt that young women were being exploited by the public nature of competition, playing before spectators and controlled by male coaches. High schools formed girls' athletic associations that focused on intramural competition in basketball, volleyball, indoor baseball, and tennis. Girls' basketball teams with six members and distinct rules date from the 1920s. Although some high schools provided interscholastic sports competition for girls during that decade, many girls' programs disappeared during the 1930s as funding dried up during the Great Depression (1929–39) (Humphrey 2002, 2; Pruter 2013, 169, 198, 244–46, 272).

As the number of state high school athletic associations increased in the 1920s, the NFHS assumed a greater role in school sports. The federation instituted a reformist agenda under secretary Charles Whitten, opposing national high school tournaments such as the University of Chicago's National Interscholastic Basketball Tournament. In 1925, the National Association of Secondary School Principals went on record as opposing interstate contests. The principals noted that travel to these events kept student-athletes out of class for days at a time. In 1927, the NFHS identified several troubling issues in high school athletics: commercialism, undue pressure to win, eligibility rules violations, neglected academics, exploitation of the athletes by the press and public, lack of sportsmanship, and overloaded schedules. Coaches were being dismissed for failing to win. Individual high school principals appeared to have little power to control these problems (Pruter 2013, 292, 295–96).

The prominent Carnegie Foundation Report on American College Athletics (1929) also looked at high school athletics. It criticized communities that "commercialized" interscholastic sports, in turn bringing about other evils that ignored student-athletes' well-being. The report also criticized postseason tournaments that diverted students' time and interests from academics. In response to growing criticism, some states, including California, abolished state championship tournaments, but other states resisted, in part because state athletic associations had been established in part to conduct state tournaments. University-sponsored state high school tournaments were cut back (Pruter 2013, 302–7).

By terminating collegiate sponsorship of interscholastic sports, the state associations reined in the expansion and commercialism of high school sports. The reforms entailed terminating national championships, curbing long trips, and reducing the exploitation of high school athletes by interests outside of the educational system. Yet the reforms had only limited scope. Most of the revenue for sports was generated by ticket sales, which motivated schools to promote winning teams with spectator appeal. The Great Depression put a hold on extracurricular activities, including interscholastic sports. Beginning in the mid-1930s, however, the New Deal's Works Progress Administration furnished thousands of high schools with field houses, stadiums, and other athletic facilities. The current system of governance of school sports was pretty much in place by the late 1930s (Pruter 2013, 310, 312–16, 326).

The postwar prosperity of the 1950s led many high schools to expand the number of interscholastic sports. But school sports began to suffer in the inner cities as migration of residents to the suburbs reduced the tax base. In communities beyond the major metropolitan areas, the bonds between town residents and their high school athletic teams represented a powerful cultural force that was accentuated as some small colleges dropped football and semiprofessional town teams disappeared. To local sports fans, the high school team represented their community, a devotion that often led to excesses (Pruter 2013, 313–17) (see chapter 4).

By this era, high schools in several states in the South and Midwest began offering interscholastic sports for girls. Young women had been competing in sports since the turn of the twentieth century. Women's field hockey, for example, was introduced in 1901 and had become popular in eastern schools during the 1920s, the same time that Iowa became known for its girls' basketball teams. However, girls' involvement in competitive sports was not widespread and remained controversial through the first half of the century. Some women educators argued against interscholastic sports for girls on the grounds that highly competitive, male-controlled programs were exploitative and promoted "masculinization." For example, women basketball players in leagues organized by men wore short-sleeved jerseys and high-cut satin pants, and the era's male journalists often sensationalized women athletes and downplayed their performance and sportsmanship. Some women educators argued instead for "female-controlled, moderate" sports. Nevertheless, those on both sides of the issue accepted that young women should participate in sports; they merely disagreed about the particular sports and level of competition that were suitable for women (Kahn 1991, 55–56, 64–65, 97; Overman and Sagert 2012, xviii).

The debate over intramural versus interscholastic girls' basketball persisted through the 1940s. Some states banned basketball tournaments for high school girls or instituted modified rules for girls' teams. Girls' sports continued on a limited basis after World War II in a sexist climate that linked "mannish" athleticism to lesbianism. Sports journalists often referred to women athletes as "Amazons," implying that they were unattractive and failed heterosexuals. Women athletes' attempts to assert their femininity—for example, by wearing hair ribbons while playing, did little to diminish the stigma attached to sports (Kahn 1991, 83–87, 164–65, 173–78, 184).

The situation finally began to change substantially with the emergence of the feminist movement in the late 1960s and 1970s and with the passage of Title IX of the Education Amendments of 1972. This legislation was revolutionary, requiring that girls and women receive equal treatment from all educational agencies that receive funding from the US Department of Education. In practice, that meant all colleges and universities as well as 16,500 local school districts, and it applied to sports programs: athletics for girls must be accorded an equal status with athletics for boys (Royals 2015, A4). "Equal status" would not be defined solely by the number of teams or sports; rather, the primary focus would be on equivalent levels of financial support and total participation rates.

Title IX required school administrators to increase funding for girls' sports, and the only way to do so often was by cutting boys' programs, provoking a backlash from the male athletic establishment. Nevertheless, the number of women and girls competing in sports doubled over the 1970s, and they began participating wrestling, ice hockey, tackle football, and other sports that previously had been considered exclusively male domains (Overman and Sagert 2012, xxiv).

In the nearly five decades since the passage of Title IX, the imbalance between boys' and girls' opportunities to play sports has diminished significantly, and girls now comprise about 40 percent of interscholastic athletes (Pusch 2014, 318, 323). Though the arguments against Title IX have been aggressive, persistent, and creative, they have very rarely been successful.

Thus, the existing program of competitive sports sponsored by secondary schools reflects tradition and popularity rather than a systematic assessment of their appropriateness for adolescents (Almond 2014a, 10–11). At the same time, school administrators' support for and subsequent takeover of student sports was based on the belief that athletics are educational. Interscholastic sports have been viewed as a means to build character, promote citizenship, and lessen juvenile delinquency as well as improve health. Early reformers sought to make public education available to all youth and to instill recent immigrants with the American ethic. Sports played a major role in this effort. Educators praised interscholastic sports for promoting school spirit and recognized that sports could be a social control mechanism (Pruter 2013, 45, 57, 59). In short, interscholastic sports were justified on didactic grounds.

But high school sports' positive values were derailed as they evolved. Bruce Svare (2004, 27), director of the National Institute for Sports Reform, comments, "With the advent of extensive playing schedules requiring significant travel, and the creation of elaborate state playoffs that are lucrative money-making endeavors for revenue sports like football and basketball, interscholastic sports lost their original purpose long ago."

An International Comparison

The United States is one of very few developed nations where athletics are intimately intertwined with the education system. Only Canada and Japan have brought competitive sports into their high schools in any way that emulates interscholastic sports in this nation (NASBE 2004). The United Kingdom is one of the few European countries that offers sports as an extracurricular activity. In Poland, schools harbor sports *clubs*. Youth sports in most developed nations exist in the form of independent clubs separate from the schools. As might be expected, the United States and Canada have far fewer such clubs.

Sports are central to the culture of American schools to a degree that is absent in other nations. Exchange students who come to the United States observe that American students place a higher priority on sports and spend more time competing in sports than do students in other countries. Students from abroad generally report that their schools offer no similar sports programs; instead, students play games on their own after school or with community-based clubs. There is no confusion about what the schools should focus on. In most countries, high school sports are taken less seriously than club sports, which means no "student-athlete" pretense, no cheerleaders, no pep rallies, and no shrines in schools devoted to the cult of athletic prowess. Typically, teachers in other nations don't serve as coaches except on community teams (Conn 2012; Ripley 2013b, 118–19, 145).

Parents in European, Asian, and South Pacific countries believe in the values of sports participation just as much as North American parents do and enroll children in community-based, state-funded sports programs to gain experience in fair competition, learn teamwork, and motivate them to achieve. Europe's sports clubs tend toward more intramural-like prep sports. The athletes do much of the organizational activity themselves. What Americans label varsity competition (i.e., an elite team representing a school) is afforded far less importance. Athletic scholarships are virtually unheard of, and talented athletes try to attract the attention of professional sports clubs, not universities (NASBE 2004; Loh 2011; Heinemann 1999, 317).

While school sports are deemphasized in Europe, sports clubs maintain relationships with a number of community organizations, including educational institutions. Scottish sports clubs often have connections to secondary and/or primary schools. Some 40 percent of German sports clubs have relationships with schools. In Flanders, Belgium, community schools are encouraged to collaborate with various local child-welfare organizations, among them sports clubs (Wicker et al. 2013, 34–38, 40–41).

In contrast, the relationships between American schools and sports clubs, which tend to be private and elitist, are often contentious (see chapter 4). In Europe, the term *club sports* generally means something quite different. With the exception of in high-level clubs, European organizations are less exclusive. Organized by age group, they focus on providing competitive activities for large numbers of young people as well as more leisurely, unstructured recreation for adults (Heinemann 1999, 323, 325; Loh 2011). European sports clubs have received a fair amount of public-sector support. Governments have a long tradition of providing sports facilities and subsidies to nonprofit clubs. Typically, support of voluntary sports clubs is mainly a responsibility of local municipalities. German municipalities (as well as the sixteen state governments and the federal government) provide financial support for the voluntary sports sector (Wicker et al. 2013, 33–34). In a country with eighty thousand sports clubs available to the public for a nominal fee, Germans of all ages can easily join clubs and compete in a variety of sports. Parents who are unemployed can get support for the annual fees for their children. Once in the club system, German children progress through the ranks, playing for teams in different age categories until turning eighteen. Beyond that, most clubs offer teams for all adults. Roughly twenty-four million of Germany's eighty million people are registered with the club system. In Denmark, half of adults and eight out of ten children are active in leisure sports, and about two-thirds of Danish children participate in sports clubs. Likewise, about two-thirds of Finns are involved in sports clubs (Heinemann 1999, 329, 332–33; Loh 2011).

Poland's sports club system is integrated into the school system, which distinguishes between student sports clubs and school sports clubs. Competitive sports is the function of *student* sports clubs and can lead young people toward professional sports careers. Recreational forms of sports activity is the purpose of *school* sports clubs. Their basic task is to promote youth health and fitness. Students can be members of both types of clubs. Schools sponsor clubs in a dozen or more sports, including track and field, soccer, basketball, and racquet sports. Student or school clubs typically have between fifty and ninety members, though they can top one hundred, and participation is equally divided between boys and girls. Students interested in athletics also can make use of community sports facilities during certain hours (Jaczynowski, Smolen, and Wiater 2012, 27–31).

Polish teachers play an important role in both types of sports clubs in the context of physical education. A good deal of cooperation takes place between teachers and clubs. Instructors conduct extracurricular activities, help organize sports events and camps, and coordinate training activities while preventing overlap of school and club activities (Jaczynowski, Smolen, and Wiater 2012, 29–31).

Student sports clubs and school sports clubs in Poland receive funds from various sources. Student clubs receive support from town, district, or county (*powiat*) authorities; sponsors; school headmasters; sports federations; parents; and donors. The school sports clubs support themselves with donations and membership fees. The basic costs of club activity include the purchase of sports equipment, travel to competitions, compensation for coaches and instructors, and bookkeeping expenses. Competitive student sports clubs also have costs associated with organizing camps and payments for athletes' licenses. In some districts, sports equipment used by students is the joint property of the schools and the clubs. Equipment used by students may be purchased out of the clubs' own funds, funds from municipal councils, or from sports unions (Jaczynowski, Smolen, and Wiater 2012, 31–32).

Of all European countries, the sports system in the United Kingdom is perhaps most like the American model, with schools offering varsity sports. But although British high schools have sports programs, they are overshadowed by club sports. The typical British school might schedule one soccer game a month. Whereas British adolescents who play on sports clubs train during the week and travel to competitive events on weekends, similar to American school athletes, British sports clubs appear to emphasize camaraderie and social activities despite the opportunities for serious competition (Loh 2011; B. Cook 2012).

Highly talented British teenage athletes can sign contracts with sports clubs and pledge their services to one club exclusively in exchange for a stipend and boarding. The club is bound to provide some sort of education to the athlete through an agreement with a vocational school or high school. When promising athletes graduate, the club may offer them two-year playing contracts; when the contracts expire, those who have not done well enough to continue playing professionally often go back to school or pick up a trade. Professional teams in Europe sponsor their own feeder systems and programs rather than relying on schools. This eliminates the controversy about whether to call sports participants "student-athletes" or "athlete-students." They are students *and* athletes. There's nothing to suggest that athletics programs must be part of an educational institution for young people to learn valuable lessons from sports (Loh 2011; Gerdy 2006, 69, 72).

Sports clubs are found in other developed nations beyond Europe. Australian club sports work outside the educational system and function well at multiple levels from recreational to elite. Unlike the United States, where school sports provide opportunities only for the talented few, the opportunities for participation are equal across skill levels. Both Australia and New Zealand have a much higher proportion of individuals participating in sports (Gatz, Messner, and Ball-Rokeach 2002, 50; Svare 2004, 54).

The sports club model is not without its problems. Not all nations provide an egalitarian environment for sports participation. In some European countries, privately owned facilities dominate, and commercial influence has expanded. Of course, this phenomenon is even more evident in the United States, driven by a dominant market economy. Both continents have sports clubs that operate as business enterprises and sell their services in the marketplace. These clubs have adopted a more professional, bureaucratic form in which staffers often freeze athletes out of the decision-making process. This emerging model stands in contrast to traditional, voluntary sports clubs (Heinemann 1999, 319–22).

Both Belgium and Germany have issues regarding the availability of sports facilities. German clubs are experiencing problems related to the condition of facilities as well as to finances. In Flanders, sports clubs are having problems with recruiting and retaining coaches. Many of these problems are tied to the Flemish clubs' relationships with local schools. Sports club participation has also been influenced by the tendency of European adolescents to choose to participate in sports outside the organized club structure (Wicker et al. 2013, 39; Heinemann 1999, 323). An increasing number of youth are spurning formal sports clubs and teams in favor of rollerblading and skateboarding activities, a phenomenon that has also gained ground in the United States (Honea 2004, 16)

As this brief review shows, the United States tends to be exceptional in terms of youth sports. Secondary schools have assumed responsibility for providing sports programs for adolescents and preadolescents with a focus on developing elite athletes (Gerdy 2014, 196). It is clearly desirable for all students to participate in sports and physical recreation. Some of the responsibility for these programs might be shifted to community sponsors, similar to the European club sports system (Gerdy 2000, 135). Indeed, through most of US history, the country has had both public and private agencies of this type, including the YMCA and city recreation departments. Such community-based sports clubs could make arrangements with schools as needed, as occurs in some European nations.

Peter Baldwin (2011) argues that despite widespread attempts to contrast the American way of life and the European social model—what has been labeled "American exceptionalism"—the two peoples are actually quite similar on a wide number of social and economic indexes. There is no reason that the United States couldn't modify its youth sports programs to incorporate the positive features of the European model.

❖ ❖ ❖

Americans should implement a "back to the future" strategy to reform school sports by returning more control to students—with appropriate adult supervision and the provision of adequate school resources to ensure success. I label this approach the *intramural/sports club model*. Elite, highly competitive sports for talented athletes should be ceded to private or community-sponsored sports clubs. School clubs and teams should focus on healthy and enjoyable recreation, with competitive tendencies kept in check. The British system provides one model.

Community resistance to shifting sports programs from interscholastic teams to European-type private clubs would likely be deep and powerful. The passion for school sports is typically driven as much by community pride as by school pride (see chapter 4). In actuality, the shift would simply mean that the school's name on athletes' jerseys would be replaced by the name of the town (Gerdy 2006, 73). School boards and administrators should convince local sports fans and parents of athletes that this approach will benefit schools and the students, and the remainder of this book provides a guide for doing so.

THE PROBLEMS WITH GOVERNANCE, FUNDING, AND PROFESSIONAL COACHES

> Management is doing things right; leadership is doing the right things.
> —Peter F. Drucker

The previous chapter leaves the impression that school sports "grow'd like Topsy," to borrow an expression from Harriet Beecher Stowe's classic, *Uncle Tom's Cabin*. There was no top-down plan of governance; sports competition proliferated from the grassroots level. The initial system of student managers didn't survive for long before school officials stepped in and assumed control. Schools quickly realized that a district- or citywide governing structure was necessary to coordinate games and tournaments. The position of athletic director was added to the education bureaucracy. Soon, state athletic associations were being formed to expand competition to that level. College athletics had created a national governing association, and in 1920 the National Federation of High School Associations (NFHS) was established to coordinate rules for high school sports, and the organization now has more than eighteen thousand members (NFHS.org).

Interscholastic sports continue to be governed by volunteer membership associations at the national and state levels. These organizations supplement and complement control by local school boards and school administrators. This governance model functions with mixed effectiveness, as national and state associations seem to do a better job of promoting sports than stemming the abuses or acting in the best interest of athletes.

The Indianapolis-based NFHS determines the rules for sixteen sports for both sexes at the high school level. The federation publishes casebooks, officials' manuals, and handbooks, but its role in interscholastic sports reaches beyond regulation. It conducts national meetings, sanctions interstate events, offers online services, sponsors professional organizations for coaches and officials, provides training, and serves as an information resource. The federation has compiled annual participation surveys since 1971. All fifty states and the District of Columbia have athletic/activity associations within the eight NFHS regional sections. (In states that have associations for both public and private schools, only the public schools are full NFHS members.)

State associations play a significant role in governing interscholastic sports. The members of these associations typically are district superintendents, school principals, athletic directors, and other officials who represent the interests of interscholastic sports. The associations are supposed to formulate rules and regulations for the well-being and protection of athletes in member schools—for example, limiting contests, providing insurance, and approving game officials. State associations produce publications and support materials that include rule books covering the sanctioned school sports (Humphrey 2002, 2; Kralovec 2003, 76).

Texas's state association, the University Interscholastic League (UIL), is typical in some ways and unique in others. The UIL (http://www.uiltexas.org) is headquartered in Austin and operates under the auspices of the University of Texas. This NFHS-affiliated body oversees sixty-four extracurricular activities in the state's public schools, some of which it has been regulating since 1920. The UIL has a twenty-eight-member legislative council. Football is the most popular sport, with eleven hundred high schools fielding teams (some of which play six-man football). Under UIL oversight, teams compete in six divisions based on school size. Each division has its own championship playoffs.

State associations vary in their approaches to governing athletics, and some associations are more progressive than others. The Michigan High School Athletic Association (MHSAA; https://www.mhsaa.com/) has established policies with the intent of blunting the impact of commercialism and professionalism. The MHSAA maintains a mileage limitation for interstate competition for school teams—a policy once common to all states and enforced through the NFHS's sanctioning program. (Several other state associations limit the distance, frequency, and/or duration of member schools' travel for interstate competition.) In addition, the Michigan association opposes all-star competitions and national championships and urges its member schools, their personnel, and booster clubs to have no involvement in such events (Jack Roberts 2007, 281–82).

Michigan schools have enforced limits on coaches' compensation. The state policy reads: "Neither faculty nor nonfaculty coaches may receive compensation for interscholastic coaching duties except through the school, and such compensation shall not exceed predetermined payments and limitations which are commensurate with compensation to classroom teachers' schedules for supplementary assignments" (Jack Roberts 2007, 281). Michigan schools also restrict live telecasts of regular-season contests, primarily to protect gate receipts for member schools.

Professional associations' function in governing interscholastic athletics is complemented by the role of laypeople, such as members of school boards. The concept of local, lay control of education lies at the heart of the American public school system, with elected and/or appointed officials determining the goals of local schools and the policies for achieving those goals. Local governing boards delegate to professional staff the responsibilities for implementing these policies (Sell 2006, 84).

The United States has about fifteen thousand school districts, each of which represents and is directly accountable to the area's citizens. School boards are typically made up of five to seven members who meet periodically to discuss various issues. Boards hire a superintendent—a professional manager akin to the chief executive officer in a corporation—and then focus on policy. School principals and other administrators carry out daily managerial tasks (Sell 2006, 72–73).

School boards have a long and daunting list of responsibilities, so it is not surprising that despite the training provided by school board associations, some boards fail to consistently produce positive results. Boards may be composed of inexperienced people who can hinder capable and knowledgeable administrators, and many issues are politically charged. Citizens' partisan demands get in the way of providing quality education. The school board is the community's education watchdog, with direct oversight of tax revenues and a crucial role in determining how this money is allocated (Sell 2006, 74–75). An important question in the present context is whether local boards are doing their jobs in regard to governing interscholastic athletics.

The superintendent is the chief administrative officer appointed by the local school board. The building principal is the professional leader of a school and as such is directly responsible to the superintendent for its successful operation. Principals manage the day-to-day activities of schools, overseeing faculty and staff and making decisions that impact overall educational success. The principal also assumes the role of school spokesperson in relation to the general public and news media as well as transmits information about the school at school board meetings. Principals oversee sports and extracurricular activities sponsored by their schools. This role involves monitoring those in attendance and addressing any problems. Principals in large schools often delegate direct responsibility for the interscholastic sports program to an athletic director.

The athletic director manages and oversees the school's interscholastic sports. (Directors may supervise sports for an entire school district, and in other cases, middle schools have athletic directors.) The high school athletic director's duties include making sure all athletes are academically and otherwise eligible; scheduling games/matches/tournaments; marketing and budgeting; hiring and evaluating coaches; dealing with conflicts between coaches, athletes, and parents; and event management. ADs spend much of their time managing sports events (Kalahar 2011). However, budget constraints are shifting this focus. A school athletic director in South Carolina commented, "I find myself studying marketing and business plans as much as I do game planning" (Drape 2006). The bottom line is that ADs must help their coaches win games to fill stadiums to generate revenue to pay for the expenses of the athletics program (Gerdy 2002, 82).

According to a 2005 survey by the National Interscholastic Athletic Administrators Association, almost half of athletic directors had additional duties, especially in smaller high schools. Most commonly, budget constraints mean that the AD also serves as an assistant principal. Some athletic directors are assigned teaching duties. Consequently, the workload can be demanding, and athletic directors have a high turnover rate. Much of their effort goes unappreciated by the local community. The head football or basketball coach rather than the principal or AD is often the most visible representative of a high school (Gerdy 2002, 94; Kalahar 2011).

Regardless of visibility, the various school administrators play a crucial role in managing interscholastic sports. They bear the unenviable burden of delivering a quality product (i.e., winning teams) while trying to protect student-athletes and appeasing the parents and rabid sports fans. Rarely do educators, student-athletes, and their parents share a philosophy of purpose for high school sports; rather, they have differing expectations (Tufte 2012, 22, 27). Administrators must take a hands-on role in controlling the excesses of interscholastic sports, while superintendents and school boards are forced to deal with the variety of financial, political, and other matters that are more pressing.

School principals rely on the expertise of athletic directors and head coaches to defend interscholastic sports. Most principals tenaciously cling to the notion that interscholastic athletics are beneficial for the school and its students. However, school sports can be counterproductive to the educational mission. The few principals who question the benefits of interscholastic sports don't want to be the first in their district to deemphasize or modify these programs. What's the solution? Carnovale (2012, 51) proposes that every high school should have an athletic board made up of teachers, coaches, and administrators to oversee programs and deal with problems. Clearly, it's a complex situation, and there are no simple answers.

One crucial area of governance that involves policy formulation, supervision, and administration across state and local levels and encompasses private as well as public sources of revenue is the funding of school sports programs.

Funding Sports: At What Cost?

While states provide almost half the funding for public schools, educational politics tend to be local. This is particularly true when it comes to funding school sports. Following the money will reveal the importance of interscholastic athletics to the local community, how available funds are spent, and the economic and educational costs (Gerdy 2014, 56–57).

Contentious discussions over school budgets are not uncommon. Budgets discussions at public meetings often bring out the worst in a community; expression of priorities usually flows in one direction, from taxpayers to school administrators. Special interests can splinter any consensus. Pressure for winning sports teams has led to a shift in budget priorities for secondary schools. Some school districts have prioritized the construction of a gymnasium or a football field over a laboratory or library. Communities rally around campaigns to build the best basketball gymnasium in Kentucky or the biggest football stadium in Texas (Pierce and Bussell 2011, 46, 58; Kralovec 2003, 3, 7). Frank Kovaleski, director of the Indiana-based National Interscholastic Athletic Administrators Association, sees much of the spending as driven by parents and sports fans who want what the neighboring community has (Wieberg 2004). Typical was a decision by the community of Minnetonka, Minnesota, to upgrade its football program to compete with powerful rival Eden Prairie, fifteen minutes to the south. The upgrade included an inflatable dome for the football field.

In Indiana, Lafayette Jefferson High School (the author's alma mater) drew up a privately financed, eight-million-dollar building project that delivered a six-thousand-seat football stadium complete with a high-end video scoreboard, plus a twenty-two-thousand-square-foot athletic complex that houses locker, weight, and training rooms. Fans could have their names inscribed on the weight room ($750,000), the football office ($30,000), or one of the lockers ($750). AD Maurice Denney, a 1965 alum, bragged, "We feel it will be the premier facility in the state of Indiana. People who come in go, 'Jeez, we're at Lafayette Jeff College'" (Wieberg 2004).

Under the current system for financing interscholastic sports, high schools model college and professional programs by operating major sports as revenue-generating businesses. In 2002, a Texas school district considered charging fifty dollars per season for seat licenses in its football stadium. The licenses would provide the buyer with the mere right to purchase season tickets (at additional cost) for a specific seat. Seat licenses are just one of several ways in which high schools are imitating college sports. In 2001, Vernon Hills High School in Illinois sold the naming rights to its new football stadium to a locally based paint manufacturer, creating Rust-Oleum Field (Walsh 2002). A recent national survey found that about one in twelve high schools offered naming rights as part of its sponsorship inventory (Pierce and Bussell 2011, 46, 58).

Public schools operate with a combination of external (publicly allocated) and internal (self-generated) funds. The most reliable source is the budgetary appropriation from general funds. But these monies may barely cover expenses, forcing schools to generate additional revenue. Public funding typically provides less than half the necessary financial support for interscholastic sports programs. A few high school athletic departments are self-sufficient, receiving little or no money from their school district offices, but they are the rare exceptions (Roan 2006).

As a rule, facility construction is financed through general obligation bonds (tied to local taxation) or through revenue bonds (secured through revenue generated by the facility). State appropriations and federal grants also are utilized to finance school facilities. In Texas and other states where a government guarantee prevents default, school bonds are generally an easy sell to the public. In the four elections preceding 2012 with bond initiatives on the ballot, voters in two-thirds of Texas's 174 districts approved borrowing a total of five billion dollars (Warbelow 2012). In Michigan, suburban Farmington Hills Harrison School District was heavily into the "better facilities by taxation" game in 2004, when voters approved a twenty-five-million-dollar bond issue to improve outdoor facilities at four middle schools and three high schools. Harrison High School would get new baseball and softball fields, synthetic turf for both its football stadium and practice fields, and a football complex with a state-of-the-art locker room and training room (Wieberg 2004).

State governments generally provide funding for public education through sales and income taxes. Locally, governments fund public schools primarily through property taxes. (Federal funds generally make up less than 10 percent of public school budgets.) Individual states have different income and sales tax levels (some have no income tax; five have no sales tax). Likewise, property taxes differ considerably across local school districts. In poorer neighborhoods, where property values are significantly lower, the revenue generated from this tax is substantially less than in wealthier areas. States commonly provide fewer resources to their high-poverty districts than their more affluent counterparts (although such inequities have been mitigated by court decisions) (Pusch 2014, 334). Funding inequities can affect interscholastic sports as well as academics.

School district funding remains the most important source of revenue for athletics but can be erratic. In 2006, on the eve of the financial crisis, more than a third of schools had experienced a decrease in the amount of funding received by their district school boards; about a fifth saw increased funding (Pierce and Bussell 2011, 46). Schools must contend with at least three factors that create difficulties in funding athletics: budget cuts from school districts, the importance placed on athletics by local communities, and Title IX compliance. Athletics administrators have to seek resources to equitably finance equipment, supplies, facilities, and coaches' salaries for women's programs. In 2009, the Florida High School Athletic Association ruled that to save money, the maximum number of sporting events for teams should be cut by 20 to 40 percent. It spared football and then decided to retain cheerleading after it was slapped with a gender-equity lawsuit (Palka 2009). When funds are inadequate, compliance with Title IX often leads to the cutting of men's programs so that an equitable number of women can participate in sports. In many instances, athletic directors literally have to beg their communities for funding to support programs (Hudson 2008).

When faced with steep declines in state funding and local tax revenues, school districts may have to eliminate sports or consider dramatic cuts despite the broad popularity of activities among parents and students. In a nationwide survey by the American Association of School Administrators, some 30 percent of school administrators said they were considering cuts to extracurricular activities for the 2008–9 school year amid the economic downturn. Schools also cut back the number of games and events to reduce travel and other expenses. Faced with budget cuts, Florida decided to reduce travel expenses and other costs of interscholastic sports but exempted football with a ten-game schedule because the sport allegedly drew enough to cover expenses (Cavanagh 2009).

Budget cuts have recently forced school districts from coast to coast to scale back on sports programs. But in most of these places, even modest cuts to athletics are viewed as temporary sacrifices, not as necessary adaptations to a new reality. In 2009, St. Lucie County District, Florida, with forty thousand students, made a 15 percent cut to its sports programs, financed at roughly two million dollars annually. The school system eliminated all middle school sports, replacing them with intramurals. In 2008–9, a California school district facing a three-million-dollar budget cut, considered eliminating all middle and high school sports programs, which cost about $250,000 annually, a proposal that roused opposition from many in the community. If the school budget is threatened, schools can use interscholastic sports to protect themselves from cutbacks by threatening to cut programs (Cavanagh 2009; Griffin 1998, 75).

Cutting sports is the most drastic response to decreased funding. Most school districts are able to maintain their sports programs through generated funds that supplement public allocations. The main source of generated funds for most secondary schools is gate receipts in the major sports. At Carroll Senior High School in Southlake, Texas, the number of fans willing to buy season tickets exceeded the number of prime seats available in the four-thousand-seat football stadium. About sixteen hundred of "green seats" in the center section were reserved for season-ticket holders, and the school maintained a waiting list for these seats. A school panel recommended that season ticket prices be increased from twelve to fifteen dollars per game (Walsh 2002).

Typically, football is the main cash cow. In the best of circumstances, it can help support other sports. Basketball is a minor revenue producer; in many cases, it takes care of itself. Nonrevenue sports such as golf, track and field, and wrestling are at the mercy of successful football programs for generated funds (Hudson 2008). In Gainesville, Florida, the high school football program funds about 75 percent of the system's athletic budget. Gainesville grossed $132,667 in game receipts at various sporting events in 2009, including: $19,000 from football season tickets, $64,000 from the football regular season, $39,000 from basketball, $7,000 from baseball, and $1,700 from soccer (Jordan 2009). Kentucky is the rare exception where basketball can generate significant revenue: the four-day Toyota Classic attracts high school basketball teams from other states and generates about sixty thousand dollars per year for the Scott County High School athletic department through sponsorships, gate receipts, concessions, and a silent auction (O'Brien 2012, 180).

Football can generate significant monies not only through gate receipts but also from connected fund-raising activities. Florida's Orange Park High School collected about $106,000 in revenue from football in 2008, including money from gate receipts, booster clubs, sponsorships, and donations. This money, along with other sports' ticket sales, goes into the school's athletic fund and helps cover a variety of costs. Money raised by players or their parents through fund-raisers usually stays with the team to cover extra items that might be needed (Palka 2009). Not surprisingly, more successful high school teams net more money. The Florida high schools that reach football championship games receive tens of thousands of dollars from the playoffs (Jordan 2009).

Some districts have turned to pay-to-play fees as a means of easing the budget crunch, although that strategy has provoked some backlash because it can create barriers to participation that disproportionately affect lower-income students. As participation fees have become more common, sports participation has declined, especially in the inner cities (Toporek 2011b; Colabianchi, Johnston, and O'Malley 2012, 4; Pruter 2013, 324–26).

With increasingly tight school budgets, athletic directors are becoming more creative about generating revenue. The actual task of fund-raising can be undertaken by ADs, coaches, students, and/or booster clubs. Fund-raising to support school sports can take the form of ongoing efforts such as game programs, concession stand sales, and the sale of sports paraphernalia, along with periodic events like car washes and raffles (Pierce and Bussell 2011, 47).

Booster clubs organized by the parents of students and local sports fans have been key community organizations. In 2006, more than half of secondary schools had experienced an increase in booster club funding, and it accounted for 10 percent of their athletic budgets (Pierce and Bussell 2011, 47). Winning teams in the major sports invigorate parent-run booster clubs, improving a club's ability to raise money. In Florida, Gainesville High School's booster club raised more than one hundred thousand dollars in 2008. The majority of the Gainesville Athletic Club's funds are related to football, and about 60 percent comes from ads in game programs. The club makes about thirty thousand dollars a year from concessions at all sporting events except football, which the band's booster club operates. The remainder of booster club funds come from membership fees, which range from fifty dollars to fifteen hundred dollars (Jordan 2009). Ballard High School in Louisville, Kentucky, uses money raised by booster clubs to support the construction and upkeep of the school's athletic facilities. Boosters paid for improvements of the football field and practice field. Ballard's baseball boosters have raised as much as sixty thousand dollars a year, the most of any booster group at the school. Softball boosters raised about twenty thousand dollars a year (Brady and Sylwester 2004).

School athletic departments are increasingly turning to less traditional sources for funding. In one survey, 57 percent of roughly 360 schools reported accepting corporate dollars to keep sports programs afloat. A spokesman for the NFHS acknowledged that more public school districts are seeking support for athletic programs from private businesses, though the association remains leery of this approach (Toporek 2011b; Gehring 2005b). The move toward corporate support appears to be growing across the country. The New York City public school system negotiated a two-year, five-hundred-thousand-dollar contract with the MSG Varsity Network, a cable channel dedicated to high school sports. During budget cutbacks, the Cleveland Browns and Cleveland Indians stepped in, donating a total of $550,000 to save athletics programs in the city's public schools from budget cuts that threatened to eliminate football and baseball (Gehring 2005b) (see chapter 9).

Another controversial source of athletic funding that is becoming more prevalent is participation fees. Given the rising costs of fielding interscholastic teams, along with the inadequacy of public allocations and the erratic nature of self-generated funds, many schools have been forced to institute a pay-to-play system, with fees ranging anywhere from twenty-five dollars to five hundred dollars for more expensive sports such as football (Wunsch and Jones 2012). During the recent financial recession, a number of schools adopted pay-to-play formats to save football. While this approach may help the schools' budgets, it causes some families to reevaluate how to invest in their child's athletic experiences (Van Milligan 2014, 41).

A recent survey found that about one-third of schools had instituted pay-to-play fees to maintain sports programs. This practice creates two tiers—students whose parents can afford the fees and those whose parents cannot—although some schools waive fees for students who can't afford them (Svare 2004, 101; Toporek 2012c). Most parents of athletes seem willing to pay sports fees and seem to worry more about the elimination of sports. School district officials, however, remain concerned about the impact of raising athletic fees on students from poor families. The schools that charge athletic fees tend to be larger, suburban schools with students from communities with higher family incomes (Cavanagh 2009).

The Loudoun County district in Northern Virginia was considering an athletic budget cut of some $12 million in fiscal 2010. The district, which had a current budget of about $745 million, planned to assess participation fees of $50 per student for each sport, with the possibility that the fees could rise depending on eventual budget decisions. In most cases, participation fees make a rather small contribution to the school athletic budget (Cavanagh 2009).

So where does all this money go? Interscholastic sports aren't cheap. School districts pay for equipment, field/court maintenance, transportation, coaches' salaries, officials' fees, insurance premiums, various medical considerations, and capital expenses (Toporek 2011b).

In 2001, the NFHS researched various school districts' budget information across the country and concluded that activity programs make up between 1 and 3 percent of the overall education budget in most school districts ("Case" 2001). During the 2004–5 school year, athletic programs in the state of Arkansas cost public school districts nearly $86 million, approximately 3 percent of overall per-pupil expenditures. In 2007, Chicago's overall public school budget was $4.6 billion, of which activity programs received $36.2 million (R. Ward 2008, 574).

One of the most significant costs that distinguishes interscholastic sports from most other activity programs is travel expenses. Colleges have always scheduled out-of-state contests, and the practice made its way to high schools in the early 1990s, when the NFHS and some state athletic associations relaxed limitations on travel mileage and interstate competition. A growing number of schools now participate in interstate tournaments, which have become larger and longer. The dramatic increase in interstate competition for high school teams has contributed to classroom absences of both student-athletes and teacher-coaches (Goldman 1991; Jack Roberts 2007, 280).

High school teams fly across the country for competition. The Beach Ball Classic, held in December in Myrtle Beach, South Carolina, features sixteen high school basketball teams from all over the United States. A Catholic high school team in Kentucky traveled to the Bahamas for a tournament (O'Brien 2012, 100–104, 110, 218). During the 2006–7 school year, the boys' basketball team from California's Lakewood Artesia High School played five games in six days during a tournament, including a game in North Carolina. In 2012, a prep school football team from Arkansas flew to California for a game. Two Florida public high schools flew their football teams to play in Texas. The trips often are paid for by boosters or by marketing firms that package these competitive events (Easterbrook 2013, 212). Such long-distance trips and whirlwind schedules can mean missed class time for athletes and can be detrimental to their health: said one former high school coach, "Arguably, playing ball in the driveway or the yard offers more benefits [to students] than traveling 500 miles for a three-day tournament" (Tufte 2012, 12). But traveling to high-profile tournaments can mean TV exposure and money for the school (Jack Roberts 2007, 279).

Interstate travel is no longer restricted solely to tournaments, with some teams routinely crossing state lines for games, sometimes via airplane Basketball teams in New Hampshire fly to Massachusetts's Nantucket Island to play games (Carnovale 2012, 19). Permian High School in Texas has spent seventy thousand dollars a year for chartered jets for the football team's travel (Bissinger 1990, 146–47). In the spacious western states, travel can be a formidable expense.

In 2012, schools averaged an estimated sixty-five thousand dollars a year for transportation for varsity and junior varsity sports teams—as much as half of the entire annual athletic budget for some smaller high schools (Wunsch and Jones 2012). When transportation costs account for a majority of the budget, the coffers often have little left to purchase uniforms and equipment or to properly pay game workers such as security personnel.

Coaching salaries constitute another significant portion of the athletics budget, whether the school is employing nonteaching coaches or paying stipends to classroom teachers. Schools normally provide coaching supplements for middle and high school coaches. In Florida, the Gainesville School District spent about $243,100 on coaching supplements at the high school for the 2008–9 school year. Some forty-seven teachers received stipends for time spent coaching high school and middle school sports. Florida's Hall County School System budgeted more than $1 million for a total of forty-three coaching supplements at six high schools. The head football coach's supplement equals 17 percent of his base teaching salary. A head baseball coach's supplement amounted to 8 percent of his base teaching salary. And in sports for which there are both girls' and boys' teams, coaches earned the same percentage in supplements regardless of gender (Jordan 2009). A significant number of Arkansas high school coaches don't teach any classes, yet their salaries come from school instruction budgets, and they make more money—up to thirty thousand dollars a year more, in some cases—than other teachers in their school districts who manage full academic schedules (Murphy 2008).

Steve Wieberg (2004) notes that by the first decade of the twenty-first century, a few high school coaches had begun earning more than one hundred thousand dollars a year. In Alabama, Hoover High School's head football coach had an official salary of ninety-three thousand dollars per year, took in between fifteen thousand and twenty-seven thousand dollars by running football summer camps on public school property, earned thirty-five hundred dollars from a local TV show, and received a new pickup truck from a car dealer every sixty thousand miles (Sailer 2007, 25–27).

Head football coaches in the southern states may be paid lucratively, but most coaching stipends offered to teachers amount to a few thousand dollars. While some schools can afford six-figure salaries for coaches in major sports, others struggle with budgetary constraints. In one school district, the AD reported having to make all assistant coaching positions at the high school level and all junior high coaches volunteer positions; each high school program also had to raise funds to pay its head coach (Winzelberg 2001; Vasco 2014).

The relative importance that schools place on athletics can be seen by comparing the salaries of coaches with those of noncoaching teachers. According to ESPN, Texas high school football coaches in Class 5A and 4A schools (with 950 or more students) were earning an average salary of $73,804, while the average salary for teachers in those same schools was around $42,400 (Shirley 2011). Such discrepancies aren't unusual in the American South, where football is king. In 2009, the average salary of seven head football coaches in Alabama's Baldwin County topped $70,000. Five years later, Alabama secondary school teachers' salaries averaged $50,000. In the Fort Worth, Texas, area, forty-six football coaches earned an average of $88,420 a year, while teachers in grades 7–12 were making $51,452 a year. The area's highest-paid coach made in excess of $114,000. In one Texas school district, which faced sweeping budget cuts in 2011, the four head football coaches made an average of $88,500 a year. Some Alabama high school football coaches' salaries are not subject to the state's open records law (Bean 2009).

School budgets are divided into an operating budget (daily activities) and a capital budget (onetime costs of building, improving, or repairing facilities). No interscholastic sport requires facilities as elaborate and costly as football—including stadiums, large locker rooms, practice fields, indoor training facilities, and weight rooms. One public high school built a six-million-dollar football training and locker facility (Easterbrook 2013, 183). But stadiums are the largest capital expense. A school district in the Pittsburgh area spent ten million dollars to renovate a stadium and build a thirteen-thousand-square-foot field house (Beem 2006). In 2004, the *Dallas Morning News* listed fifteen new or pending high school stadiums in the area with a combined price tag of $179.2 million. That same year, Georgia's Valdosta High School completed a $7.5 million facelift of its 10,300-seat stadium. The stadium upgrade—along with a new fine arts center for the high school and replacement of a local elementary school—was financed by a 1 percent sales tax earmarked for capital improvements in education (Wieberg 2004).

Texas school districts have raised millions from bond issues to build lavish football stadiums. Nearly one hundred high school stadiums opened in Texas between 2007 and 2012. In the East Texas district of Tatum, where federal standards classify almost 60 percent of students as economically disadvantaged, the school district has recently passed six bond issues totaling $73 million, including $16 million for sports facilities. The 4,600-seat stadium at the 464-student high school has a three-story press box, and the football team trains in an indoor facility with a seventy-yard practice field. By 2012, ten Texas high schools had stadiums with 16,000 or more seats, and more than five hundred had artificial turf fields (Warbelow 2012).

The stadium-building boom includes a penchant for fancy scoreboards and video systems costing as much as $750,000. School officials argue that revenue from scoreboard advertising eases the financial burden of football. One high school bought scoreboards comparable to those at second-tier football-playing colleges for its two stadiums (Wieberg 2004). Texas's Carthage High School Bulldogs play in a stadium upgraded in 2012 with a twelve-hundred-square-foot video scoreboard. The scoreboard, a stand-alone ballot item, won with 69 percent approval. The high school serves 750 students.

Allen High School's football team plays in Texas's most expensive stadium, a sixty-million-dollar facility with a high-tech scoreboard, Wi-Fi, and 18,000 seats. More than a hundred Texas high schools now have video scoreboards. At the same time, the Texas state legislature slashed $5.4 billion from the two-year budget for schools (Warbelow 2012).

These figures regarding operating budgets and capital expenses underscore the point that tackle football is far and away the most expensive high school sport. More students might be able to participate in school sports if the inordinate expenses of football were redistributed. The costs can be extravagant. In addition to capital expenses, school football teams have half a dozen or more coaches, all of whom typically receive stipends. Some high schools hire professional nonteaching coaches at full salaries. Reconditioning helmets, a service for which many teams pay every year, can cost more than $1,550, an amount that will increase as a result of new safety standards. The cost of medical supplies for a high school football team can top six thousand dollars each year. A team in Texas spent six thousand dollars on film processing during one season. Maintaining grass fields can run more than twenty thousand dollars a year (Bissinger 1990, 146; Ripley 2013a).

The cost of football equipment and uniforms delivers a major financial hit to a school's athletic budget. The average cost of outfitting a high football player in 2010 was around $500 and has subsequently increased. The most expensive items are helmets ($200) and shoulder pads ($150). New high-tech helmets purported to reduce concussion risk can cost up to $400. Pads have about a ten-year lifespan. With squads including fifty players or more, these expenses can exceed $25,000 each year. Some parents and coaches are advocating additional pads to protect players' thoraxes as a consequence of the emerging risks of life-threatening injuries to internal organs. The cost? Between ninety and one hundred dollars per player. Other team sports require far less expensive gear. It costs $250 to $300 to outfit each baseball player, a lesser amount for basketball players, and squads in these sports are significantly smaller. In swimming and some other sports, equipment and costs are minimal, as team members often purchase and retain their own suits and caps (Schmidle 2017, 41; R. Ryan 2010).

Much of the cost of interscholastic football results from the fact that games are staged as public entertainment. High school games involve up to a hundred players plus dozens of coaches, trainers, and equipment staff. They are played in pricey stadiums offering substantial amenities for thousands of fans, journalists, and radio and television crews. When games are televised, they require satellite uplinks, with vans and power-generation trucks (Easterbrook 2013, 268). Despite admission fees to games and money spent on concessions, game programs, and the like, the bottom line for most high school football programs is red (Palka 2009).

In Northeast Florida, football can bring in more than $100,000. At Fletcher High School in Neptune Beach, football ticket sales brought in around $90,000 in 2008, with program advertisements and donations netting another $15,700. The football program reportedly cost the school about $76,700, excluding coaches' pay and security. The district paid $33,856 for coaches' supplemental pay and some $10,768 in security costs. Schools routinely subsidize football expenses—for example, by paying transportation costs out of a field trip fund (Palka 2009). School officials may claim that football programs more than pay for themselves, but close analysis often finds unreported costs.

Most parents and taxpayers have little understanding of the real costs of school athletics, which can be distributed among different budget lines or buried in an undifferentiated total budget. Buried costs can include insurance, employee benefits, and debt service as well as transportation expenses. Insurance costs for athletics are usually meshed with the total insurance bill. There are buried costs for sports-related contractual services such as referees and team physicians. For home games, schools generally must hire officials, provide security, and clean up the venue. When teacher-coaches travel on school days, schools must hire substitute teachers to cover classes as well as pay for buses, meals and hotels the for players, the band, and the cheerleaders (Ripley 2013a,). The costs of maintaining gyms and fields as well as other operational expenses normally aren't specifically tied to athletic programs; when they are, athletics can account for as much as 10 percent of the school budget (Gerdy 2014, 137–38; Gerdy 2006, 30). Critics of spending charge that the full cost of school athletics is neither publicly disclosed nor fully analyzed, and in many school districts, sports expenditures are so entrenched that not even the people in charge realize the actual cost. Coaches administer their individual budgets, but administrators have oversight and must approve each expenditure. Athletic directors may have to manage as many as ten different budgets.

Interscholastic sports programs are eating up school budgets like never before, and little is being done to maintain the spirit of amateurism. There are inequities among major and minor sports and between curricular (academic) and extracurricular programs. As Ken Reed (2015, 97–98) points out, continuing to pour money into interscholastic athletics during a tight budget situation while cutting back physical education is the equivalent of offering the three Rs only for the intellectually gifted. While a disproportionate amount of money is being spent on interscholastic athletics, intramural sports remain a low priority (Gerdy 2002, 209). In truth, we have a costly system of interscholastic sports that benefits a distinct minority of students.

The athletics spending spiral comes at a time when education funding has been tightening. In Georgia, state legislators made $180 million in education cuts in the fiscal 2005 budget—and that was before the economic downturn. Valdosta's city school system saw $3.5 million in state funding reductions over three years, and its class sizes crept upward. The school district nonetheless budgeted $319,000 for football. By the time the team made it to the 5A state championship game, the school had spent a little more than $419,000 on the sport, not counting another $100,000 in booster-funded renovations to the weight room and a multimillion-dollar stadium project (Wieberg 2004).

One public high school in California spent seven times as much on its athletic programs as on textbooks. In some cases, high schools have eliminated teaching positions as a result of budget cuts but did not eliminate or reduce athletic programs. Meanwhile, taxpayers continue to support multi-million-dollar bond issues to finance new athletic facilities (Kralovec 2003, 68; Svare 2004, 102). In Arkansas, where a great deal of financial resources are devoted to interscholastic athletics, many of the state's schools are struggling academically and have dilapidated buildings. After allegations that some schools had funded athletics with money set aside for computer technology, the state board of education enacted new rules requiring school districts to submit annual reports on all publicly funded expenditures related to athletics (Murphy 2008).

Texas's obsession with high school football has had a deleterious effect on academics. School boards typically pay coaches more than other teachers even as coaches teach fewer classes. Some school districts paid six-figure stipends to coaches while cutting health benefits for teachers and reducing funding for textbooks (Wieberg 2004). Two weeks into one school year in the early 1990s, the Dallas Independent School District laid off 245 teachers—most of them secondary school teachers in core subjects and elementary school teachers. Administrators implemented a small reduction in the district's athletic budget, reducing the number of middle school coaches and equipment, but did not touch the budget for high school sports (Miracle and Rees 1994, 21, 167).

Texas ranks at the top among states in economic performance, yet its per-pupil expenditures ranked forty-ninth among the states in 2015 (alec.org). In 2013, the American Legislative Exchange Council awarded the state a D– in state academic standards and Ds in identifying and retaining exceptional teachers. On the overall question of whether its education policies provide high-quality educational options to all students, Texas received a C. The state's eighth-graders scored near the bottom on the National Assessment of Educational Progress scale equivalent scores in 2009. Budget decisions are but one factor that creates inequities in school academic programs, but lavish high school football expenditures clearly play a role (see chapter 6).

The basic policy question concerns whether the funding of interscholastic athletics represents a wise use of taxpayers' money. Varsity football programs are singularly expensive. The staffing of coaching positions across a dozen or more school sports constitutes a major line item in the operating budget. In 2009, one school district in Michigan with 16,500 students spent three million dollars on salaries and pensions for athletic coaches and staff (Gantert 2010). The current professional coaching model not only crimps school budgets but can cause additional problems.

Amanda Ripley (2013a) has described what occurred in the spring of 2012, when the State of Texas threatened to shut down Premont Independent School District for academic failure and financial mismanagement. To cut costs, the district had already laid off employees and closed the middle school campus, moving its classes to the high school building. The elementary school hadn't employed an art or a music teacher in years, and the high school had shut down its mold-infested science labs. Yet the high school still funded football, basketball, volleyball, track, tennis, cheerleading, and baseball teams. Football cost about $1,300 per player, while math cost $618 per student. For the price of one football season, the district could have hired a full-time elementary school teacher for an entire year. Despite the fact that the football team had won just one game the previous season and hadn't been to the playoffs in roughly a decade, no consideration was given to the option of eliminating the sport.

When the state threatened to shut down the district, the superintendent suspended all sports, including football, after realizing that doing so could save $150,000 in one year. A third of this amount was being paid to teachers as coaching stipends, while $27,000 went to athletic supplies, $15,000 to insurance, $13,000 to referees, and $12,000 to transportation. He explained his decision to the principal of the district's high school, emphasizing that eliminating sports would save money and refocus attention on academics. The principal agreed. The school made other changes as well: giving teachers more time for training and planning and aligning the curriculum with more-rigorous state standards (Ripley 2013a).

The first school year without football was quiet: "There were no Friday night games to look forward to, no players and their parents cheered onto the field on opening night, no cheerleaders making signs in the hallway, no football practice 10 or more hours a week" (Ripley 2013a, 73–74). Only the basketball team was allowed to complete its season, though its tournament schedule was diminished. More than a dozen student-athletes transferred, including four volleyball players and a football player. Most went to a school ten miles away where they could play sports. Two teachers who had been coaches also left. To boost morale, the high school principal began holding sports-free pep rallies every Friday. Classes competed against each other in drum-offs and team-building exercises in the school gym. There were additional upsides. Administrators commented that the fall semester was more peaceful, with additional energy devoted to planning and lessons and to after-school tutoring. Whereas just 50 percent of students had passed their classes the preceding fall, 80 percent did so in the absence of football. About 160 people attended parent-teacher night, up from 6 the year before. Through some combination of new leadership, the threat of closure, and a renewed emphasis on academics, Premont's culture changed.

Suspending sports proved a crucial part of the equation. The money not spent on athletics was used to give teachers raises, and communities across Texas raised four hundred thousand dollars to renovate the science labs. For the first time in many years, Premont had a healthy operating balance and no debt. During the following spring semester, the school brought back baseball, track, and tennis with the caveat that the teams could participate in just one travel tournament a season. The following fall, Premont reinstated the volleyball and cross-country teams, in addition to basketball, baseball, track, and tennis but not football. In May 2013, the state announced that the Premont Independent School District could stay open (Ripley 2013a).

The Professional Coach: Problems and Issues

According to the NFHS, about 750,000 men and women coach interscholastic sports in the United States (Pruter 2013). Though this phenomenon seems unremarkable to us, the American system of hiring school coaches is exceptional and results largely from the way interscholastic sports evolved (see chapter 2), with coaching becoming a parallel profession to teaching in the nation's secondary schools. More recently, a growing number of high schools have returned to the earlier practice of hiring coaches from outside the teaching ranks.

High school coaching became an attractive profession for male teachers and later for women. Many former school and college athletes become coaches to remain close to the sport they played. Successful coaches realize a sense of professional fulfillment and have the opportunity to impact the lives of young adults. Coaches serve as teachers, disciplinarians, counselors, leaders, and parent figures. How coaches choose to fulfill these roles shapes the experiences of student-athletes. Such mentors can be a positive influence on students (Butterfield and Brown 1991, 123–28), but negative consequences can also occur if passion turns to obsession or the pressure to win becomes all-consuming. High school coaches have been caricatured as "grown men devoting too much time and energy to sixteen- to eighteen-year-old students in an attempt to win contests against other sixteen- to eighteen-year-olds also coached by grown men who willingly sacrifice their social lives"—and frequently their ethics (Tufte 2012, ix).

Though most of the twentieth century, high school coaching remained a largely male domain. This pattern changed dramatically with the passage of Title IX legislation in 1972. Title IX increased sports opportunities for female students and created a parallel need for more coaches, opening up positions for women. The male coaching establishment initially offered strong resistance to Title IX, and women had to fight for their right to coach. When some schools had difficulty finding coaches to cover the increased number of teams, they revived the practice of hiring nonteachers off the street to staff coaching positions (Winzelberg 2001).

The teacher/coach remained the norm in secondary schools for some time. A survey in the mid-1990s found that a typical high school with eight hundred or more students had about a third of its faculty involved in coaching, although the numbers were lower for some schools and higher for a few others (Cotton 1996, 42–43). Over the following two decades, hiring coaches from outside the school staff became more pervasive. Fewer teachers may be willing to take on coaching assignments as a consequence of increased classroom responsibilities and imposed paperwork. Coaching requires long hours—sometimes thirty or more per week. Football coaches in Texas meet with team members at 6:45 a.m., before classes start, analyze Friday's game film until late in the night, and have four-hour meetings on Sunday afternoons (Levy 2015, 14, 129). Thus, in areas where teaching salaries are adequate, many teachers now pass up the extra money from coaching stipends. Among other reasons teachers cite for not wanting to coach, the most notable may be meddlesome parents trying to will their children to stardom on the playing fields (Winzelberg 2001).

Educators recognize that there are inherent teacher-coach conflicts: when teaching staff are hired as interscholastic coaches, the incentives and responsibilities of coaching can compromise classroom responsibilities. In truth, there are distinct problems associated both with classroom teachers coaching and with hiring nonteachers as coaches.

Traditionally, physical education teachers were the staff members most likely to coach interscholastic sports. As the number of teams increased, with multiple sports in season, physical educators could no longer fulfill all the coaching responsibilities. Male teachers from other disciplines, notably the social sciences, increasingly were recruited to fill coaching positions (Austell 2010, 2). As Ohio State history professor Steven Conn (2012) relates, "I do a magic trick on the first day of class whenever I teach a big introductory survey. I point to a student at random and predict: 'I can guess the first name of your high school history teacher.' Fingers on temples, brow furrowed, I announce: 'Coach.' I haven't been wrong yet."

For the most part, teachers have handled the dual responsibilities of the classroom and the athletic arena, but educators cite instances where classes have been compromised to accommodate coaching responsibilities. Physical educators have employed the cliché "throwing out the ball" to describe what goes on in gym classes taught by teacher-coaches with little interest in providing instruction. The author's high school physical education class was taught by the head basketball coach, who emptied a bag of basketballs onto the gym floor and then retired to his office during class. There are teachers who coach and coaches who teach—the ones called "coach" by students—primarily in high-profile sports such as football and basketball. Head coaches in these sports aren't hired for their classroom teaching ability; they're expected to win games, adjust their priorities accordingly, and are accommodated by sympathetic school administrators (Cotton 1996, 42–43).

Coaches commonly have their teaching responsibilities or schedules modified during semesters when they have coaching duties. Head football coaches who teach may be relieved of one or two classes. High school history teachers who coach major sports may finish all their teaching responsibilities before lunch. In Texas, some assistant football coaches teach only two classes, leaving them the entire afternoon to devote to coaching duties. Many schools schedule an "athletic period" that is considered part of the teaching load. Although Arkansas requires head football coaches to teach academic courses, one in eight didn't teach a single class during the 2007–8 school year, and even many of those who did teach didn't spend much of their day in the classroom (Kralovec 2003, 67; Levy 2015, 14, 94; Murphy 2008). According to Bissinger (1990, 148), before crucial games, Texas teachers who coached football often did not meet their classes; instead, the students watched movies.

Head coaches in the major sports are primarily responsible for orchestrating a public display for local sports fans and promoting a positive institutional image through these displays. Coaches recognize their other major responsibility as generating revenue by conducting winning programs. Male coaches commonly face more pressure than women coaches because their coaching performances are more visible in the community. While effective coaching performances are viewed as critical for job security, ineffective teaching may generate little feedback. Few parents complain about a coach's performance in the classroom. Predictably, teacher-coaches—in reality, coach-teachers—can experience cognitive dissonance and heightened tension when attempting to effectively fulfill the expressed expectations of both roles (Figone 1994; Austell 2010, 5).

Given the reality that teacher-coaches perceive and expressly receive mandates to produce winning teams, individuals occupying these dual positions inevitably seek to either minimize or eliminate inherent role conflicts. They may experience reduced trust among colleagues when unfavorable evaluations regarding their teaching are expressed, but they are seldom fired for their lack of academic repute or teaching effectiveness. Thus, professional survival requires that they devote a majority of their time and energy to coaching. Coaches often receive empathy from school principals when attempting to negotiate role conflict, and a disproportionate number of school administrators are former coaches (Foley 1990, 122; Figone 1994).

But support from sympathetic administrators goes only so far. High school principals, athletic directors, and school boards feel mounting pressure to make coaching changes when a team in a major sport doesn't win consistently. Capable coaches can have losing seasons, and mediocre coaches can win games with talented athletes, fans blame coaches for losing seasons. The result is that high school coaching tenures (like their college counterparts) are getting shorter. Typical is the case of a high school in Abilene, Texas, that fired the football coach after he compiled a 9–11 record over two seasons (Tufte 2012, 53; Buchanan 2006, 20). The sports pages of the nation's newspapers are replete with similar accounts of high school coaches losing their jobs when they fail to win consistently. Avid sports fans are not appeased by the reality that for every winning team, there must also be a losing team. Breaking even isn't good enough. Initial pressure to fire a coach usually comes from the community, and school administrators often capitulate to public sentiment.

The bottom line is that the coaching role is subject to more public scrutiny and pressure than the teaching role. The institutional redefinition of these roles and the resulting role conflicts directly affect students in general and student-athletes in particular. Some coaches regard academic requirements as little more than barriers to implementing their program. Under these conditions, athletes may be induced to take academic shortcuts. Coaches often side with athletes against their teachers regarding standards for achievement. When academically marginal student-athletes are enrolled in courses taught by colleagues not involved in coaching, the expectation is that the student-athlete's inadequate academic performance will be overlooked or at least evaluated in a more lenient manner. The student in question often isn't shielded from these conflicts (Figone 1994).

The hedging on academic eligibility can occasionally escalate to outright cheating, defined as altering the mutually agreed-upon conditions for playing a contest to favor one side. The metaphor of a level playing field suggests that the conditions for competition are fair and nominally equal for everyone, but despite the high-sounding rhetoric, sports competition rarely commences at a point of equality, and those involved in sports know it. Moreover, administrators, coaches, parents, and students routinely seek ways to manipulate variables to boost their side's chances, violating the principle of equality of chance beyond differences in skill and strategy but often viewing such practices merely as "getting a competitive edge." In some sports, illegal acts are accepted as part of the game, a phenomenon labeled "normative cheating" (Eitzen 1995). At lower levels of competition, such as sandlot games, cheating is less likely to occur because it destroys the goodwill and cooperation required to continue the game. In organized sports, with formally scheduled contests and a contractual obligation to compete, competitors may follow or break the rules according to their strategic self-interests, leading to widespread violations (Morgan 1994, 230).

Reports of cheating have become common in interscholastic sports. Journalist Matt Baker (2013) reported a series of scandals in Oklahoma. In the Jenks Public School District, a high school football coach allegedly "facilitated the living arrangements" between an recruited player and a team manager, while a booster attempted to pay players and the coach and became involved in the transfer of one player. At another Oklahoma high school, more than forty student-athletes in four sports, including at least seven starters on the football team, participated while ineligible for academic reasons, residency, or recruiting issues. A Tulsa football coach/athletic director and other school officials failed to conduct grade checks for five weeks and let a football player practice with the team even though he wasn't enrolled at the school. After the coach resigned, board members, school officials, and players said that they hoped he would return. Similar scandals have occurred across the country.

While undue pressure on coaches can compromise their teaching role and undermine the education of student-athletes, the hiring of outside coaches has created a parallel set of problems. Writing about Texas high school football, Gray Levy (2015, 281) asserts, "Nothing has caused more separation between education and athletics than the outsourcing of coaches away from professional educators." Historically, the primary identification for coaches as part of the educational community centered on the concept that coaches are teachers. But in many communities, the coach-as-educator model has "gone the way of the leather football helmet and the two-handed set shot" (Gerdy 2006, 211–12). A growing number of coaches are not classroom educators and may never have set foot in the classroom as a licensed teacher. Texas has taken the practice a step further: some high school football coaches are hired by booster clubs, meaning that principals have little control over these individuals (Easterbrook 2013, 230).

There's a clear trend toward high school coaches who are not employed as teachers. According to the New York State Athletic Association, with fewer teachers taking on coaching positions, the number of nonteacher coaches in the public schools went from virtually 0 to more than 20 percent during the last quarter of the twentieth century (Winzelberg 2001), a phenomenon that was repeated nationwide. Many of these coaches have little formal training or certification, and they are not integrated into the educational community in any meaningful way. The only school facilities these coaches occupy are the locker rooms and athletic fields, courts, or gyms. According to a 2005 survey, only 53 percent of the middle school and high school head coaches in one county in Pennsylvania were teachers. The NFHS estimated in 2014 that as many as half of the nation's high school coaches were not teachers (Gerdy 2002, 100, 2006, 40–41, 2014, 156).

School administrators have scrambled to find qualified individuals to coach and no longer limit searches to classrooms. Notices of available coaching positions are posted online, though in many cases little money is allocated for a comprehensive search. Larry Doyle, the former AD at Marina High School in California, said he would like to hang a "help wanted" sign in front of the school. One of the places school administrators are finding coaches is community sports leagues, but the staffing problems persist (Reilley 1991; Winzelberg 2001).

Classroom teachers are averse to taking on coaching responsibilities for a variety of reasons. Many teachers don't want to deal with the politics of high school coaching and feel that they have more control over the classroom than when coaching. Coaches have to answer to parents, boosters, and even players in addition to the superintendent, principal, and athletic director. Interscholastic sports teams have been plagued by increased pressure to win with less focus on fundamentals, fun, and sportsmanship. Parents want results in the arena and college scholarships for their children (Vasco 2014).

According to Bill Vasco (2014) teachers are inclined to bypass coaching for a variety of reasons. (1) Time commitment: winning requires enormous investments of time—practices sessions, film meetings, strength and speed workouts, attending camps and clinics, and summer sessions. (2) Red tape and additional commitments: coaching certifications, rules meetings, CPR/AED training, first aid training, background checks, booster club meetings, athletic council meetings, fund-raising events. (3) Public scrutiny: not only from parents but also from news and entertainment media; the proliferation of social media has intensified this scrutiny. (4) Low pay for assistant coaching positions and minor sports: when coaching pays only about two thousand dollars, teachers prefer to pursue other avenues for making extra income. (5) Increased classroom responsibilities: as the demands of teaching have grown, teachers are unwilling or unable to add any more commitments to their load.

External regulations facilitate the hiring of nonteachers to coach. A number of states don't require interscholastic coaches to have teaching certificates, leading to an increase in off-the-street coaches. The New York Board of Regents amended its regulations to remove the preference for certified teachers over nonteachers when hiring coaches. Nonteacher coaches can now earn a professional coaching certificate by taking certain educational, first aid, and CPR courses and by amassing three years' coaching experience in a specific sport in a state interschool athletic program (Winzelberg 2001).

Despite these concessions, some coaching positions have remained unfilled. Although dropping a sport because no coach can be found (as opposed to because of budget constraints) is unusual, it occurs and has become more common in the post–Title IX era. When Bay Shore High School in Suffolk County, New York, could not find a boys' gymnastics coach in 2000, the school's gymnasts could not compete as a team, though they could still enter meets as individuals (Winzelberg 2001).

Despite the growing difficulties in securing qualified coaches, most school administrators believe that having teachers coach school sports helps to maintain a healthy relationship between athletics and academics. Yet the primary influence—either positive or negative—that coaches exert on student-athletes comes not in the classroom but on the fields and courts. One study found that most college students interviewed about their high school sports experiences had problems with coaches (Garcia 2015, 121, 131). In fact, the most prevalent negative aspect of their high school sports participation was the problematic relationship with a coach. Nevertheless, students also described coaches in such positive terms as "helpful," "supportive," having a "good coaching style," and as good mentors or role models.

One student recalled, "My senior year coach ... made me absolutely hate the sport, he absolutely burnt me out.... We had a lot of talent on our team ... but his coaching style and how he ran the team was miserable and made no sense. He would punish people for doing the right things, reverse psychology, but it didn't work. The whole team got pissed at each other." Problematic relationships with coaches resulted from a punitive coaching style, lack of competence, lack of interest in the students, favoritism, personality conflicts, and frequent coach turnover. This suggests that if high schools can provide coaches with better teaching and mentoring skills and techniques, students' athletic experiences will be more enjoyable and more valuable (Garcia 2015, 131–33) (see chapter 8).

We expect coaches to be positive role models, and indeed, impressionable young athletes are influenced by the demeanor of these adult mentors. Unfortunately, not all interscholastic coaches meet these expectations. Keith O'Brien (2012, 8) describes a Kentucky basketball coach at courtside during a closely fought game: "His face . . . burned red as he screamed at his boys in the final, frantic moments of the game. The veins in his neck were bulging as if pumping crude oil through his towering six-foot-four frame. And he wasn't merely sweating; [he] was drenched, and his damp hair was disheveled from all the times he had grabbed his face in horror." Moreover, "Cursing isn't uncommon in high school locker rooms and sideline huddles. Some coaches make a craft out of it, somehow turning obscenities into artistry" (44). In a pregame meeting, a Catholic high school basketball coach proclaims, "Boys, it's ass-kicking time" before leading his players in the Lord's Prayer (226).

High school coaches can be a key factor in provoking verbal intimidation, physical intimidation, and violence by athletes. Verbal aggression can be a precursor to physical aggression. Football coaches at one Texas high school showed their players a video in which former professional boxer and convicted felon Mike Tyson, known for biting off a piece of his opponent's ear during a championship bout, described his mind-set before fights: "Every punch I throw with bad intentions at a vital area" (Levy 2015, 236). Prior to a game against the Golden Eagles, a high school coach in Iowa spray painted a chicken gold and had his players stomp it to death in the locker room (Eitzen 1995).

After a San Antonio high school basketball game in which one player fractured an opponent's nose and gave him a concussion, the coach was overheard saying, "It's about time someone drew some blood" (J. Lee and Lee 2009, 101). In a high school locker room in Maryland, the football coach yelled, "I want someone hurt! I want some kid's mother crying in the stands because her son was carted off the field! Unless someone from that team is taken off injured in the second half, you will do punishment drills at 6 a.m. tomorrow!" The admonition was peppered with obscenities. The coach's exhortation resulted in two opposing players getting seriously hurt (Bercovici 2012).

Injuring opponents so badly that they can't continue to play has become a basic strategy in football and other contact sports. Los Angeles Rams defensive coordinator Gregg Williams instructed his players before one game, "Kill the head, the body will die!," a coded message to injure the opposing team's quarterback (Almond 2014a, 140–41). Awareness of such tactics carries down to the high school level, and not just in football. Basketball and ice hockey coaches have been known to employ physically intimidating players as "enforcers." A study of high school athletes found that one in sixteen injuries occurring in competition were related to illegal activity; lighter-weight athletes sustained a higher proportion of injuries during play ruled as illegal (Yard and Comstock 2011, 185).

Such incidents are not typical among high school coaches, but they illustrate how hypercompetitiveness—a term coined by German psychoanalyst Karen Horney in the 1930s to denote a very strong desire to compete and win as a means of enhancing a sense of self-worth—and the culture of violence have engulfed interscholastic athletics, notably the major school sports and specifically contact sports. The coaching profession is aware of the problems and has attempted to promote appropriate behaviors among coaches. The NFHS offers a fundamentals-of-interscholastic-coaching course that can be taken either online or in person to provide guidance about promoting a healthy and age-appropriate sports experience ("Case" 2001). The profession can claim its share of positive role models. As legendary basketball coach John Wooden said in 1966, "I'm an educator, and I try to teach decency through intercollegiate basketball. Virtue cannot be learned from a playbook or from chalk talks by the coach. It comes from example" (Jenkins 2014, 6).

The more insidious problem is the divorce between athletics and academics, often abetted by pressured coaches (see chapter 6). Schools would be well advised to find ways to make coaching attractive so that teachers are more willing to accept such assignments. School boards should consider implementing stricter oversight measures to govern coaches who are not members of the teaching staff. And administrators must ensure that coaches (and teachers) aren't allowed to compromise a student-athlete's education simply to maintain athletic eligibility. Short of implementing these correctives, concerned educators have every right to question the present system of professional coaching.

◆ ◆ ◆

Converting school sports to a locally managed intramural/sports club model would eliminate the need for the NFHS and much of the state-level school sports bureaucracy. Reconfigured state associations could assist in coordinating and facilitating competition as needed, while students themselves would determine their participation in particular activities. A school would have no obligation to field a team in any given sport. The rules for competing in traditional sports are established, and competitors could agree on playing by the existing rules or modify them. The officiating would be handled at the local level, with adult volunteers or students serving as officials. Tennis and similar sports would rely on students to practice sportsmanship and adhere to the rules without line judges or other officials. Athlete eligibility would be determined by participating schools. Area schools would form leagues or conferences as needed and coordinate game/meet schedules.

The traditional school athletic director would be replaced by an intramural sports director. High schools and middle schools would follow the college intramural model, staffing the program with student volunteers and thus providing them with valuable managerial experience. Modest stipends would be available for teachers who serve as intramural or club coaches. Vetted adult volunteers from the surrounding community could also fill these positions. Intramural teams and sports clubs could operate with either paid or amateur coaches. Hiking clubs and cycling clubs wouldn't need coaches but might need adult supervisors.

The operating budgets under the intramural/sports club model would be much more modest, motivating schools to get out of the sports entertainment business. Spectators wouldn't be encouraged to attend student sports events. Revenue from ticket sales would disappear, but very few high schools currently generate more in such revenue than they spend on sports. Departing from the interscholastic sports model would also result in huge savings on spectator accommodations, elaborate uniforms, costly equipment, referees, facility maintenance, and so on. Sports clubs would be free to initiate fundraising drives.

Shifting from tackle football to flag football, which requires minimal protective equipment, would result in significant savings. Some players might want to wear soft helmets; however, the game can be played without protective gear. Flag belts are a minor expense. For team sports played indoors or in temperate weather, athletes can be outfitted in pinnies (nylon pullover vests) with distinct colors distinguishing teams. School names on uniforms would be superfluous. Flag football games wouldn't require a team physician on call (although staff present should be trained in first aid protocol).

The retention of coaches would depend on meeting student-athletes' needs. Teacher-coaches' jobs wouldn't depend on winning seasons. School principals would no longer be burdened with complaints from community members about a team's record or their child's amount of playing time. All students could participate in activities, whether competitive or noncompetitive. No team or club would require more than one or two coaches, and teachers could coach more than one activity, schedules allowing. Coaches' meetings would be collectively attended and devoted to coordinating the overall program.

In short, the current problems with governance, finance, and coaching would be reduced significantly by adopting an intramural/sports club model—and students would benefit greatly from this modification.

4

HOW PARENTS, BOOSTERS, AND SPORTS FANS DRIVE THE AGENDA

> You will suffer humiliation when the sports team from my area defeats the sports team from your area.
> —*The Onion*

The cherished emblem of American education is local control. This model of governance is premised on the belief that those closest to the actual operation of schools are most knowledgeable about and invested in the welfare and success of the teachers and students. The actual management of public schools is by elected or appointed representatives serving on governing bodies—that is, school boards. Local control intersects with state and federal efforts to influence the structure and operation of academic programs in public schools. The nation's schools are influenced by policies emanating from all three levels of government.

The system of governing the nation's schools derives from the US Constitution, which doesn't explicitly mention education. The Tenth Amendment has been interpreted as delegating primary authority and control over the regulation and operation of public schools to the individual states. School governance varies from state to state, with some states exerting more direct control over public schools than others. Control of schools intersects with the concept of states' rights and incorporates feelings of skepticism directed at federally administered programs. In recent years, control of public schools has become a source of tension and conflict that are part of broader political and ideological schism and debate related to the federal government's role in citizens' lives.

Local control of schools offers several advantages but is also the source of many of the nation's problems relating to education. The one aspect of control that is imperative to most people is local management of school finance. While this system can be responsive to local needs and sensitive to fiscal resources, it has created problems as a consequence of inequitable funding. State control over school finance would lead to a more balanced distribution of resources by ameliorating the practice of financing schools largely through locally levied property taxes. Some educators argue that the federal government should assume more responsibility for the financing of public schools, as is the case in most developed nations with the top-performing students (Tucker 2013, 3, 45).

American education has been described as a system in which everyone has all the brakes and no one has any of the motors—the opposite of a system governed by a strong national ministry of education that has the power to set direction and goals, to decide on strategies, and to implement those strategies. This metaphor discounts the revved-up motor promoting interscholastic sports in many American communities, which can simultaneously apply the brakes to funding for academics (Tucker 2013, 13).

Most local school boards are composed of honest, responsible citizens who care about their community and the children in it, people who contribute time and energy in a spirit of community service. But some boards do not answer to this description. Some school board members lack college degrees or even high school diplomas. Some board members are clearly more interested in winning basketball or football teams than in students' test scores (Tucker 2013, 22–23). The historical development of interscholastic sports in secondary schools interfaces with the strong school-community bond in ways that can be functional or dysfunctional. The emphasis on sports can create pride in the schools as well as distort the fundamental purpose of schools.

Community has two meanings: a group of people living in the same place who interact, and the feelings of fellowship with others that result from sharing attitudes, interests, and goals. A sense of community doesn't rely on geographic proximity. Community can be based on shared identities among a group of individuals. It constitutes a sense of us, of who we are. Both meanings of *community* are relevant to a discussion of school-sponsored sports, which can provide for a shared social experience and shared identity (Hughson, Inglis, and Free 2005, 63–64). Gray Levy (2015, 54) observes that in Texas, "schools represent communities as well as provide education." Texas is not unique among the states in this regard.

High schools are the social center of many communities, with parents and alumni directly involved with school programs—and more often with sports than with other activities. Interscholastic sports are appreciated for more than their pure entertainment value. High school teams have come to represent a sense of pride that transfers to the surrounding community. Cheering for the team operates at the intersection of small-town local pride and national patriotism, promoting civic rituals and public spectacles. The national anthem is played at sporting events. Downtown parades are held on game day, and high school athletes are revered as local heroes. Sports constitute an important point of contact between the high school and the community (N. Adams and Bettis 2003, 15, 17; Austell 2010, 5).

School sports are a font of small-town partisanship: *If our team beats your team, then our school beats your school, and our community beats your community.* The entire district basks in the reflected glory of a winning team. Team sports such as football and basketball are the particular bearers of community prestige. Towns and cities across the nation feature signs and billboards celebrating the success of local high school teams (Miracle and Rees 1994, 157–58). A fan commends a successful Kentucky basketball coach, "The people of Scott County now smile a little bigger, stand a little taller, and *look* for people they can tell where they are from" (O'Brien 2012, 3–4). *Boosterism* commonly refers to the act of boosting or promoting community organizations with the goal of improving public perception. The practice has been closely associated with small-town America. High school sports enhance boosterism.

Schools came to realize that they would benefit from providing something the local population could identify with. Sports can serve as a unifying force within the community. School administrators, ever public relations conscious, have come to view interscholastic sports as a link to the community at large, a way to sell the overall school program to the taxpaying citizenry. Schools in effect manipulate the local community by giving the citizens what they want: winning sports teams. Administrators have assumed that this trade-off would make it easier to get bond issues passed and increase tax revenues (Butterfield and Brown 1991; Miracle and Rees 1994, 167).

The positive side of this relationship from a sociological perspective is the community bonding that results. Across the nation, local citizens gather to watch football, basketball, and other school sports events. In doing so, they establish a sense of collective identity that unifies the school and the community and binds them with cultural traditions. Spectator sports function as a ritual event that creates shared beliefs and traditions. Athletic events provide the context in which Americans are most likely to feel a union with a broad range of others. Players and spectators are as one. More people assemble for high school games than any other community event. In many small towns and rural areas, high school sports are the only game in town. Local residents find it easier to identify with local high school teams than college or professional teams. All-star exhibition games generate less emotional involvement or interest than do games between teams representing local rivals, thereby demonstrating the importance of sports followers' need for identification (Miracle and Rees 1994, 13, 20, 157, 162).

In towns across the nation, spectator sports provide the main medium for a sense of place and bonding, integrating members of different social classes.

Football is the first major sport of the school year, adding to its importance as a school activity. Attending a high school football game on a Friday night provides immediate evidence of the depth of school and community involvement, bringing together students, parents, alumni, and other community members. There are pregame rallies, parking lot gatherings, and school dances and other postgame social affairs. All of these diverse constituencies are unified around a common theme (Miracle and Rees 1994, 67–68; Braig 2004, 352).

As Levy (2015, 80) explains, "Small towns don't support their school and kids out of boredom but because small-town . . . social life revolves around the high school in a way it doesn't in bigger cities. As with church, school events allow . . . residents to catch up with neighbors and recognize their kids. It's simply a civic duty to attend community events." Football fans in Texas towns describe going to games as "like going to church" (Bissinger 1990, xi). A similar mind-set occurs in Kentucky with basketball, where one high school coach appeared at a local church so that the congregation could pray for the team prior to the regional tournament (O'Brien 2012, 240).

Contemporary high school sports supply the bonds and emotional needs that natural communities provided throughout most of history. Spectator sports create a sense of community that allows people to imagine that they have a common past, a common interest, and a common future. These interpretive communities exist in the collective imagination—they are, in effect, "consumer tribes." Whether or not the members know each other intimately, they share consumption habits and interests. Sports fans constitute imagined communities that define themselves by paying to attend sporting events and purchasing team paraphernalia. They are defined above all else by what they consume. This is the keystone of their identity (Meir 2007, 335–36).

High school sports bridge the generation gap in a society that is becoming more age-segregated. Parents and grandparents of students root for local teams. Sports conjure up fans' memories of their own youth and an uncomplicated fondness for the alma mater. Schools stage events where alumni teams play ritualized games against students. At the same time, there are indications of growing apathy toward spectator sports among the younger generation. Fewer students are attending high school games (B. Cook 2012). At some high schools, crowds consist mostly of alums and parents of players. At some Kentucky basketball games, the student sections weren't filled (O'Brien 2012, 82), yet the adult community of fans shows no signs of dissipating.

Parents of high school students reflect the values of the majority culture, and they have a vested interest in their own children. Athletes' parents sway local school administrators' decision making, often in hopes that children will receive college athletic scholarships or even become professional athletes.

School administrators have to deal with more issues associated with sports than with academic success or failure. At some high schools, most parent conferences are scheduled to discuss athletics. The athletic director may be on the telephone with parents more than the principal and the teachers combined (Roan 2006; Tufte 2012, 14, 37). Calls from sports parents have become a nuisance. In one New York school district, the athletic department implemented a three-strikes policy for parents who cross the line. The first time parents call, the athlete gets a warning. The second time, the athlete with the problem parents is suspended for a game or two; the third time that parents violate the policy, the child is off the team (Winzelberg 2001).

Athletic directors are routinely confronted by parents complaining about their children's playing time. A former high school coach commented, "The ideal scenario for many parents is: the team wins and my child plays a vital role in these victories. Anything short of that, and the parents become dissatisfied" (Tufte 2012, 59). At sporting events, parents of athletes carry clipboards and stopwatches, keeping track of playing time. A veteran coach was forced to resign after the parents of two basketball players who felt their children weren't getting enough playing time launched a campaign to get the coach fired (Carnovale 2012, 12, 45; Tufte 2012, 44, 59). A Kentucky high school principal observes, "You might have a kid who's just academically not getting it done, and you'll never hear from the parents. But ... bench them? And they're writing the newspapers about how out of control things are" (O'Brien 2012, 72–73). A few parents have sued coaches over a child's lack of playing time, and some coaches now carry liability insurance (G. Cook 2003, 13–14).

The problems involving athletes' parents exemplify the intense relationship between school sports and the local citizenry. According to former high school coach John Tufte (2012, 63), people in the community are consistently dissatisfied with one thing or another about high school sports and assign blame to coaches, principals, and even superintendents. In some communities, school boards select the high school football coach and make other important decisions affecting major sports. School boards that don't seem concerned about a decline in academics will fire a superintendent if they are disappointed by the football team's lack of success (Hannel, Gartman, and Karpel 2014, 48). Superintendents bear ultimate responsibility for school programs but normally cede oversight of interscholastic sports to athletic directors and head coaches, who may operate with relative freedom and independence from institutional controls.

As schools forge links with external groups, athletic directors and coaches become more accountable to alumni and boosters than to academic administrators, including principals. High school ADs report spending a significant amount of time dealing with community and public relations: holding press conferences, communicating with members of the media, managing websites, addressing community groups, and so forth. Allowing those outside the education profession to dictate standards has created a situation in which schools must chase sports championships no matter the cost to education. School officials may be reluctant to stand up to members of the community who wish to promote interscholastic sports at the expense of other school activities (Figone 1994; Humphrey 2002, 40–41; Griffin 1998, 74).

When a victory by adolescents in the athletic arena becomes the principal focus of community concern, high school sports arguably have been blown out of proportion. Community members, parents, and even some school officials applaud talented athletes on the field of play but turn a blind eye to athletes' academic problems. People seem less interested in what high school sports do for the athletes than what athletes do for the community members (Miracle and Rees 1994, 158, 172–73; Gerdy 2000, 97).

Do adults in the local community who care about football scores in late October show any interest in the reading or writing ability of the students? In the words of former University of Alabama football coach Paul "Bear" Bryant, "Fifty thousand people don't come to watch an English class." Similarly, according to Tufte (2012, 117), "Our citizens do not spend Friday nights huddled together in bleachers to talk about the newly tenured tenth grade math teacher and her outstanding approaches to teaching geometry by using new technology. No, the folks in the bleachers are watching high school sports—and they care deeply about both the people involved and the outcome of the games." This misplaced focus can have significant consequences for schools and students.

School consolidation is a signature issue that affects both sports and academics. Proponents of consolidation argue that combining smaller school districts into larger ones lead to savings, more overall efficiency, and a better academic experience for students (Clinchy 1998). However, ingrained loyalty to a local team can fuel resistance to school consolidation. In hundreds of rural areas where scattered farms surround tiny county seats, the local high school, with its arbitrarily drawn district lines, is the central focus of community life. The southern states in particular harbor a disproportionate number of small autonomous school districts. Rural Texans have passionately opposed school consolidation even when it made good economic sense because it threatened the community's identification with the high school football program (R. Roberts and Olson 1989, 215).

While rural areas resist consolidation, some metropolitan areas have been reluctant to build regional high schools because they wish to maintain their advantage in sports. Michigan State professor Valerie Lee (2010), a leading scholar on school organization and size, has found that a full curriculum can be offered and students will learn better in schools with enrollments between six hundred and nine hundred students. The town of Allen, Texas, has a population of eighty-five thousand and a single high school with an enrollment of nearly six thousand. Eliahu Sussman (2011, 20) asks, "Does the reluctance to build more regional high schools have to do with maintaining an advantage in football?" Clearly, drawing athletic talent from a student population in the thousands has its advantage. When it comes to making decisions about improving local schools, sports often trump academics.

Consequences of misplaced priorities reach beyond the school into the larger community. John Gerdy (2006, 58) observes, "For a society to thrive, there must exist among its citizenry a basic set of behavioral norms, ethical standards, and humanistic values. Most discussions of civil society center upon what binds a community." This should include a sense of civic responsibility. Social scientists express a growing concern that the American preoccupation with sports entertainment is undermining civic engagement. One of the mandates of public schools is to promote civic education. Critics question whether schools are doing as good a job of promoting civics classes as they are of fielding football and basketball teams. Schools arguably feed into the national preoccupation with entertainment culture. A little escapism isn't necessarily harmful, but sports addiction can lure us into mindless stupor and civic neglect (Gerdy 2006, 51–52).

Noted author James Michener (1987, 70) points out that spectators contribute nothing to the common good while they are sitting and watching. Peter G. Stromberg (2009, 162) elaborates, "In contemporary society, entertainment opportunities are ubiquitous and constantly expanding. Those caught in the grip may be completely under its sway, and abandon other commitments." He observes that a precipitous decline in civic engagement has occurred. In a classic case of sports appearing more important to members of a community than civic responsibility, although just thirty-eight thousand voters turned out for a 1999 Dallas mayoral election, later that evening, well over forty-five thousand people attended the Texas Rangers baseball game in suburban Arlington (Wann et al. 2001, 203).

The past few decades have seen declines in voting rates as well as trust in government, trends that have been accompanied by drops in civic knowledge and participation in civic organizations. Membership in groups such as the League of Women Voters has fallen. Popular culture has had a negative influence on civic life among the younger generation so that they don't view political participation as cool. Adolescents are devoting an enormous amount of time and energy to activities that have little to do with civic involvement or academic achievement (Lewis et al. 2002, 53–54, 56–57, 61). This trend could be reversed if schools committed to strong academics and civic education. As the noted social activist Marian Wright Edelman reminds us, democracy is not a spectator sport ("Edelman Finds" 2011).

Critics charge that spectator sports represent a misguided emphasis on entertainment culture at the cost of intellectual culture and meaningful civic activism. Being a compulsive sports fan offers little of long-term substance or meaning. It entices us to escape our problems and ignore vital issues. We invest our efforts and emotions into following sports stars and teams rather than improving our lives through reading, hobbies, or meaningful conversation. Idly watching sports on TV is easier than becoming involved in community activities (N. Adams and Bettis 2003, 25; Gerdy 2002, 22–23). Almond (2014a, 73) views football as the ultimate middle-class indulgence, distracting the working class from civic obligations and indoctrinating them into the ethic of consumer capitalism while promoting individualist and materialist values.

So how did high schools get into the entertainment business, expressly sponsoring public sporting events? The short answer is that they imitated colleges with big-time athletics programs. The public initially was drawn to professional and college sports; high schools followed this trend. The past hundred years has been characterized as the Age of the Spectator. Live sporting events remain a major component of this culture. Many high schools now operate as if they have an obligation to provide sports entertainment for the local community (Miracle and Rees 1994, 49; Reed 2015, 92–93).

Ideally, sports in a school setting should be developmental and serve a broad range of students. However, the focus of interscholastic sports has strayed from its educational purposes. Schools may claim to sponsor basketball and football to facilitate wholesome physical activity for students, but in reality, these events entertain local sports enthusiasts. The entertainment model encompasses both the type of activity and the social context in which it occurs (Stromberg 2009, 5). The presence of public address systems, electronic scoreboards, marching bands and cheerleading squads attests to the fact that school sports have been transformed into public performance. There would be no need for these appurtenances without the presence of spectators. The influence of electronic and print media has reinforced the sports entertainment model at the high school level and sidetracked the developmental objectives of school sports (Reed 2015, 162).

Participation in sports becomes a performance when the actions of the athletes and the nature of the competition are staged for public rather than private consumption. This form of involvement becomes sports for the Other.

The gratification in competing is attendant upon the acclaim of the crowd, conveying hero status to the winners and star performers. Sports become theater; athletes play to the audience. Football features end zone celebrations (although officially discouraged); basketball players dunk the ball for dramatic effect (Allen and Fahey 1977, 166; Hyland 1990, 110). As the late novelist John Fowles (1977, 190) observed, "Audience corrupts even more than power."

Should schools even be in the sports entertainment business, particularly when so many of the values and attitudes of entertainment culture run counter to those of education (Gerdy 2006, 42–43)? Former basketball all-American and member of the US Congress Tom McMillen (1992, 207) declares, "As a result of misplaced priorities, we have allowed vast entertainment complexes to reshape our schools and deflect them from their true educational missions. It is sheer folly to think that school officials have the time, energy, or resources to educate their charges and to run . . . entertainment empires at the same time."

The case can be made that interscholastic sports adversely affect civic responsibility while distorting the mission of the public schools. As Gerdy (2014, 178) points out, "An educational institution's most important value and driving principle should not be entertainment, but rather an unquestionable commitment to education, academic excellence, and the positive social development of the students." Steve Almond (2014b), a self-proclaimed football fan, puts it more bluntly: "What is a . . . commercialized form of athletic combat doing in our public schools? In an era when parents lament rising class sizes, crumbling facilities and underpaid teachers, why are taxpayers underwriting a form of entertainment?"

Almond's questions deserve answers. Entertaining spectators is the tail wagging the dog of interscholastic sports. Thus, it is important to understand the phenomenon of spectatorism and how it affects schools.

Spectatorism

English humorist Jerome K. Jerome quipped, "I like work: it fascinates me. I can sit and look at it for hours." Substitute *sport* for *work* and the witticism would apply to the majority of contemporary adults and many adolescents. We are more inclined to be sports viewers than doers. Spectatoritis has become a national epidemic. The term *couch potato* was coined to describe those of us who watch too much television. We have become a nation of TV addicts, in large part as a result of sports. As sports grow in popularity, the majority of us are inclined to watch the performances of the talented minority either on the couch or in the bleachers. Commercial television doesn't warrant all the blame for the shift toward sports spectatorism. Public schools and colleges have contributed to this epidemic (Stillwell and Willgoose 1997, 4; Gerdy 2002, 115–19). In Indiana, where I grew up, basketball is king, and the seating capacity of some high school gymnasiums exceeds the town's population.

Why do schools promote spectator sports at the expense of participant sports? The message conveyed to most students and alumni is that watching others engage in physical activity is better than actually engaging. Not all school sports attract a large number of spectators, but football and basketball routinely draw crowds. Schools hold pep rallies encouraging students to "support the team" yet limit intramural and recreational sports offerings. A distinct minority of students participate in sports in large high schools. At the same time, local communities devote a tremendous amount of energy and resources to supporting school-sponsored spectator sports while public recreation programs languish. Physical educators counsel that we need to provide opportunities for mass physical recreation as well as settings for viewing sports, but this message appears to fall on deaf ears. There remains little doubt that spectator sports override participant sports.

This issue has important implications for schools. One of the Cardinal Principles of Secondary Education is worthy use of leisure. In the best sense, leisure should provide an opportunity for the individual to become refreshed and rejuvenated. Leisure time activity without cultural significance fails to satisfy these needs. A liberal education encompasses the arts and literature, both of which have implications for worthy use of leisure. What about school sports? Do these activities contribute to a liberal education and promote worthy use of leisure? If so, more students should be encouraged to participate.

Spectatorism has important health implications. There is growing concern that schools aren't putting more effort into promoting participant sports, with their obvious physical benefits. Health professionals worry that the increasingly popular habit of watching sports has transformed many adolescents and young adults into bleacher creatures. According to a study in the *Sports Journal*, those individuals who regularly patronize spectator sports demonstrate significantly higher health risk behaviors than non-sports-fans. These behaviors include high fat consumption and increased alcohol consumption. Sports fans have higher body mass indexes on average. The United States is doing a poor job of promoting lifelong sports participation. Not surprisingly, data from 2012 show that the United States has one of the most obese populations among thirty-four developed nations (Reed 2015, 92–95). Nearly a third of high school students are overweight. Schools could shift their focus to ameliorate these problems.

Being a sports spectator encourages unhealthy eating habits. The nation has witnessed a recent campaign to develop healthier school lunches, but this effort doesn't extend to the sports arena. Concession stands in gymnasiums, ballparks, and stadiums are purveyors of junk food—typically including soft drinks, french fries, nachos, funnel cakes, corn chips, candy, and snow cones. To make matters worse, sports venues prohibit patrons from bringing in their own food and drinks. At a recent high school basketball tournament at Rupp Arena in Lexington, Kentucky (seating capacity twenty-three thousand), the crowd of spectators consumed sixteen hundred pounds of hot dogs, sixty-seven hundred gallons of soft drinks, eighty-two hundred boxes of popcorn, and nearly twenty-one thousand servings of ice cream (O'Brien 2012, 255).

Spectator sports are not without their advocates. The late Christopher Lasch (1977), a contrarian social critic, maintained that while no one denies the desirability of participation in sports, we measure ourselves against standards derived from watching athletes who have mastered a sport. By entering imaginatively into their world, moreover, we experience in heightened form the pain of defeat and the triumph of persistence in the face of adversity. An athletic performance, like other performances, calls up a rich train of associations and fantasies, shaping our unconscious perceptions of life. He argued that spectatorship is no more passive than daydreaming—provided that the audience understands the performance and that the performance is of such quality that it elicits an emotional response. Lasch extolled the vicarious nature of sports, noting that excellence in sports can operate as a reference point for identification, emulation, meaningful dialogue, discriminating criticism, and shared appreciations (see Hemphill 1995, 52).

Lasch (1977) contended that the need for greater participation in sports is entirely irrelevant to a discussion of their cultural significance. We might just as well assess the future of American music by counting the number of amateur musicians. In both cases, participation can be an eminently satisfying experience, but in neither case does the level of participation tell us much about the status of the art. Watching sports clearly offers some value—most obviously, it is enjoyable, an escape from the ordinary. Watching sports can be exhilarating, drawing us together and making us feel we are part of something larger than ourselves. The sports audience is an organic part of the entertainment experience. Real-time sports are one of the major draws for live audiences.

Other cultural critics have disagreed with Lasch's assessment, characterizing spectator sports as the junk food of the mind. They accuse schools of promoting tackle football and other activities that are lowbrow and brutal, lacking in refinement in comparison to pursuits such as attending a concert or dramatic presentation. Sports are seen as standardized, repetitive, and superficial activity—little more than mindless escapism. Viewing such activity doesn't broaden one's cultural perspective. Instead, enthusiasts become immersed in the arcane trivia of sports (Wann et al. 2001, 205). This concern extends to the younger generation engrossed in their electronic devices. Professor Dana Gioia (2008, 56) observes, "A child who spends a month mastering ... NBA Live on Xbox has not been awakened and transformed the way that child would be spending the time rehearsing a play or learning to draw." Such entertainment "promises us a predictable pleasure—humor, thrills, emotional titillation, or even the odd delight of being vicariously terrified; it exploits and manipulates who we are rather than challenges us with a vision of who we might become."

Examining the nature of entertainment culture enables a better understanding of the issue of spectatorism and how it affects young adults. The term *entertainment* implies an activity that provides a particular kind of pleasure: diversion, amusement, lightness—enjoyable occupation without seriousness. As a consequence of recent advances in technology and the availability of leisure time, entertainment plays a much more significant role in everyday life today than it did in the past, and institutions and opportunities for entertainment have proliferated (Stromberg 2009, 6, 8).

Entertainment is so woven into the fabric of our existence that we rarely stop to think about our relentless quest to be entertained. That quest lies at the hub of our culture and arguably constitutes the most influential ideological system not only in the United States but most developed nations, particularly those that embrace some form of consumer capitalism. *Entertainment* is a broad term that includes consumption behavior closely tied to advertising. Indeed, entertainment and consumption are often two sides of the same ideological coin, providing escape, sensation, and instant gratification. An activity must pull people in to be entertaining. Yet consumer capitalism can also breed a sense of boredom, the development of a nagging feeling of emptiness and discontent in the absence of a stimulation from something new and exciting (Stromberg 2009, 6, 9, 142).

The undeniable pleasures of entertainment bring with them some potentially significant social and psychological costs, including ethical and mental health implications. Entertainment can divert us from our day-to-day reality, can deflect our minds from not only tedious but serious concerns. Entertainment begins to dominate other standards of value in society. It becomes part of the process of finding meanings that ground us in the world. Entertainment and the pleasures it generates have become fundamental to our vision of the good life, working to create and sustain many of our fundamental ideas, practices, and values (Stromberg 2009, 6, 9, 2011, 738).

We can be caught up, transformed by entertainment. Spectator sports provide a classic instance of obsessive entertainment. Many Americans plan their days, weekends, and even vacations around sports. We watch sports on television at home, at restaurants, bars, and friends' homes. We listen to sports talk radio. These habits go beyond escapism and begin to resemble addiction. At some point, the exposure moves beyond harmless to chronic physical inactivity and mindless stupor. Conversation languishes when the game telecast begins. Rather than interacting with others, we focus entirely on the screen (Gerdy 2002, 22). Such obsessions can corrode relationships within the family if some members do not share in the passion. Retired sportswriter Kevin Quirk (1997) titled his book on fandom, *Not Now Honey, I'm Watching the Game*.

No one is suggesting that we cease watching sports, just that we do so in moderation. Being a compulsive sports viewer offers little of long-term substance or meaning. It entices us to escape our problems and ignore important issues. We invest our efforts and emotions into following sports stars and teams rather than improving our lives through reading, hobbies, or meaningful discussions. It becomes easier to sit idly and watch sports than become involved in community culture and recreation. The passion for sports can become all-consuming (Gerdy 2002, 22–23).

From an educational perspective, concern is growing about the adverse effects of entertainment culture on the talented athletes' self-perceptions. One effect of sports culture on social mores is the increasing dominance of fame and celebrity as models of personhood. Athletes compete not only for the love of the game but also to garner attention. Public adulation is a powerful motivator. The crowd may not be essential to the athletic experience, but it does contribute a significant element (K. Miller et al. 2006, 10). High school football players comment on the thrill of performing before large crowds. School athletes become local celebrities. They acquire a following of fans, see their names in the local newspapers, receive mention on local television news, and are discussed on sports talk shows. Advertising exploits celebrity culture. Critics charge that celebrity status promotes self-centeredness, materialism, escapism, and cynicism and undermines the communal ethos (Stromberg 2009, 27, 30; Lewis et al. 2002, 54). School administrators have a choice: they can exploit sports celebrity culture or attempt to ameliorate the adverse ramifications. The detrimental effects of sports culture on athletes and audience escalate when spectatorism morphs into rabid fandom.

Fandom

There are sports spectators and there are sports fans—two distinct but not mutually exclusive groups. People attend sporting events for a variety of reasons: because they were given a free ticket or simply to enjoy the action. They are not necessarily fans. A partisan fan is someone with an abiding interest in a team or athlete, an enthusiastic devotee. Traditionally, the public audience for sports consisted largely of men, but the number of women sports fans has grown. Fans may include those who played sports during their youth and acquired a passion for and sense of the game, able to make discriminating judgments. One of the virtues of contemporary sports lies in their capacity to appeal to a knowledgeable audience (Lasch 1985, 53).

Sports can seem as important to those who follow them as to those who compete. Sports events provide a focal point for the lives of dedicated followers. Fans will suffer discomfort, deprivation, and expense to demonstrate support for their favorite team. In return, the fans claim a source of social identity, and the team experiences feelings of pride or disappointment in its performance from among the fans. The relationship between fans and athletes is a central feature of modern sports (M. Lee 1985, 38, 41). Fans commonly associate themselves with teams that represent high schools, colleges, and cities, and/or countries.

Partisan followers maintain their support for extended periods and are emotionally involved with the outcomes of contests and seasons. Sports fans arrange personal schedules and relationships around sporting events and modify and decorate their clothing to identify with a team. Fan behaviors include attending sporting events, watching sports on TV, listening to sports on radio, reading the sports section of the newspaper, discussing sports with friends, and purchasing sports paraphernalia (Wann et al. 2001, 2, 11). These behaviors exemplify the psychological importance of sports and highlight the importance of team success to individuals' lives. Identification with a sports team not only facilitates escape from the frustration and monotony of daily routine but constitutes an affirmation of self—of one's beliefs, attitudes, and identity. The performance of a favorite team is experienced as a direct reflection on one's worth (M. Lee 1985, 45; Gerdy 2002, 57).

Sports scholars identify both positive and negative features of fandom. Among the positives are the strong social bonds among spectators. Sociologists refer to rituals of interaction, and those related to sports occur in an excited crowd. An energy of interaction can become associated with symbols, institutions, moods, and attitudes. In contemporary society, large-scale gatherings compete with the print and electronic entertainment media.

On-the-scene rituals strengthen ties to fellow humans and to ideas. This suggests that spectator sports can be more than entertainment. Sports rituals provide a cultural process through which values and commitments are generated (Stromberg 2009, 11, 13, 161).

The rituals that have become a part of athletic events exemplify the passions of fandom. Outside the stadium before a football game team buses "park at the formal arched entrance of the stadium, where await thousands of spectators, the cheerleaders, the dance squad and the regimental marching band, a cadets' organization. The team then stages a slow walk to the entrance to the athletic complex where they will dress. As this happens, cheerleaders somersault, brass instruments oompah a few familiar ostinatos, and adoring supporters clap while calling out player's names" (Easterbrook 2013, 43).

Fandom extends beyond the sports arena and beyond the sports season. Discussions of games at sports bars, barbershops, and similar venues suggests that sports fans as a group share a level of solidarity that reaches into their everyday lives. A high school basketball team's varsity preseason scrimmage fills the gym with fans. When one Kentucky basketball team played in the state tournament, the county courthouse closed at noon on game day, and the schools dismissed classes at 10:30 in the morning (Cottingham 2012, 180; O'Brien 2012, 1, 3, 235). Local businesses in small Texas towns close on Friday nights during high school football games. People get off work early to make the trip to away games. Sports fans follow state and national rankings via the Internet or radio and television (Levy 2015, 58; Tufte 2012, 6).

Nowhere in the nation is the local community's dedication to school sports more palpable than in the case of Texas high school football: "There's nothing to replace it. It's an integral part of what made the community strong. You take it away and it's almost like you strip the identity of the people" (Bissinger 1990, 41, 43). In the words of Joe N. Patoski and Suzy Banks (1999, 110), "It's a game ... a community bond, the state religion, the biggest show in town every Friday night in the fall, ... a revered symbol, an inspirational rallying point that offers a rare moment ... in which all races, religions, and economic strata put aside their differences to get behind the home team."

High schools across the state keep waiting lists for season tickets, which some families have purchased for twenty-five or thirty years—long after their children graduated and moved away. New residents scramble for season tickets. In one community, four hundred families entered a lottery for seventy seats. Thousands of fans travel hundreds of miles to attend away games. One fan in a small town bragged he hadn't missed a high school football game in thirty-one years. Fans show up to watch the football team's practice sessions (Bishop 2011; Levy 2015, 13, 48, 89, 243).

In the late 1980s in the West Texas town of Odessa (population eighty thousand), twenty thousand fans attended Friday night high school football games, and as many as one in fifteen Texas residents attend, play, coach, or otherwise take part in activities at a high school football game (Bissinger 1990, xi; "Sports Marketing" 2014). In one suburban district with two high schools, sixty or so adults work at each varsity football game, including officials, police officers, parking attendants, concession workers, ticket agents, ambulance attendants, and a physician. Media people fill the press box; an electrician and a stadium manager are on duty. Fans' relationship with the high school team is more personal than their relationship with college or pro teams. These are "their boys," representing their town (Miracle and Rees 1994, 164–65; Levy 2015, x).

Fandom is fully integrated into school and community life. On game day, flags with school colors hang from virtually every business in town. Mothers of players decorate the team's locker room. Boosters in one community presented the team with a giant cookie decorated as a football field. High school teachers dress in the school colors on game days. Local souvenir shops sell T-shirts, hats, helmets, jackets, and pajama pants in the high school colors. A high school booster club in Texas holds an annual watermelon feed. In some towns, coaches' and players' families get together for a potluck meal following the games (Levy 2015, 90, 117, 186; Bishop 2011).

Tailgate parties offer another popular venue for combining feasting and football. Though they began at college sports events, they soon gained popularity with high school fans. Texas high school administrators encourage students to organize pregame tailgate parties (Popke 2006). The students set up grills in the stadium parking lot and invite fans to the festivities. Tailgate parties aren't unique to Texas; they're a growing phenomenon across the country. Parking lot parties at Ohio high schools date back to 2003. Tailgate parties have spread to sporting events other than football, including basketball, hockey, soccer, and baseball.

Students, alumni, businesses, and members of the community set up tents in parking lots, fields, or streets near the stadium to cook out, play games, socialize, binge drink, and enjoy live music. Tailgate parties start at noon on game day in some towns and often continue during games for those who don't have tickets but still show up to take part in the socializing and excitement. Campers and tents on the scene play television or radio feeds of the game. With names such as Future Tailgaters of America and Friends of Football, sponsoring groups charge from five dollars to twenty dollars for admission and may attract hundreds of people. At some schools, band members and the athletic department join forces to sponsor tailgate parties (Levy 2015, 72; Gordon 2012).

These gatherings are generally viewed as safe and fun but are increasingly attracting sports marketers and becoming venues for the consumption of junk food and alcohol. Schools and municipalities have reported violations of open-container ordinances, public intoxication, underage drinking, public urination, lewd behavior, driving under the influence, and destruction of public and private property (J. Lee and Lee 2009, 52–53). Tailgate parties represent yet another source of concern for schools that promote spectator sports.

Booster clubs—organizations formed to promote interscholastic sports by raising money and coordinating events—offer a more enduring and entrenched form of community support. Such clubs are uniquely popular in American high schools and universities. High school booster clubs are generally organized and run by local sports fans. Booster clubs supplement public revenue by providing financial assistance for school sports. Clubs may build new playing or practice fields, donate or equip weight rooms, and provide labor for various projects. They also sponsor annual postseason awards banquets. The funds boosters raise have been used to supplement coaches' salaries and provide incentives like the use of an automobile. Some high school booster clubs have more than a thousand members. Each club typically has an executive committee made up of a president and one or more vice presidents, a secretary, and a treasurer. There also may be a liaison for each sport or activity. Most clubs also have a school administrator, coach, or program director as a nonvoting board member and adviser (DeNisco 2014, 75).

Sports programs in a growing number of school districts rely on the support of parent-run booster clubs. As budgets tighten, these clubs provide basic necessities from player uniforms to travel money for games and tournaments. High school football stadiums may have fund-raising tables staffed by booster club members. Budget cuts in recent years have led to the expansion of booster clubs in middle schools (Levy 2015, 104; DeNisco 2014, 73–74).

According to the executive director of the National Booster Club Training Council, an average school booster club raises about seventeen thousand dollars per year, but such community organizations have raised as much as $1 million for local high schools. Fairfax County Public Schools in Northern Virginia has more than two dozen high schools, each with an athletic booster club that raises between $75,000 and $250,000 annually. The Hoover, Alabama, football booster club has raised approximately $300,000 per year. In some towns, marching bands have separate booster clubs: Houston's Stratford High School has four booster clubs—for athletics, band, choir, and theater—that have raised about $100,000 per year to fund scholarships, trips to competitions, and various projects such as a tennis court upgrade. In 2014, the athletic booster club began a $10,000 football field beautification project that included planting trees and installing a drip irrigation system. Some high schools have as many as seven booster clubs (DeNisco 2014, 74; Sailer 2007, 25–27).

Economic disparities between schools, even those in the same district, impact booster club fund-raising, as parents from wealthier schools tend to organize and donate to booster clubs more often than do parents from poorer schools. A high school athletic booster club in an affluent district of Montgomery County, Maryland, raised $110,000 for a video scoreboard in 2013, while a few miles away another high school was unable to raise $14,000 (DeNisco 2014, 76).

The relationship between schools and booster clubs is symbiotic but can also be discordant. High school coaches in the major sports are in the debt of local booster clubs. While these clubs raise funds for school programs, their members can interfere with teams—for example, by pressuring coaches to start certain players (Foley 1990, 123–25). In addition although school administrators regulate the use of school property and can choose whether to endorse booster clubs or accept donations, schools cannot disband booster clubs or control their money. At least three dozen booster club members have received criminal convictions for embezzlement since 2011, with the amount of money stolen ranging as high as $439,000. In 2012, reports of corruption led the Ohio Attorney General's Office to open an investigation of the state's booster clubs (DeNisco 2014, 75–76).

Critics assert that booster clubs are shallow forms of community support based on rabid fandom and partisanship and raise legitimate questions about priorities. Some school districts have booster clubs but no parent-teacher association. Some school districts don't accept booster club funds for new gymnasiums or other capital projects that are considered the responsibility of the district, county, or state (DeNisco 2014, 76).

Sports fandom remains problematic for educators, and some observers have questioned whether team loyalty has positive outcomes on balance. Highly competitive spectator sports—especially basketball and football—encourage rabid identification with teams and towns, a phenomenon that has important psychological implications for individuals and may foster negative sentiments toward out-groups. Support for school teams harbors the implicit assumption that "we" are better than "they" (M. Lee 1985, 38–41).

Winning sports teams are often claimed to unify communities, but when overdone, loyalty can result in divisiveness. Sports create intercity and interschool rivalries. Communities are brought together for a common cause—to enjoy a sporting event—but then root against each other. The action on the field may be violent and uncivil, and this temperament occasionally carries over into the stands. The fervor surrounding sports has a tendency to mutate into a form of tribalism. A Texas high school football fan and former player crows, "I was ready to put the pads back on after forty years, go out, and knock the shit out of someone and say, 'I am from La Marque and damn proud of it!'" (Gerdy 2014, 142–44; Levy 2015, 7).

Gerdy (2002, 57) comments, "It seems as if our 'fandom' has crossed over a line where it is no longer simply about a pleasant evening out, but rather an affirmation of self, of one's beliefs, attitudes, and identity, that the performance of your favorite team is a direct reflection on your worth as a human being." When a particular team wins, it becomes an indication and a validation of a person's and a community's values. This mind-set promotes a win-at-all-costs mentality in which an athletic event no longer constitutes an occasion where a group of people pull together for a purpose or common cause. Too often the action on the field and in the stands becomes uncivil. (At a music concert, in contrast, the entire audience cheers for the same outcome—a great performance.) The nature of athletic competition can divide rather than unite (Gerdy 2002, 58). There are discriminating fans and then there are rabid partisans.

Conscientious school administrators attempt to influence and shape the ethical and aesthetic sensibilities of sports fans. Schools promote codes of conduct for spectators, with mixed results. Booing and jeering are not uncommon among crowds at sports events. Problems in controlling high school games are exacerbated by the proximity of unruly fans, notably in basketball arenas, and when officials lose control of the game. Despite attempts to manage crowds at sporting events, fan misbehavior is widely reported (Donaldson 2014).

During one girls' high school ice hockey game in Massachusetts, an athlete's father in the crowd was caught was shining a laser into the eyes of the opposing team's goalie. With tacit approval from school administrators, one Texas high school allowed a fan to rev a chainsaw right before the kickoff of football games, alluding to a movie, *Texas Chainsaw Massacre* (Carnovale 2012, 49; Levy 2015, 239). Some high school cheers encourage gratuitous violence:

A-T-T-A-C-K
Attack the quarterback
And knock him flat, right on his back
Pow! (Bennett 1990, 6)

On the first play of one Texas high school football game, a player was ejected for punching an opposing player; some fans began verbally attacking coaches and players. After one Southern California high school football game in which a runner's helmet was knocked off during a tackle, and a member of the opposing team attempted to kick him in the head, parents from one school attacked members of the opposing football team in the locker room, pushing past the security guard to strike four players in the face or grab them by the neck (Levy 2015, 24; "After Prep" 2015).

The presence of security personnel at athletic events has become routine. Fans of opposing teams are kept apart by design. In some instances, fear of crowd violence has required games to be played in neutral locations or at unannounced times. In January 2005, California's Salinas Union High School District officials planned to hold a high school basketball game in an empty gym after a coach received intimidating phone calls, though the decision was reversed after fans protested (Miracle and Rees 1994, 169; Buchanan 2006, 21).

Sports fandom can be beneficial, even indispensable and can run the gamut from a few parents watching a tennis match to twenty thousand screaming fans at a state championship football game. But it can also have a downside. Football and basketball fans in particular can wield significant local power, even costing principals and coaches their jobs when they fail to meet expectations. And students get the message: sports are what is important.

A reformer might envision a system where the nation's towns and cities organize amateur or semipro sports teams, as occurred historically in many areas of the country. This would relieve local schools of the burden to sponsor sports teams as a rallying point for community identity. But this alternative seems unlikely to be implemented. Instead, the trend is toward private, community-sponsored youth sports clubs.

Private Sports Clubs

Interscholastic athletics aren't the only sports programs available for teens and preteens. Private sports clubs are increasingly perceived as a rival to school sports. Like interscholastic sports, club sports tend to be highly competitive and selective, focusing on talented athletes. Young athletes do not always need to choose between school or community-sponsored teams but in some cases can play on both, even in the same sport (Miracle and Rees 1994, 207).

However, a growing number of young athletes play exclusively on non-school teams—a predictable development in a climate of increasing time commitment and specialization. The top club teams claim to offer teen athletes more exposure to college coaches. College recruiters looking for the top athletes attend the regional or national tournaments where elite clubs compete. For some time, students participating in golf, tennis, ice hockey, and gymnastics have been drawn to club sports because their high schools either didn't field teams or didn't offer competitive teams with official league play. Soccer players, swimmers, and to a lesser extent basketball and baseball players are making the switch to community-based clubs (Gehring 2004c, 13).

Many private soccer clubs affiliated with US Soccer, the national governing body, are moving from seven-month to ten-month schedules, effectively preventing thousands of club players from playing on their high school teams. Highly motivated soccer players and their parents are increasingly convinced that club soccer is the most likely path to a college scholarship. This trend is being encouraged by the promoters of the national Olympic soccer team, citing the need for intense, extended training to be competitive (B. Cook 2012). A growing concern is the eroding relationship between high school programs and community-based programs, given the rising influence and prestige of club sports that encourage young athletes to devote themselves to that one activity year round.

The Amateur Athletic Union (AAU) has long sponsored youth sports and now has more than five hundred thousand participants in a variety of programs. The AAU's 57 associations annually sanction more than 34 sports programs, 250 national championships, and more than 10,000 local events (www.aausports.org). School athletes are being recruited by AAU coaches, some of whom pressure their athletes to drop school sports. Because of the intense schedules of AAU teams, the coaches don't want their athletes playing school sports during the club season. Consequently, an increasing number of talented young athletes focus solely on their AAU team commitments. Those who follow local sports are convinced that this practice has diminished both the level of competition and popularity of high school sports ("What Effect" 2014, 46). The influence of private sports clubs and elite travel teams reaches beyond the local community. Programs under the auspices of the AAU have become one of the nation's most competitive and popular venues for young athletes looking to showcase their skills in national tournaments.

Club teams can have a significant impact on sports participation in high schools and middle schools. Since practice traditionally occurs after school, it is difficult for kids who play on travel teams to do school sports during the club seasons. Some swim club athletes arrive for practice at 5:00 a.m. during the school year. Swim teams also schedule after-school practices (Gehring 2004c, 13–14). Moreover, the number of games or meets that a young athlete attends on private teams is often significantly greater than the number of high school games, and practice sessions may be held more frequently than for interscholastic sports. Young athletes find it nearly impossible to juggle the responsibilities of playing for both club and interscholastic teams ("What Effect" 2014, 46–47).

School sports administrators attuned to the rapidly changing environment have voiced some reservations, and interscholastic coaches have expressed growing concerns about the influence of private teams. The competition between high school and elite club coaches in California became so intense that the assistant executive director of California Interscholastic Federation, the governing body for the state's high school athletic programs, sought to bring the various parties together to seek some sort of balance (Gehring 2004c, 13–14). But sports clubs have little incentive to seek a compromise with schools.

Conversely, educators who decry the adverse effects of interscholastic sports on academics argue that shifting the responsibility for conducting elite sports programs from the schools to outside clubs might be in the best interests of the schools, student-athletes, and coaches. Local sports fans undoubtedly would resist such a shift, although the difference between cheering for the high school team and a local club team made up of the same athletes with a different sponsor doesn't seem terribly significant (Gerdy 2014, 126–27, 229).

Former basketball coach Len Stevens believes that club sports would solve a lot of problems with interscholastic sports and allow schools to focus on education. Following this format, high schools would still sponsor intramural sports, primarily for recreation and physical exercise. Parents and young athletes who want the experience of high-end competition and believe the road to a college education is through sports could realize these goals through club sports (B. Cook 2012).

Private community-based sports teams offer a wide range of opportunities to teenage athletes, but current practices have created their own set of problems and triggered growing concerns. For parents and educators whose major focus is the best interests of the athlete, troubling issues have emerged. The trend toward club sports can be seen as part of the broader phenomenon in which youngsters begin to specialize before they have had the opportunity to try a range of sports. Club teams can be just as authoritarian, hypercompetitive, and restrictive as interscholastic sports. Playing on private sports clubs also can be prohibitively expensive. Parents of club athletes may spend more than three thousand dollars a year on fees and travel costs. Some parents hire private trainers and personal coaches for their teenage athletes. These efforts are fed by the hope of college scholarships, but in truth, only a small fraction of teenage athletes will earn an athletic scholarship. And the other drawbacks include the fact that youngsters pushed too hard and too early in a single sport are candidates for burnout and overuse injuries (Gehring 2004c, 13–14).

Educators and community leaders might consider other sports club models (see chapter 2). However, American communities or school districts do not seem inclined to adopt alternative approaches to student sports. Most likely, the competition between interscholastic sports and private club sports will continue in the short term.

◆ ◆ ◆

Secondary schools should get out of the sports entertainment business. If parents and friends of student-athletes wish to view competitive events, schools can develop a sideline protocol similar to what some youth sports leagues have implemented (e.g., spectators and athletes remain on opposite sides of fields and courts during competition). But there is no reason for schools to encourage spectators by investing in extensive seating and expensive sports arenas. Capital funds should be devoted to constructing and maintaining recreational facilities for participants, not amenities for fans or media such as concession stands, press boxes, and elaborate electronic scoreboards.

Critics of interscholastic sports are convinced that moving sports out of school settings is less likely than in-house reform, as such a proposal would send shock waves through the community. But there are clearly potential advantages to implementing such a policy. Transferring highly competitive sports programs from public schools to community organizations and private clubs wouldn't lessen the positive aspects of participation or spectatorship. Indeed, sports might play a larger role in community life. Local citizens could build the necessary organizations and strengthen the link between schools and communities (Kralovec 2003, 6, 80; Pruter 2013, 327). Existing school sports facilities would be made available to the entire community when not in use (and vice versa), as there is little justification for public facilities standing empty.

Etta Kralovec (2003, 68) has proposed that "the funding, organizational support, and structure for competitive sports programs for young people should be provided by community organizations other than the public schools. The benefits for school budgets and school schedules would be enormous." Gerdy (2002, 231–32) notes that if schools eliminated interscholastic sports, "elite sports activities and training would simply shift to other local sponsoring agencies. Local organizations and youth groups that receive no public funding would develop and sponsor more athletic programs." Professional sports teams would begin to sponsor their own feeder systems and programs, thereby freeing schools to expand intramural sports programs.

Whannel (1993, 111) uniquely proposes that the idea of having schools switch from emphasizing big single-sports events accommodating large numbers of spectators to multisport, mass peoples' festivals. This is another way to integrate school sports into the community and involve more students. In fact, a number of elementary and middle schools do sponsor sports days or field days, consistent with this model. These events can involve teams integrated with students from more than one school and offer a way for students to make new friends rather than view other schools as adversaries. Likewise, "parking lot parties" could bring people together rather than foment rivalries. Under a similar strategy, communities would adopt the European model of age-integrated sports clubs that involve entire families. Such sports clubs could replace booster clubs.

These reforms would radically alter school culture and reframe the role of student-athletes among their peers.

SPORTS CULTURE RULES IN THE AMERICAN HIGH SCHOOL

> The ... crew coach, Bill Stowe, explained to me that there were only
> two kinds of men on campus, perhaps in the world—Jocks and Pukes.
> —Robert Lipsyte

Culture is defined as the way people interact based on shared beliefs, values, and activities. High schools have their own distinct culture. Adults who've attended high school could enter a local school today and recognize its elements from their own experience. The grammar of schooling—the shifting of students into groups of twenty-five or so and the moving of students from teacher to teacher and subject to subject according to a prescribed schedule, punctuated by the ringing of bells—would be familiar. Visitors who left high school years ago could negotiate crowded hallways filled with chattering students, noting posters and announcements taped to the walls about the upcoming big game and the next school dance. References to the student council, yearbook, drama club, and band performances would be familiar even to those who didn't participate in these activities. Varsity team members would be recognized by their stylized letter jackets in school colors (Hoffman 2002–3).

High school is a kind of secular church, a place of institutional rituals and ceremonies that match the stages of a young person's life. Society provides these rites of passage as mechanisms for orderly transitions. Ritualized performances in the public schools reinforce expectations of behavior. The value of these rituals depends on cultural consistency; thus, freshmen students are oriented to important school traditions. The school might be the only institution in modern society where adolescents can participate in rite-of-passage experiences that mark their transition from childhood to adulthood. The process of growing up and the act of going to high school are profoundly intertwined. The importance and virtue of students' involvement in school activities are reinforced at home and in the community (Hoffman 2002–3).

Sociologists distinguish between rites of *passage* and rites of *intensification*. The former are organized around individuals, while the latter center on groups. Intensification rites in high school serve to restore an interactive balance among group members faced with change. Such rites include homecoming, pep rallies, the senior prom, and honors day. Most students participate is these activities. Their engagement indicates the degree to which they are connected to, involved with, and invested in school. Students who are more engaged are less likely to drop out of school and more likely to graduate (Hoffman 2002–3; Gerdy 2014, 95–96).

The high school yearbook documents elements of high school culture as well as constitutes a significant element of the school traditions it reflects. The yearbook is a piece of material culture, an artifact that can be used as data to interpret high school customs and rituals. A document intended to tell the story of the school year, it is simultaneously a book of memory, history, and reference (Hoffman 2002–3). Contemporary student yearbooks reflect the nominal emphasis on academics. Few if any pages are devoted to honor roll students, while a large number of pages devoted to extracurricular activities—most notably, interscholastic sports—demonstrates their importance. A century ago, high school yearbooks devoted about 5 percent of their pages to school athletics, a number that rose to nearly a third at the beginning of the twenty-first century (Kralovec 2003, 69–70; Svare 2004, 99, 103).

The status accorded sports bolsters the idea that academics isn't everything and may not even be the most important thing to students. Identity as an athlete garners such a level of importance within adolescent subculture—reinforced by the school and community—that the chances are slim that academic performance will appear significant. Interscholastic sports provide what may be schools' only collective goal, given that student academic achievement is framed as an individual goal (Miracle and Rees 1994, 68). Etta Kralovec (2003, 15) describes a lighted signboard on the front lawn of a public high school, the product of a community fund-raising effort. The signboard provides information regarding upcoming school events, announcing a wrestling meet, a soccer game, and a junior varsity football game but omits the school play and other nonathletic activities.

The various forms of recognition accorded athletic performance illustrate the importance of achievement in this area relative to academics. A sports hall of fame is a common feature of American high schools, usually located in a visible area of the school such as the main corridor or lobby adjacent to the gym. Such tributes are the joint efforts of the school athletic department and local booster groups. Their purpose is to immortalize former athletes. Artifacts include trophies, photos, and memorabilia. Rituals of recognition may include an elaborate induction ceremony and banquet each year. Some high school athletic associations sponsor statewide halls of fame. But if high schools are principally about education, why do they not have an academic hall of fame or alumni hall of fame honoring students who have distinguished themselves in other arenas? (Svare 2004, 95–96).

The trophy case is a form of recognition found in the entrance foyers of most American schools. Visiting a New Jersey high school, Bernard Lefkowitz (1998, 121) observed,

> In the hall right across from the principal's office were the glass cases displaying shelf after shelf of sports trophies, a glittering tribute to Glen Ridge's athletic triumphs. The cases could not contain the entire display, and the overflow adorned the shelves of the school's main office and the library, a cornucopia of bats and gloves and baseballs and footballs and plaques and cups and statuettes. Nowhere visible was last year's student honor roll.

Sociologist James Coleman noted that a visitor to an American high school who scrutinized the trophy case would be confronted with a curious fact: "The gold and silver cups, with rare exception, symbolize victory in athletic contests, not scholastic ones.... Altogether, the trophy case would suggest to the innocent guest that he was entering an athletic club, not an educational institution" (Ripley 2013a, 75). Cups or ribbons won by the debate team, if allocated space in the trophy case, are smaller and less prominently displayed.

Interscholastic athletics bring together the student body. Boys' athletics are the most important and most attended events at high schools. Large numbers of students do not attend debates or science fairs. Even stage productions and concerts don't garner the attendance of football and basketball games. Female students garner the most visibility at boys' athletic events in the role of cheerleaders and members of dance squads. They likewise perform in front of the student body at pep rallies. The only other school event where female students are afforded such prominence is as the homecoming queen or member of the court, and this ceremony is often tied to football. Females achieve high status in high schools via support roles for male athletes—either as cheerleaders or their dates. Female athletes are less likely to enjoy comparable status (Eder 1995, 32–34, 37; Miracle and Rees 1994, 70–72).

Male power and gender inequity are institutional features of American high schools. The homecoming ritual valorizes male athletes, and the boy selected as homecoming king is often a popular athlete. Likewise, male athletes are the main focus during pep rallies. This public recognition and status leads to privileged treatment. Athletes may have more contact with teachers and other authority figures. In time, these privileges accrue into social goods (such as college admission and employment) that reinscribe social class distinctions. Schools' policies and practices allocate privilege and advantages to males and subordination and disadvantages to females as a consequence of to the outsized importance accorded boys' sports (Tonso 2002; Fortuna 2011, 6).

The social production of difference, even in high schools serving relatively homogeneous student populations, suggests the centrality of privilege as an ordering principle in American education. Research indicates that schools set the stage for the production of oppositional peer groups and the development of hierarchical relationships between students from different groups. High school culture is ruled by hierarchies. Adolescents form cliques and rank them. Emphasis on students who participate in interscholastic sports can alienate those who don't participate, particularly among recent immigrants who are not familiar with American high school sports. Athletics can thus marginalize as well as assimilate students (Tonso 2002; Grey 1992, 255–56).

Schools promote peer culture. Friends figure into every conversation when students describe the essential ingredients of their high school experience and what would be most memorable for them. Students speak about their friends more than any other aspect of their lives. Differences are based less on gender, race, grade level, or academic skill than on social groupings such as athletes versus nonathletes (Hoffman 2002–3).

A large comprehensive high school can foster competition, conformity, and intolerance that can escalate into a kind of mean-spiritedness. A well-known instance is when hostile peer groups polarize as jocks versus nerds. These rifts infect both the academic and social environment. Evidence indicates that the problem begins in middle school, where nerds may be harassed. Studiousness is denigrated because it shifts up the grading curve and forces others, including jocks, to work harder to get good grades. Victims of harassment rarely complain to their parents, their siblings, or their friends and generally accept the reality that complaining to a teacher is self-defeating and will only exacerbate the situation (Terzian 2004, 42–45; P. Peterson 2010, 25).

Not all students have bought into the traditional school hierarchy. Groups of high school students with hip lifestyles may view sports as kid stuff. Some athletes may envy the hip males in school, who don't have to follow the strict training rules that prohibit drugs, tobacco, and late hours. A few athletes may break the training rules and secretly be admired by teammates for getting away with violations. Athletes occasionally are suspended from teams for breaking the rules (Foley 1990, 129–31).

Another oppositional group in high schools are the burnouts, rebellious teenagers who adopt a lifestyle that does not accord with the schools' middle-class ideals. They often come from working-class homes and are enrolled primarily in general and vocational courses. Burnouts engage in antiestablishment behaviors, such as disrupting class and truancy. The all-out rebels smoke pot and use other drugs, drink beer and hard liquor, skip classes, and occasionally have run-ins with the police. Burnouts reject the cultural authority of the school and feel largely rejected. As hostile behaviors perpetrated by the in-group increase, so may incidents by the threatened out-group. Such a scenario is consistent with reports regarding the Columbine High School shooters, who were said to resent the popularity of the sports clique and reacted in a dramatically antisocial manner (Tonso 2002, 439).

Many athletes, conversely, enthusiastically espouse the establishment attitude: an acceptance of the school as the all-encompassing social context. The distinct subculture of jocks aren't merely students affiliated with sports but rather student-athletes in the leading crowd whose lifestyle embraces a broader ideal associated with sports in American culture (Tonso 2002, 439).

Jock Culture

Though often used interchangeably, *jock* and *athlete* have markedly different connotations in the adolescent lexicon and are associated with conspicuously different behavior profiles. Student-athletes are admired for their athletic accomplishments and glorified in popular culture. At the same time, male athletes may be designated *jocks*, a label perceived by many as a derogatory term that connotes ignorance (evident in the derivative, *dumb jock*). Together, these personae represent the two faces of school athletics. Studies confirm the distinctions between status as an athlete and jock identity, although they constitute overlapping constructs (K. Miller et al. 2005, 180–90, 2006, 3).

In a survey of high school students, the image of athlete was almost universally complimentary. Students emphasized athletes' well-roundedness, modesty, and talent. Female students overwhelmingly characterized athletes as dedicated, motivated, determined, disciplined, and focused. Male students similarly emphasized athletes' commitment, dedication, determination, work ethic, versatility, and ability. In contrast, students identified jocks with the terms *simple-minded, egotistical, cocky, vain,* and *bullying* and particularly with the sport of football (K. Miller et al. 2006).

Even before high school games were shown on television, school teams were ranked nationally by *USA Today*, and journalists covered high school athletes' announcements of college choice, high school athletes had a certain social stature. In the post–World War I era, interscholastic athletics became a form of public entertainment and spawned a new icon, the high school sports hero, who garnered praise from local politicians, businessmen, news reporters, and the community at large. Many athletes were idolized by their fellow students. In their 1929 classic, *Middletown: A Study in Modern American Culture*, Robert S. Lynd and Helen Merrell Lynd observed that high schoolers in the 1920s reserved their highest respect for successful athletes (see Zimmerman 1999).

Not even on college campuses does being involved in sports define who one is to the extent that it does in high school. Participants in high-profile sports tend to be rewarded with significant social status both informally from peers and more formally from the official school apparatus. Because a high school's image can depends on its male athletes, they may be treated as celebrities, even demigods, deemed untouchable. Some male athletes receive preferential treatment from teachers and other authority figures (K. Miller et al. 2006, 10; Williams 2015).

The predominance and visibility of sports in schools encourage some students, regardless of their gender or athleticism, to define their identities in relation to the most popular athletes and their cliques. Star athletes may be venerated by their peers and comprise the core members of a school's in crowd. They attract friends who tend to share their elevated social status and gain membership in the more exclusive peer groups. As the in-group grows in relative prestige, those not in the clique may feel increasingly insecure, left out, or even threatened (Kreager 2007; Langbein and Bess 2002, 439).

Many boys not involved in sports envy the popularity of jocks, while some girls long to date these icons of physical prowess, viewing them as the ultimate catch. Such female adoration can lead jocks to believe that women are at their beck and call. Given the preferential treatment by fellow students as well as school authorities, male athletes may develop an exaggerated sense of self-importance (Williams 2015).

When the jocks are accorded unchallenged privilege, they enforce the social code at their schools. They often appear to run the school or at least dominate the public space, a state of affairs encapsulated by the expression "Jocks rule." One former high school baseball player described muscular football players in their varsity letter jackets striding through a crowd of students and pushing others out of the way because they're the "main guys." Sports fans observe high school football players strutting and pointing at themselves on the field in imitation of egotistical professional athletes (Zimmerman 1999; K. Miller et al. 2006; Easterbrook 2013, 214).

Off the field, jocks at times pick on other kids, particularly those who are different. This practice, if tolerated by school authorities, can lead to tragedy.

Prior to the 1999 mass shooting at Colorado's Columbine High School, varsity athletes misbehaved with impunity: one football player teased a girl about her breasts during class, while another player taunted a Jewish student by singing about Hitler. Columbine football players routinely shoved other students into lockers (L. Adams and Russakoff 1999, A1).

In Texas, high school football players are often objects of envy, with access to the best parties and the best girls, strutting proudly through the halls of the school as if it were their own private kingdom. According to one football player in the 1980s, "You walk around, you break all the rules. The teachers and administrators, they see you, the just don't say anything to you. It was just like we owned it. Everybody looked up to us; it was just a great life" (Bissinger 1990, 127). According to H. G. Bissinger, if a football player "and his friends felt like missing class and going to the lunchroom, they went to the lunchroom. If they were bored and felt like leaving class early before the bell, they just got up and walked out before the bell. If they felt like walking around the halls without the required hall pass, they walked around the halls without the required pass. If they felt like leaving school, even though it was a closed campus, to go out for lunch or go home, they left school" (1990, 291–92).

The prestige of high school jocks may be buttressed by various traditions, customs, and ceremonies. The school calendar includes days when sports teams dress up in Hawaiian clothes or pajamas to draw attention to their status. Schools award athletes letter jackets or sweaters that advertise membership on varsity teams. These garments often display patches indicating the wearers are district or state champions, a confirmation of their status. During team introductions at a Kentucky high school basketball game, the home team turns off the lights in the gym, NBA-style, as each player's name is announced. Basketball players sign autographs, and television reporters interview them following the game. High school jocks' status may be further reinforced by members of the community who patronize the better athletes, extending favors, offering them jobs (O'Brien 2012, 16, 121, 170).

The high point of an outstanding high school athlete's career is the public commitment to sign with a college. One Kentucky high school teacher released her class to attend a signing ceremony, while students in other classes excused themselves to attend. The signees sat at a table beneath photos of previous state champions and posed for photos with parents and coaches while the cameras rolled. Their sense of self-importance was manifest. Athletes courted by scouts and college coaches were overheard referring to them derisively as "jersey chasers." A former high school coach observed, "High school sports have become a breeding ground for narcissism among our adolescent student athletes" (Tufte 2012, 51).

With the negative connotations of jock culture in mind, some scholars and sportswriters are questioning the effect of school sports on minority athletes. Steve Almond (2014a, 110–11) notes that in sports such as football and basketball, two-thirds of the players are African American, thus fueling insidious stereotypes that such young men are inherently animalistic. Watching black men in mock combat has become one of our most profitable and popular forms of entertainment, leading Almond to ask, "Does it relieve the racial guilt of white Americans to lavish so much money and adulation on a few African American men? Is it an oblique form of financial restitution?" He continues, "What does it mean that we ... think nothing of calling them 'studs' and 'beasts' and 'specimens'?" African American sports columnist Shaun Powell (2008, 8–11) decries that the image of black athletes has such negative connotations: flamboyant, mouthy, gangsta rap images, putting on shows in the end zone, and other racially stereotypical behaviors.

Jock identity may lead to a disrespect for established norms and adherence to a counterethic that combines elements of exaggerated masculinity, risk-taking, and personal exemption from ordinary rules. Jock misbehavior reaches beyond their physical domination of school hallways. A growing body of research has found troubling links between jock identity and such problem behaviors as heavy drinking and binge drinking, sexual risk taking, violence, and bullying. The emerging picture suggests a "toxic jock" effect. A two-year analysis of school misconduct and changes in school grades found that adolescents who identified with the label *jock* reported more subsequent misconduct than those who did not (although such findings have been inconsistent). The effect varies based on gender and ethnicity. Female and to a lesser extent African American athletes who self-identified as jocks reported lower grades than did their nonjock peers. Sports participation had less effect on girls' misconduct in school than on that of boys. Girls participating in sports may acquire an athlete identity, whereas the male students are more susceptible to developing a jock identity. Girls of all races are less likely to perceive themselves as jocks; female athletes are also less involved in contact sports (K. Miller et al. 2005, 187–89, 2007).

A study of six hundred New York adolescents found that jock identity was associated with significantly more incidents of delinquency across genders and races, although an intervening variable may muddle the findings. Boys who get into trouble may be filtered out of sports at some point, while girls who get into trouble are filtered into sports because they are disproportionately amenable to violating conventional gender norms regarding assertiveness, competition, and physicality (K. Miller et al. 2005, 190, 2007) (see chapter 8).

High schools would clearly be best served by structuring environments where the positive attributes of sports participation prevailed and the jock characteristics were eradicated, and a few schools have done so. The Paideia School, founded in 1971 as a liberal alternative to the white-flight academies in Atlanta, sought to preempt jock culture by requiring every student to participate on a sports team and by instilling the mantra, 'I'm not a jock, I'm an athlete.' The system seems generally to have worked despite some struggles. When both the boys' and girls' basketball teams reached the Georgia state finals, hero worship reared its familiar head (Adler 1999).

At a Texas high school, following the suspension of interscholastic sports (except basketball) for budget reasons, the principal began holding sports-free pep rallies every Friday. Classes competed against each other in "drum-offs" and team-building exercises in the school gym. There were unanticipated benefits from the suspension. A speech teacher noticed a definite decline in misbehavior among students. The principal commented, "The first 12 weeks of school were the most peaceful beginning weeks I've ever witnessed at a high school" (Ripley 2013a, 76).

As these two examples indicate, school trustees and administrators need to structure an environment where the positive attributes of athletic participation supplant the negative aspects of jock culture. Striking a balance between sports and other facets of school culture conveys to students a sense of what school is about, what they should invest their efforts in, support, and feel good about.

School Spirit

What is school spirit, and why do we cultivate it? There are three distinct, interrelated dimensions of spirit in a high school setting. First, school spirit means that students contribute time and energy to academic, social, and extracurricular activities. Next, school spirit signifies a particular state of mind—prominently, loyalty to one's school and a striving for a kind of social harmony. Finally, spirit indicates a feeling of pride in one's school, a relishing of the traditions (Terzian 2004).

Specific attitudes and behaviors indicative of school spirit include involvement in school clubs and organizations, a desire to attend school events such as pep rallies, and to support the sports teams. Visible symbols of school spirit encompass personal apparel referencing the school: school colors or name, images of the team mascot, decals and bumper stickers on automobiles. School spirit extends to the larger community and is manifested in alumni support, pride, and commitment, often revolving around athletics (Reifman 2004, 18).

Students crave an ideal that will bond them and mitigate the effect of separate academic tracks, curricular specialization, and the growing sense of anonymity caused by large enrollments. This approach to creating spirit emphasizes a shared sense of purpose and interests, such as rooting at football or basketball games, although this may not be sufficient. Frequent complaints about the perceived absence of school spirit indicate that not all high school students embrace this elusive ideal. Students and school administrators fairly consistently express concern about the lack of school spirit (Terzian 2004).

Educational scholars and practitioners have voiced particular concerns that the proliferation of large comprehensive high schools with thousands of students contributes to alienation. School administrators stress school spirit to mitigate feelings of detachment and obscurity and create a sense of community and strive to bolster social cohesion via homerooms, student assemblies, supervised clubs, and various other activities. At best, school spirit appears to offer a way to lift the veil of anonymity and perhaps to remedy some of the symptoms of student alienation. Studies indicate that school spirit thrives in high schools when a significant percentage of enrolled students are involved in co-curricular and extracurricular activities (Terzian 2004).

Sports play a prominent role in creating school spirit. Athletics have been touted for inspiring students to think of themselves as unified members of their school. This relationship has several dimensions. Students may find sports exciting and stimulating, which sets these activities apart from much of the rest of school offerings. Whether as athletes or as spectators, students' involvement in sports allows them to rise above the humdrum monotony of the school environment (Miracle and Rees 1994, 224).

Interscholastic sports generate calendar rituals. Homecoming—the custom of welcoming back alumni—is another tradition that began at the college level and moved to high schools. Usually held in late September or early October, during football season on a week when there is a home game, high school homecomings focus on a central event such as a banquet and include various activities for both students and alumni. Parades feature the school marching bands and athletes. A homecoming king, queen, and court are crowned at halftime of the football game, and there is usually a dance. Some schools organize a homecoming pep rally with a bonfire in the school parking lot (Foley 1990, 116–17).

Pep rallies are a tradition of assembling students and others in a large area such as the gymnasium prior to a sports event. Classes may be dismissed so students can attend. The purpose of such gatherings is to excite students for an upcoming game and to cheer on the team. Cheerleaders lead boisterous chants and perform dance moves. The school's band or drumline plays upbeat music. Seated on the raised platform are the school principal and coaches. Team captains take the stage and garner support for the team. A large picture of the school mascot is displayed, along with victory slogans, and students wave signs. In Texas during football season, some high schools hold weekly pep rallies (Foley 1990, 116–17; Miracle and Rees 1994, 57–58).

According to Gray Levy (2015, 96) at a Tuesday evening pep rally in Texas, the stands on one side of the school gym were packed with community members rattling noisemakers. The football team sat in folding chairs on the gym floor, while the band played, cheerleaders danced and cheered, a highlight film was shown, and the head football coach revved up the crowd. On Thursday morning, fans lined both sides of the road as the football team departed for a midweek playoff game. A Kentucky high school's annual Thanksgiving pep rally includes a procession of the fall sports athletes, a rendition of the national anthem, a performance by the cheerleading squad dancing to techno music, a teacher-student volleyball game, a presentation of the class presidents, and a hip-hop performance by a group of senior boys that mimics the cheerleaders' attire and demeanor (O'Brien 2012, 3).

Efforts to foster school (or team) spirit are apparent in the other rituals, ceremonies, and hoopla that increasingly augment athletic events, especially football and basketball. A growing number of high school football teams have adopted elaborate procedures for taking the field, in imitation of college teams, that include running through inflatable tunnels with smoke-filled exits. Cheerleaders and members of drill teams line up in parallel rows at the tunnel exit. Male students bearing school flags stand nearby. The band plays a fight song as the team bursts out of the tunnel and sprints the length of the field (Levy 2015, 118). And the pregame showmanship also features flashing electronic scoreboards and hyperbolic rhetoric broadcast over public address systems to excite fans.

All of these developments do not address the central questions of whether interscholastic sports are effective in generating school spirit and whether schools should even be seeking this particular expression of spirit? Some advocates of school sports strongly believe that winning teams and their proud traditions enhance the value of a high school education. New students must be taught the importance of such allegiances because indifference to these ideals will yield an impersonal and fragmented environment (Terzian 2004).

But there are grounds on which to challenge this approach to generating school spirit. Student attendance at school athletic contests is declining—according to one recent study, fewer than 10 percent of students attended high school games (Sacks 2012). Critics also question whether the forms of orchestrated enthusiasm at football and basketball games translate into genuine school spirit beyond the arena. When local residents rally around high school teams, this seems to enhance community spirit, but does the same hold true for students? The relationship between sports and school spirit appears to be a mixed bag. While interscholastic sports are touted for creating a sense of community and feelings of loyalty, they also can create an us-versus-them mentality in relation to other schools (Griffin 1998, 72). Moreover, the adulation of school athletes may create discord within schools.

Can schools be effective in the absence of school spirit generated by sports? Do schools without interscholastic sports programs harbor school spirit? One high school that was too small to field major sports teams compensated by competing in statewide music competitions, creating student pride in the school's musicians. The most popular students were the leading musicians rather than star athletes (Sitkowski 2008, 26). Both trade schools and schools that rely on online courses sponsor few extracurricular activities: Do such institutions suffer from lack of school spirit? Does it make any difference to the students?

The Anachronism of Cheerleading

Although interscholastic athletes (typically males) occupy center stage and receive the lion's share of attention, members of another, primarily female, group, cheerleaders, are assigned responsibility for generating spirit. Orchestrated enthusiasm, such as prompted cheering at sporting events, comes across as inauthentic. Critics regard it as shallow boosterism, gratuitous enthusiasm. Genuine expression of fervor (excitement, enthusiasm) is intrinsically motivated and unprompted. Thus, cheerleading can be seen as a contrivance. This is not a novel perspective. A. Lawrence Lowell, who served as president of Harvard University from 1909 to 1933, described cheerleading as "the worst means of expressing emotion ever invented" (Lurie 2014) The early promoters of college athletics convinced themselves that it might be beneficial to recruit squads of students to lead the attending fans in cheers from the sidelines, a distinctly American ritual that later filtered down to the nation's high schools. Organized cheering at athletic events might best be viewed as a sequence of ritual acts framed as supporting the team.

Historical accounts suggest that organized cheerleading began at the University of Minnesota in the 1890s and soon gained popularity at Ivy League colleges. Cheerleading was institutionalized on college campuses in the early twentieth century. The overwhelming majority of college cheerleaders were males, and women did not begin joining cheerleading squads until the 1920s. Cheerleading flourished along with football, as campuses around the nation began building giant stadiums to accommodate spectators. In the 1930s, cheerleaders began using megaphones to excite crowds. By the 1940s, cheerleaders were working the crowds in the nation's high schools. After World War II, the image and perception of cheerleading began to change. While the head cheerleader typically was a male, cheerleading squads were mostly female. Ultimately, high school cheerleading became a feminine subsidiary of masculine athletics. The selection of school cheerleaders was tied to the notion of ideal femininity (Bennett 1990; Munro 2006, 22–23; N. Adams and Bettis 2003, 29; Bettis and Adams 2006, 22–23).

Today, virtually every middle and high school in the nation sponsors cheerleading squads. Sports cheerleading at the amateur level currently has more than three million participants, 97 percent of them female. Some predominantly Latino high schools have as many as fifty cheerleaders, although the typical school squad is much smaller (Sailer 2007, 26). The practice of cheerleading is widely supported by school administrators and the community. Schools conduct tryouts and interviews for the cheerleading squad; some even provide cheerleading preparation classes. Auditions may have student judges but are essentially controlled by the staff, either in person or by proxy. Because there is so much competition for positions on the squads, judges wield immense power and easily obtain compliance and submission from aspiring cheerleaders (Bennett 1990). Parents have filed suits against school districts claiming that the selection process wasn't fair (N. Adams and Bettis 2003, 121, 124–25).

Cheerleading has been a high-status activity, often the most visible space for female students to inhabit. Girls have recognized and coveted the prestige associated with the activity. Being on the cheerleading squad conferred a special cachet. Cheerleaders formed cliques and sat together in the school cafeteria. Like football players in their game jerseys, the cheerleaders walked school halls and classrooms in their outfits, flaunting their status. In contrast, the leading female actor in the school play doesn't wear her costume offstage; the academically gifted girl doesn't display her report card sewn onto the front of her sweater (N. Adams and Bettis 2003, 2–5; Bennett 1990).

Some girls see cheerleading as a route to popularity, and some boys regard cheerleaders as the ultimate prize, with dating a cheerleader serving as an affirmation of masculinity and coolness. Some males view cheerleaders as status as well as sexual objects; at the same time, other students disparage cheerleaders as stuck up or even sluts (Foley 1990, 115; Bennett 1990; Bettis and Adams 2006, 127).

Recent cultural developments have affected the perceptions of female cheerleaders. Radical changes to ideas about the roles and expectations of women during the 1960s and 1970s led to greater participation by adolescent girls in sports and other traditionally male activities. However, prior to Title IX, cheerleading often was the only organized extracurricular physical activity for high school girls of the 1970s (N. Adams and Bettis 2003, 58–59).

Title IX's regulations took effect in 1975 and resulted in a significant transformation. As schools were required to sponsor more girls' sports, some in the male sports establishment responded by redefining cheerleading as a sport, a tactic bolstered by second-wave feminism's support for competition among women. The emphasis on competing both remasculinized cheerleading and maintained its market appeal among a new generation of girls with more options for athletic involvement. Advocates of the redefinition of cheerleading have argued that the activity's emphasis on athleticism and competition exemplifies the emerging elasticity in gender roles (Grindstaff and West 2005, 71; Munro 2006, 25).

Under Title IX, cheerleading had to meet certain guidelines to be recognized as a sport: its overarching mission had to be not presentations at male teams' competitions but rather competition against other squads on a regular season and postseason qualification basis (in much the same structure as gymnastics) and had to conduct regular, coach-supervised practices in preparation for such competition. The cheerleading teams could occasionally put on exhibitions at boys' or men's sports events, but these exhibitions could not be the cheerleaders' primary purpose (Boyce 2008).

Two dozen states eventually granted high school cheerleading Title IX status, and by 2004, roughly half the country's state high school associations promoted competitive cheerleading as a sport. Some schools began referring to such squads as "stunt teams" (Grindstaff and West 2005, 2, 9). Florida's high school athletic association recognized cheerleading as a sport in 2007; however, cheerleading squads enjoyed smaller expenditures for coaching, facilities, insurance, transportation, and uniforms than did boys' sports (Boyce 2008).

Cheerleading teams in states whose high school athletic associations do not sanction cheerleading have to cover their own costs, often running to hundreds of dollars monthly. Girls on these cheerleading squads fund-raise, but most of the financial burden of cheering falls on parents, who can spend in excess of a thousand dollars on cheerleading activities. Cheerleaders' uniforms cost more than one hundred dollars, and some schools require each girl to purchase three sets. Sleeves for the uniforms cost twenty-five dollars apiece, as do pom-poms. Jackets, backpacks, and shoes cost around sixty dollars each.

And the hours of practice mean that cheerleaders don't have time for regular after-school jobs, leaving parents to foot the bill (Fowler 2016).

The legal controversy about the status of cheerleading has persisted. In 2012, a US circuit court affirmed a lower court ruling that the elimination of volleyball by a school could not be counteracted by the elevation of cheerleading because "cheerleading is not a sport for the purposes of determining compliance with Title IX." As the court explained, neither the NCAA nor the US Department of Education recognizes cheerleading as a sport (M. Ryan 2012–13, 5). The Women's Sports Foundation, too, has refused to recognize cheerleading as a sport. Many feminists feel that high school girls, like their male counterparts, would be better served by competing on sports teams. Thus, while cheerleading obviously contains an element of athleticism, it is not universally considered a sport. Those who disagree with the circuit court ruling point out that the aesthetic performance demands of cheerleading are not unlike those of figure skating (N. Adams and Bettis 2003, 13).

Promoters of cheerleading worried that young women would prefer to participate in other activities, but such concerns have proven unfounded. Cheerleading has remained a popular activity. As cheerleading has become more competitive, it has incorporated the strategies of interscholastic sports. Cheerleading squads practice every day after school, with some squads holding additional practice sessions during school hours. Teenage cheerleaders can spend as many hours a week practicing as do varsity athletes. Cheerleaders may also enroll in private tumbling lessons. Cheerleading teams now hire outside choreographers to teach dance moves, many of which aren't performed at pep rallies or on the sidelines but in competition, and choreographers commonly charge between two thousand and five thousand dollars for a two-day camp (Fowler 2016).

Cheerleading camps and national associations date back to the 1950s. Jeff Webb, a former college cheerleader who advocated incorporating more gymnastics into the activity, founded the Universal Cheerleaders Association in 1974 (www.uca.varsity.com). The organization has subsequently held hundreds of competitions, clinics, and camps with a focus on acrobatic stunts and pyramids. In 1980, the association held the first National High School Cheerleading Championship. By the mid-1980s, some 150,000 young women were participating in cheerleading clinics each year. The competitive cheerleading establishment foregrounds the activity's sports-like features while minimizing its feminine aspects (N. Adams and Bettis 2003, 5–6, 11; Lurie 2014; Grindstaff and West 2005, 12).

The advent of cheer competitions led to the development of competitive routines that integrate cheerleading, dance, and stunts involving intense physical exertion—tumbling, pyramids, and jumps (Boyce 2008). As the stunts became more athletic and competitive, cheerleading squads began training year-round and incorporated weight training. The Universal Cheerleading Association claimed that as a result of girls' increasing participation in athletics, cheering itself was becoming more overtly physical and athletic. This emphasis also led to more injuries. Organizations sponsoring competition eventually developed safety guidelines and rules for the sport (Munro 2006, 30; N. Adams and Bettis 2003, 5, 48–49).

If commercial interest is any indication, cheerleading experienced a renaissance around the turn of the twenty-first century. By 2001, ESPN was broadcasting more than a dozen cheerleading championships each year, and the biggest film of that summer was *Bring It On*, about a competitive high school cheer squad in Southern California. Two cheerleader reality TV shows debuted in the first decade of the twenty-first century, and scores of cheerleading specials aired on cable television (Grindstaff and West 2005, 2). *American Cheerleader* magazine released its first issue in 1995. Texas has the nation's largest cheerleading market, and the cheerleader magazines that are now available include *Texas Cheerleader*. Some four dozen companies and businesses cater solely to cheerleading (Munro 2006, 21; N. Adams and Bettis 2003, 7).

Both competitive and sideline cheerleading endure in the post–Title IX era, and squads are based not only in schools but in private cheerleading clubs. Competitive squads normally don't cheer for other athletic teams but compete solely in state and national tournaments, making *cheerleading* a misnomer for their activities (N. Adams and Bettis 2003, 39). Sideline cheerleaders continue to work the crowds at pep rallies, football stadiums, and basketball arenas.

While sideline cheerleaders and football players perform in the same arena, the gendered meanings of the two roles are worlds apart, leading some critics to characterize cheerleaders as football players' "perky heterosexual helpmates" (Pascoe 2007, 117–18). Progressive educators argue that girls should be playing sports, not cheering from the sidelines, but many schools and parents encourage girls to assume this auxiliary role. Sarah, a high school student relates, "I wanted to play football. . . . But my mom didn't [want me to], and I think that's why I didn't get to play. So I became a cheerleader"—what she saw as the closest thing to playing football (117–18).

Current school practices perpetuate the traditional gender divide in the nation's sports arena. When girls compete, they do so against other girls. But it is also common for boys to compete against each other while girls cheer them on. The boys are ensconced in pads and helmets and battle heroically on the field, while the girls are on the sidelines in skimpy outfits imploring the boys, "Hold that line" and "Move that ball!" After a touchdown is scored, female cheerleaders have been observed getting on their knees and bowing down to the male players. Cheerleaders often don't even face the game; they face the spectators. Some sports aficionados argue that cheerleaders detract from the game (Ryan 2012–13, 2; N. Adams and Bettis 2003, 1–2, 132).

High school cheerleaders' responsibilities have extended beyond the field of play. At many schools, they have been responsible for decorating the hallways, performing at pep rallies, and painting paper signs for football players to run through as they enter the arena (N. Adams and Bettis 2003, 15). High school girls who don't make the cheerleading squad may join the pep squad, which helps spark crowd enthusiasm at games and publicize athletics by decorating the school and town with sports-related slogans and paraphernalia (Foley 1990, 116). At Odessa High School in West Texas in the 1980s, each girl on the pep squad, the Pepettes, brought sweets for "her player" every week before the game. In addition, each Pepette made a large sign for her player's front yard for the duration of the football season, signaling his status as a football player to the community. Some girls spent more than one hundred dollars on signs festooned with twinkling lights. The girls also constructed scrapbooks for their players that included collections of news clippings (Bissinger 1990, 45).

Cheerleading constitutes what social scientists label emotional labor, defined as "the management of feeling to create a publicly observable facial and bodily display" (Munro 2006, 26). Cheerleaders are required to sustain an outward countenance that produces the proper state of mind in others. Cheerleaders express enthusiasm and rally the crowd by performing happiness and constantly moving—jumping and executing dynamic arm, hand, and head motions that are considered feminine terrain. Cheerleaders are expected to motivate others to be spirited, which means that they must appear spirited and charismatic regardless of their particular personal feelings at the time. In short, cheerleading is performance (Grindstaff and West 2005, 14).

The performance aspect of sideline cheerleaders' personae is obvious in comparison to their appearance and behavior in private cheer practices. In this setting, they often wear loose-fitting clothes, their hair may not be tied with bows or held down with hair spray, they may be without makeup, and they aren't obliged to smile. The shrinking number of male cheerleaders highlights the tension between conventional notions of performance and notions of heterosexual masculinity. Some heterosexual men are resistant to the elements of cheerleading associated with femininity (Munro 2006, 30; Grindstaff and West 2005, 15).

Cheerleading continues to occupy contested space in American culture. The relative positions of status groups in schools has shifted. While jocks remain popular, cheerleaders are less exalted, perhaps because girls are now playing more sports. The continuing debate about cheerleading reveals the process by which cultural dualities between masculinity and femininity are contested and reconstructed as well as the degree to which cheerleading resists occupying either side of the divide (Grindstaff and West 2005, 1).

Popular representations of the cheerleader remain contradictory. In some settings, cheerleaders represent the pinnacle of popularity, while in others they are the target of scorn and ridicule. Adults in the community typically construct cheerleaders as the "good girls" whose sole rationale for joining the squad has to do with school spirit and motivation. The school cheerleader is a recognized symbol of youthful prestige, wholesome attractiveness, peer leadership, and popularity. At the same time, the cheerleader has become a symbol of mindless enthusiasm, objectified sexuality, and promiscuous availability. Cheerleading is associated with shallowness and narcissism. Detractors maintain that the conformity and confused priorities behind costumes and routines really don't represent anything (Grindstaff and West 2005, 2; Bettis and Adams 2006, 103; Munro 2006, 21, 23).

Sociologists observe that cheerleading symbolizes a dominant ideology of how females should look and act in contemporary society. Cheerleading clearly embodies taken-for-granted beliefs about "natural" gender difference and performs these distinctions through scripted public displays. Observational studies suggest that girls don't inherently embody the feminine ideal of the cheerleader. Rather, they learn to execute this ideal in accordance with the cultural stereotype. Cheerleading, like beauty pageants, represents versions of ideal womanhood and sends the message that a girl's worth is based primarily on her appearance. Cheerleaders, however acrobatic, are required to maintain the image of femininity (N. Adams and Bettis 2003, 113, 136; Grindstaff and West 2005, 3; Bettis and Adams 2006, 103; Munro 2006, 30).

Cheerleading symbolizes objectified sexuality if not promiscuous availability, but this facet of cheerleading is typically unacknowledged. Cheerleading provides a school-sanctioned space where males can gaze on young women. Because they literally stand out in the crowd, cheerleaders are prime targets for sexual assessment if not harassment. Cheerleaders perform in short skirts and provocative lipstick. Many contemporary cheerleader moves are sexually suggestive. Routines that promote ogling include kicking their legs into the air, snapping their fingers, swaying their hips, and doing breast juts. Middle school cheerleaders put their hands on the sides of their pelvic bones and sway their hips. High school cheerleaders perform pelvic thrusts.

Some cheerleaders' outfits would constitute a violation of school dress codes (Boyce 2008; N. Adams and Bettis 2003, 29, 83–84; Bettis and Adams 2006, 127–28; Levy 2015, 22).

The prevailing notion of the contemporary American cheerleader is that of a slender, fit, attractive, heterosexual young woman who is alluring in the abstract but untouchable in reality. A New Jersey high school cheerleader proclaims, "I'm sexy, I'm cute, I'm popular to boot. That's what cheerleaders are." A certain amount of sexual provocation is allowed, as long as it doesn't cross over into vulgarity, although it is difficult to define what crosses the line (Munro 2006, 28, 30). Cheerleading activity conveys a clear indication of sexual availability, yet such access is explicitly forbidden. Thus, cheerleading is a form of sexual teasing controlled and cultivated by schools. This message is not likely to be lost on males and may contribute to misogyny among male students. Detractors charge that school cheerleading is an attempt to hide sexual exploitation behind a veil of enthusiasm for sports (Bennett 1990).

Another troubling dimension of the cheerleader persona involves the fact that the requirements for holding a cheerleading position are precisely what American society expects from a delightful little girl: upbeat, acquiescent, fun to be with, satisfied with trifles. The high school cheerleader is thus portrayed in a way that denies her maturity in age or experience. A preschool girl who wears skirts that allow her underwear to show is not considered unusual, but an adolescent with an adult figure joyously displaying simulated underwear is certainly erotic (Bennett 1990).

In a word, female cheerleaders are infantilized. They are dressed as toddlers in short skirts, brightly colored and visible undergarments, and hair ribbons and are encouraged to verbally emulate preschoolers by performing songs and yells that feature nonsense words, rhymes, and spelled-out words (Bennett 1990).

The sexualizing of school cheerleaders was amplified by the introduction of professional cheerleading squads in the 1970s—perhaps most notably, the Dallas Cowboys Cheerleaders, who became the prototype of the sexy cheerleader. The sexual connotations of cheerleading have been further exploited in popular films and pornography(Bettis and Adams 2006, 131; N. Adams and Bettis 2003, 74; Lurie 2014).

There are growing concerns about the health implications and safety of cheerleading. Female cheerleaders not only share the risk factors for eating disorders that affect other young females but face additional issues. Revealing costumes may exacerbate body consciousness, and lower body weights make lifts and other stunts easier. Coaches may enforce weight standards, and some cheerleading teams require group weigh-ins. One study found that high school cheerleaders exhibit more body dissatisfaction and more eating disorders than do college cheerleaders (Boyce 2008).

In addition, the increased emphasis on stunts has resulted in rising injury rates among cheerleaders, and they, like male athletes, may be pressured to perform with injuries such as broken wrists and fingers and torn ligaments. Ankle injuries are the most common, followed by the neck, lower back, knee, and wrist. A large majority of injuries occur during practice, as is the case in football. Catastrophic cheerleading injuries are most likely to occur during pyramids and basket catches and to result from tumbling moves, basing, and falls. A large percentage of falls involved more than one participant. While risks are inherent to sideline cheerleading, competitive cheerleading harbors a distinct set of concerns, as the presentations are judged on several criteria including athleticism and degree of risk (N. Adams and Bettis 2003, 63; Bagnulo 2012, 293–94; Boyce 2008).

Cheerleading ranks low compared to school sports in overall injuries but is second to football in the number of catastrophic injuries, and those cheerleading injuries have included skull and cervical fractures and even a handful of fatalities. Cheerleading injuries account for about half of all catastrophic injuries to high school female athletes, and high school cheerleading accounts for some 65 percent of all female catastrophic sports injuries. Moreover, the rate of injuries may be underreported (N. Adams and Bettis 2003, 53–54; Bagnulo 2012, 295).

In one study of twenty-two high school sports, seventeen had higher injury rates than cheerleading, but only gymnastics had more injuries that caused athletes to be benched for at least three weeks: 11 percent of injuries sidelined cheerleaders for three weeks or more, and 5 percent of injuries proved season- or career-ending. Researchers recommend that evidence-based efforts to prevent cheerleading injuries be aimed at specific activities that put cheerleaders at risk for the most severe injuries (Venosa 2015). Concussions are a particular concern: 70 percent of cheerleader concussions occurred during stunts when cheerleaders were lifted into the air, whereas 16 percent occurred during pyramid formations and 9 percent during tumbling. Cheerleading injuries have led to their fair share of lawsuits, although schools generally are immune from liability short of outright negligence (Boyce 2008).

Given the expansion of opportunities for girls to participate in legitimate sports and the radical transformation of women's roles in society, many athletic young women have abandoned the sidelines to share center stage with their male peers, leaving cheerleading as something of an anachronism. In a society that is moving toward encouraging women to derive their sense of worth not from physical appearance but from values and accomplishments, schools should seriously consider eliminating what progressive educators recognize as a mindless and sexist holdover from the past.

Marching Bands: The Thrall of Football

The nation's secondary schools sponsor music education programs that include both curricular and extracurricular activities. High school music courses are generally electives that attract a significant number of students, who participate in concert bands, jazz bands, choirs, and theatrical performances that include music. Marching bands have become the most visible component of the music extracurriculum, with an estimated two million US students participating as of 2007 (Cohen 2007). School orchestras and bands have been a part of music education for more than a century, while marching bands have a distinct history.

Marching bands began with traveling musicians who performed together at festivals and celebrations, and this tradition persists via marching bands' participation in street parades. Perhaps most notably, New Orleans's "main line" or "first line" brass bands play a prominent role in Mardi Gras celebrations and funeral processions. High school and college marching bands also perform at such events as the annual Rose Bowl Parade and Macy's Thanksgiving Day Parade.

Another form of marching band, the military band, arose as a consequence of the development of national armies. Musicians initially directed the movement of troops on the battlefield, but as communications technology developed, military marching bands moved increasingly into ceremonial roles. Many military traditions survive in modern college and high school marching bands—for example, they march in formation and respond to commands such as "about face" and "forward march." Marching bands may employ a drum major who carries a baton or mace. Some bands incorporate the nuances of the drum and bugle corps or even carry dummy rifles. Uniforms of school marching bands (and some first line bands) resemble military uniforms. The traditional music of the marching band is the military march.

In the seventeenth century, composers began writing music especially for marching bands, which typically featured brass, woodwind, and percussion instruments. Such bands became common in the United States during the following century. George Washington wrote about a parade at Valley Forge that featured a military band of fifes and drums. The US Military Academy Band was organized in 1815. John Philip Sousa became conductor of the US Marine Band in 1880, touring the world and becoming known as the March

King, a title he earned by writing more than a hundred marches. Military bands played at graduation ceremonies at Harvard, Princeton, and other colleges and universities (see Garty 2003).

The first uniformed college marching band may have been founded at the University of Wisconsin in the 1880s. Purdue University's All-American Marching Band was organized in 1886. These bands were visible ambassadors of school spirit. Pep rallies and homecoming parades came to depend more and more on marching bands, and by the early twentieth century, college bands had begun playing at halftimes of football games. The bands enlivened these occasions and got people on their feet, clapping and cheering for the home team (Garty 2003). Over time, college marching bands developed more and more ways to entertain the audience and to showcase their music and marching maneuvers.

Band uniforms featured shakos, pith helmets, feather plumes, gloves, and sometimes gauntlets, sashes, and/or capes; uniforms displayed school names. Marching bands evolved from carrying the national flag to carrying school colors and decorative swing flags that added sparkle on the field. Field formations date back to the early 1900s, when the Marching Illini at the University of Illinois formed a block *I* in parades and halftime shows (see Garty 2003). Soon marching bands were executing formations that suggested pictorial images and geometric shapes as well as letters. Today's marching bands employ drill writers and visual coordinators, along with choreographers who write scripts for the band's maneuvers. Some of these scripts rival football playbooks in thickness (Lane 2001, 104–5).

High schools began organizing marching bands based on the college model just as high school sports imitated intercollegiate athletics, and high school marching bands began performing at school athletic events, including football halftimes. Today the great majority of high schools feature marching bands that perform at athletic events. To a considerable extent, the prominence of interscholastic athletics has shaped marching band programs. Directors of large bands have a staff comparable to coaching staffs of major sports, and schools may give physical education credits for participation in the marching band. And like sports, bands have a feeder system in which students may begin training for the marching band while in elementary school (Sussman 2011, 23; Foley 1990, 114).

This close association with athletics had both plusses and minuses. A high school administrator in Michigan observed, "If your band program's successful and your football team wins, that's the image your school has, even though your standardized test scores may not be the highest.... It's a shame, but it's the rules we play under" (Wieberg 2004). According to a Texas high school band director, football games are "one area where we really reach the community. One of the most visible activities our school does is have a football game every Friday night. That's what our community sees, and that somehow relates to the climate of the entire school. We're out there to support that team, and the community, in turn, supports us. In addition, we also support the community through store openings, pep rallies, Veteran's Day celebrations, holiday parades, and so on" (Sussman 2011, 25). And there is nothing wrong with band students performing at public events in the community—within limits.

But school bands are routinely appropriated to serve the needs of varsity sports, often to the detriment of the musicians. School funds are reallocated in favor of athletics, facilities are hijacked, and music rehearsals are rescheduled to accommodate the needs of sports teams and coaches. The favoritism affects music education at a basic level. The band program's core ensemble is the concert band. While concert bands can be justified for their intrinsic contribution to a liberal education, school marching bands are, for the most part, organized to serve one purpose—entertaining crowds at athletic events. This leads to internal inequities in the school music program. The school marching band has a much greater importance and visibility than the school orchestra, as is reflected in the substantial expenditures for special uniforms, instruments, and paraphernalia (Grey 1992, 261).

Many of these expenses are passed along to students' families. Some instruments can cost thousands of dollars. One high school band director in Mississippi recently spent fifty-five thousand dollars on six sousaphones. Band members may also be asked to pay fees of several hundred dollars a year (Fowler 2016).

Serious musicians complain that the emphasis on marching bands can distort music education and ask whether the optimal way to master an instrument in a group setting is to spend hours on an athletic field playing very loudly while executing stylized steps and performing closely choreographed maneuvers. Does rehearsing the same constricted genre of music from June to November support the overall development of music students? Marching band members spend as much time memorizing moves in formation as they do memorizing musical scores. These students might be better off playing in a stage band, absorbing the intricacies of sound production and air flow and being introduced to a range of musical forms (Lane 2001, 157–58).

Music educators charge that marching band members are not involved primarily in getting a music education but are an entertainment adjunct to the football team (Deford 2013). Professional musician and former athlete John Gerdy (2015) believes that "it is fair to say that those big marching bands are just as much about supporting the spectacle of football as they are about pure music." Gerdy adds, "If I were a serious musician, I'd get more value out of a music group that is solely about the music as opposed to having to satisfy expectations regarding providing an element of spectacle." According to one professional bandleader, the visual spectacle of a marching band upstages the music: the eye-catching maneuvers are often accompanied by mediocre music with musicians often out of sync and hitting the wrong notes. Sports fans primarily appreciate the spectacle. When a marching band performs on an athletic field, the notes emanating from each musician's instrument (traveling at the speed of sound) reach the other musicians at slightly different intervals, complicating musicians' efforts to stay in sync. If the distance between musicians and the audience is large, listeners may perceive waves to be out of phase. While band directors are aware of this phenomenon and try to compensate, the synchronization of the score is often compromised. Given the nature of this environment, it's not surprising that the visual spectacle takes precedence over the quality of the music. If music were the principal reason that bands performed at athletic contests, the band would limit its performance to playing music in the stands, the typical format at basketball games.

Playing in a marching band can have troubling repercussions for band members. Marching bands often practice for hours in small rooms at volumes intended for football stadium audiences. Studies show that marching band members endure long-term exposure to sound levels of more than 100 decibels, an intensity at which unprotected ears can be damaged in just fifteen minutes according to the National Institute for Occupational Safety and Health. High school band members report developing headaches and tinnitus (ringing in the ears), while the long-term effects of the damage may be irreversible and may not be noticed for years. A few bands require percussionists to wear earplugs, but they can prevent students from hearing instructions and the nuances of the music. In addition, horn players have been known to damage their lips by playing too loud for too long (Cohen 2007).

Many high school students may be afraid to complain about marching band culture, though some are not: wrote one student on an online blog ("To March" 2010), "Marching Band is expensive, it's all the same stuff for 3–5 months, it teaches bad playing habits, it dissuades students from continuing in band, it is very time consuming, and frankly can be argued that it is very unmusical in its concept." Some students argue that music teachers and band directors should focus on enhancing players' sense of musicality, rhythmic accuracy, intonation, and other basics (Cohen 2007).

Parents, for their part, complain about the length and frequency of practice sessions. At some schools, marching band practice runs till 10:00 p.m. on school nights, interfering with homework. Some high school bands practice for an hour at the beginning and end of each school day (Sussman 2011, 26). And in many cases, all of this rehearsing is for a stadium performance that lasts as little as minutes. (In Texas, however, high school football halftimes may run twenty-eight minutes, and some bands also perform postgame concerts under the scoreboard.) Band practices often take place during the summer, with intensive "band camps" filling up the weeks before school starts. Practicing eight hours a day for two weeks in the summer heat can leave students exhausted (Levy 2015, 119–20; Fowler 2016).

Attendance at band camps may be mandatory. One Pennsylvania district required all music students to attend summer band camp and participate in marching band at football games: those who refused were prohibited from joining the concert band, the symphonic band, the jazz band, and the school orchestra. When one parent complained that this requirement constituted extortion, schools in the district protested that excusing students from marching band would result in smaller bands that made less of an impression at halftime (Deford 2013).

Indeed, a school may take great pride in the size of its marching band. Kentucky's Scott County High School boasts that its two-hundred-member marching band is the largest in the state (O'Brien 2012, 195). Texas's Allen High School proudly declares that its six-hundred-member band is the nation's largest (Levy 2015, 219; Bishop 2011; Sussman 2011, 20). But there is no music-related reason why bands must be so large: the average concert orchestra has between forty and seventy players, and even some larger collegiate symphony bands have no more than about one hundred members. Are a dozen sousaphones really necessary? Do they enhance the quality of the music, or do they simply provide a visual spectacle?

Parents are an important component of the band program, from chaperoning buses to sewing buttons on uniforms to handing out food and water to band members. "Pit dads" help move heavy equipment and the steel tower from which the assistant director presides over practice, while "box parents" oversee uniform boxes (Sussman 2011, 25; Lane 2001, 104, 157).

Many students and community members clearly appreciate school marching bands. In one Ohio town, female "spirit squad" acknowledge marching band musicians by planting wooden "bandie" cutouts on their front lawns—the same practice used to acknowledge football players in some places. Coaches and administrators occasionally hold formal appreciation ceremonies for marching bands (Atkin 1998; Foley 1990, 114; Gordon 2012).

In a growing number of towns, bands have their own booster clubs, with membership fees ranging into the hundreds of dollars. One Texas high school has a 250-member marching band supported by a booster club that has raised more than $150,000 per year. A Mississippi high school's band boosters bought an eighteen-wheel trailer to transport equipment to parades, away games, and competitions. High schools without booster clubs may put pressure on band members to raise funds (Levy 2015, 112–3; Fowler 2016).

The competitive ethos that has become pervasive in interscholastic sports has made its way into the band arena, with high school marching bands taking part in competitions at the local, district, and state levels. Judging reflects precision movement as much as music. The Bands of America Grand National Championships, held in Indianapolis, include one hundred of the nation's best high school bands (Lane 2001, 163; "Bands of America" n.d.).

High school marching bands also travel to appear in high-profile parades. One Ohio high school band has appeared in parades in Miami, Atlanta, Pittsburgh, Cleveland, Chicago, and New York, including three Macy's Thanksgiving Day Parades. The travel expenses can be formidable. High schools have been known to spend exorbitant sums so their marching bands can participate in presidential inaugural parades (Atkin 1998).

The benefits of music education are well established and widely acknowledged. Mastering a musical instrument requires perseverance, discipline, and hard work. Marching bands offer a way to include a significant number of students in a school activity and require many of the same sorts of teamwork skills as athletic teams do. Students who take part in band and orchestra, like participants in other extracurricular activities, are less likely to drop out of school. And music can become a lifelong leisure activity that provides pleasure and a sense of accomplishment.

However, high school athletics have a way of subordinating and co-opting curricular and extracurricular activities. Music education suffers when it becomes the handmaiden of varsity sports. School administrators and district board members must ensure that school activities are conducted in the best interests of students and are not appropriated by external interests that can sabotage their educational mission. Music educators should take the lead in restoring school band programs to their legitimate function. If community members wish to by entertained by high school musicians, they should attend school concerts.

◆ ◆ ◆

School cultures should not be dominated by sports. Rather, schools should be honoring scholars, not placing football players on a pedestal. Adolescents will choose their own heroes, but educators have the responsibility to help clarify values. Schools should honor not only accomplished athletes but also members of the debate team, science fair participants, talented musicians, and honor roll students. And these groups will overlap.

School administrators and teachers should discourage jock culture and its abuses. Status groups and cliques will persist among students, but by removing themselves from the sports entertainment business, schools can go a long way toward eliminating the phenomenon of privileged athletes who feel that the rules don't apply to them. Rabid sports fans in the community should be induced to look elsewhere for heroes to venerate. Adolescents should not be treated as celebrities.

Sideline cheerleading should be phased out, eliminating the objectifying, sexualizing, and infantilizing of young women. Students who wish to pursue competitive cheerleading can find nonschool avenues to accommodate their interests, while those interested in acrobatics should be steered into gymnastics programs.

School bands should receive support in their own right, not as an adjunct to spectator sports (see Gerdy 2014). If music educators see an educational value in marching bands, then schools can sponsor these activities. Student musicians can march in civic parades within the parameters of the school budget.

THE TROUBLED RELATIONSHIP BETWEEN INTERSCHOLASTIC SPORTS AND ACADEMICS

> While it's a shame when Johnny can't read, it's not so bad if he can really play!
> —Robert McCabe

The American experience has been infused with episodic reports and studies lamenting the status of educational achievement. Recent findings are often based on comparisons with other developed nations. These critical assessments invariably trigger reform agendas. A reform effort was launched in the mid 1980s following the publication of the widely heralded report, *A Nation at Risk* (1983). This document, drawing on national and international test data, accused the nation's system of public education of being awash in "a rising tide of mediocrity" and thus constituting a severe threat to the present and future economic health of the nation. The crux of the reform effort was centered on the establishment and implementation of nationally approved, uniform, world-class academic standards at the state and local levels. The federal government vigorously advocated a system of national and comparative international standardized testing. The reformers questioned the idea that students should be "socially promoted" to the next grade without first passing grade-level tests (Clinchy 1998, 272–77).

A rejuvenated reform agenda led to passage of the No Child Left Behind Act in 2001. NCLB instituted reforms based on the premise that setting high standards and establishing measurable goals could improve individual outcomes in education. The act required states to develop assessments in basic skills in order to receive federal school funding. Each individual state was to develop its own standards. The implementation of the act produced disappointing results over time. The emphasis on standardized tests proved an unreliable means of assessing student learning and had other unintended consequences. The implemented standards had the effect of narrowing the curriculum, and made it more difficult for teachers to connect classroom activities to their students' needs and interests (Hursh 2007, 295–98).

In 2009, the National Governors Association and the Council of Chief State School Officers presented a fresh proposal promoting the Common Core State Standards Initiative. The initiative detailed what students should know in English, arts, and mathematics at the end of each grade. Common Core sought to establish consistent educational standards across the states but soon became immersed in partisan politics. A growing number of (mostly conservative) states that initially adopted Common Core since voted to repeal or replace it.

While this recent attempt at educational reform has become a political football, few of these reform efforts have addressed the influence of interscholastic sports on student achievement. A notable exception was the 2004 report of the National Association of State Boards of Education (NASBE), *Athletics and Achievement*. The report followed a three-year, $1.4 million study that focused on a wide range of issues related to athletics' role in the twenty-first-century high school, including the effect of sports participation on students' grade point averages and whether athletes received favorable treatment from teachers. The report, which resulted from a collaboration between the NASBE and the NCAA and the National Federation of State High School Associations, concluded that an overemphasis on sports can undermine a high school's academic mission. More specifically, the NASBE report found a "significant fragmentation" in state policies governing interscholastic sports and noted a need for state boards of education to guarantee that interscholastic athletics didn't take precedence over student academic performance (see Hoff 2006, 9).

Athletics versus Academics

The NASBE report set the stage for a timely book by journalist Amanda Ripley, *The Smartest Kids in the World* (2013b), which compared the American educational system with those from other developed nations. Ripley's assessment was based on the Program for International Student Assessment (PISA), which tests fifteen-year-olds in math, reading, and science. Based on tests taken in 2012 by six thousand American students from 161 randomly selected schools, the United States ranked at best in the middle of the pack among the thirty-four Organization for Economic Coordination and Development (OECD) nations—twenty-seventh in mathematics, twentieth in science, and seventeenth in reading (OECD 2012).

Ripley (2013b, 118–19) labels the "unholy alliance between schools and sports" a major contributing factor in the relatively poor performance of

American students. In her view, school boards and secondary school administrators have generated a lopsided focus on varsity sports, devoting significant resources to sports programs at the expense of academics. Student-athletes spend inordinate amounts of time and energy training for and competing in school sports, often to the detriment of their academic development.

Ripley is not opposed to school sports (she played soccer growing up in New Jersey from age seven through most of high school); rather, she objects to their overemphasis relative to academics. For all the inherent values of school sports, they siphon resources and attention from classroom learning. Most school sports have lower student-mentor ratios than do math and reading classes. The average high school football team has between forty and fifty players and six coaches. The school's reading instructor might have one teaching aide for a class of twenty-five or more. In the midst of a budget crisis, one Texas high school spent $1,300 per year per football player and $618 per math student. Another school was spending $328 per student for math instruction and more than four times as much per cheerleader, even though the school district's strategic plan claimed that math was the primary focus. A survey in Alabama in the late 1980s found that of the nearly 400 high schools in the state, 370 had football teams but only 286 offered a foreign language and fewer than 100 offered full-fledged computer courses (Ripley 2013a; Gerdy 2002, 81, 93). Given tightened school budgets, there is little doubt that such disparities continue today.

The consequences of such misplaced priorities are readily apparent. Ripley (2013b, 118–19) found that more than twenty countries had better high school graduation rates than the United States. More than 90 percent of South Korean students graduated from high school, compared to less than 80 percent of American students in many states, though the graduation rate for the United States improved to 84 percent by 2014–15 (US Department of Education 2017). Given this imbalance, the relative importance placed on school athletics should be the subject of serious discussion.

In a provocative article in *The Atlantic*, "The Case against High-School Sports" (2013a), Ripley argues that Americans' obsession with high school sports—the rankings, the trophies, the ceremonies, the misplaced pride, and especially the funding and staffing distortions—has been a significant factor in the academic failure of our secondary schools. Not surprisingly, the article generated a spirited rejoinder from the athletic establishment as well as some academics and educators.

The Atlantic printed a rebuttal in which sociologist Daniel H. Bowen and education professor Colin Hitt (2013) made six major assertions:

- School-sponsored sports appear to provide benefits that seem to increase, not detract from, academic success.
- Schools' commitment to athletics facilitates or reflects greater social capital.
- Athletes have lower dropout rates than other students.
- Based on students' test scores, coaches are just as effective in the classroom as noncoaching teachers.
- Studies show that athletes score higher on aptitude tests and have higher GPAs than nonathletes.

(Bowen and Hitt also argue that participation in athletics keeps at-risk students from becoming juvenile delinquents. This issue is discussed in chapter 8.) A close examination of these claims demonstrates that they are based on faulty premises and/or that the supporting evidence is less than convincing. For example, Bowen and Hitt cherry-pick their data by comparing test scores taken from students in Massachusetts, who score near the top on national achievement tests, with scores from students in other high-performing countries. A comparison using the scores of students from Mississippi would produce very different (and equally skewed) results. The appropriate comparison is the one Ripley makes—scores for national samples.

Moreover, Bowen and Hitt fail to acknowledge other independent variables that influence academic achievement. Sociologists are well aware that family characteristics and socioeconomic status are among the strongest predictors of students' academic achievement, and Massachusetts is among the states with the highest average family incomes. A more valid comparison would be between schools with and without varsity sports programs, holding family income and other relevant variables constant.

Bowen and Hitt (2013) argue that success in sports programs facilitates the creation of "social capital within a school's community" and define social capital as "the norms, the social networks, and the relationships between adults and children that are of value for the child's growing up." There is no question that high school football builds social capital in Texas towns. However, there is little evidence that a cohesive community with an avid interest in school sports is equally interested in supporting academics. And the core issue is whether school sports are essential for generating social capital. And the answer is no. Charter schools and other institutions that lack varsity sports programs, including elementary schools, generate community cohesion and school spirit around academics (Ripley 2013a). Moreover, it is also not clear that social capital generated by sports has a positive effect on a school's primary mission.

Bowen and Hitt (2013) claim that a commitment to athletics correlates with lower dropout rates, since sports participation keeps some kids from dropping out. However, the numerous studies on this subject have produced mixed results. Most studies linking participation in sports to academic achievement fail to determine whether the relationship is causal, and some better-designed studies suggest that there is a selection bias: higher-achieving students are more inclined to participate in extracurricular activities.

In addition, just because the athletes are staying in school, doesn't mean they're learning: according to Keith O'Brien (2012, 13), for two Kentucky high school basketball players, school "was just a means to an end. Get through the day, then they could play." In his estimation, "the boys seemed to have very little interest in school at all." And another group of high school basketball players were absent from class supposedly as a result of illness but then showed up for basketball practice in the afternoon (195). A high school in Florida known as an athletic powerhouse was characterized as a "dropout factory," with only half of the freshman class graduating four years later (Farrey 2008, 325–26).

Bowen and Hitt also cite data from a Florida study indicating that coaches are just as effective at raising students' test scores as noncoaching teachers. Once again, however, the study is not rigorous enough to support Bowen and Hitt's assertion. Validating their argument would require creating matched samples of students of similar academic ability taking the same classes taught by coaches and noncoaches and compare their scores on a common exam both before and after taking the class.

Finally, Bowen and Hitt cite studies showing that athletes have higher GPAs and score higher on aptitude tests than do nonathletes. Though studies have indeed found a modest correlation between sports participation and higher academic achievement (see Fejgin 1994; R. Ward 2008), they have not established causation: it is not clear whether sports participation improves grades or better students are more inclined to play sports (see Broh 2002, 70, 76; K. Miller et al. 2005, 179).

The reasons for the linkage between athletics and academic performance are to some degree pragmatic; student-athletes who have disciplinary problems or who perform poorly in the classroom risk being dropped from the team. Academic eligibility requirements likely account for the finding that athletes have lower rates of absenteeism and higher GPAs during their playing seasons than out of season, suggesting an extrinsic motivation to make good grades. After surveying the literature, Gerdy (2000, 132) found no convincing evidence to indicate that sports transform poor students into good students. At best, interscholastic athletics may stimulate academic aspirations but does nothing to provide students with the academic skills needed to fulfill those aspirations.

Moreover, grades may reflect a variety of factors beyond academic achievement. Some high school teachers routinely pass underperforming athletes to keep them eligible, and in other cases coaches pressure teachers to change grades of failing student-athletes (Gerdy 2000, 96–97). At one Texas high school, football players received answer sheets for tests or were given passing grades without taking exams (Bissinger 1990, 295).

The perception is that talented athletes continue to be passed along from grade to grade regardless of whether they meet the academic qualifications to advance. Student-athletes' grades are changed without supporting documents, and athletes with college prospects are allowed to graduate without meeting minimal requirements (Winfrey 2010, 156). In one case, a retired federal judge was called upon to investigate a high school in Alabama following a complaint by a math teacher that a school administrator had "rounded up" the Algebra II grade of a senior football hero so that he could play for the University of Alabama (Sailer 2007, 25).

McNeal (1998) has found that students with higher standardized test scores are significantly more likely to participate in extracurricular activities with the exception of athletics, cheerleading, and vocational clubs. However, a slightly different pattern emerges for GPA, a more direct measure of classroom performance. Students with higher grades are generally more likely to participate in athletics, cheerleading, and vocational activities. The finding for athletics may be affected by screening mechanisms (i.e., no pass, no play) that prohibit students with the lowest academic credentials from participating. Another study of students participating in a range of extracurricular activities found the lowest academic performance among "athletics only" participants (Miracle and Rees 1994, 144).

Once again, self-selection of the better students into sports may explain why athletes score higher than nonathletes on aptitude tests. There's another type of selection bias: not all seniors (or juniors) take the ACT or SAT. In some high schools, less than half of all seniors take these aptitude tests, thus skewing the data. Ripley (2013a) reported that at one upper-middle-class high school, only 17 percent of juniors and seniors took at least one advanced placement test. School administrators appreciate that the more select the group taking these tests, the better the school appears on measured aptitude. For a valid comparison, similar percentages of athletes and nonathletes would have to take the test.

A study of Texas high schools found statistically significant negative associations between money spent for athletics and various aggregate-level student outcomes. In particular, increases in district-level athletic expenditures per pupil reduced college entrance exam scores, lowered the percentage of students who scored high on college entrance exams, and decreased students' willingness to take such exams (R. Ward 2008, 564).

Finally, Bowen and Hitt gloss over the differences in academic performance between male and female athletes as well as between athletes in minor sports and those in major sports. Most critical observers recognize that the problem centers on male athletes in revenue sports. Being a member of the high school golf or swimming team has a minimally adverse effect on student-athletes' performance in the classroom. It's also relevant to note that athletes may be provided tutoring and assistance above and beyond that offered to other students. In some high schools, athletes are required to turn in a weekly grade sheet to their coaches during the school year. Why aren't all students' grades monitored? (Levy 2015, 129).

On a common sense level, one wonders what possible beneficial effects shooting baskets, smashing into tackling dummies, or swimming laps could have on test preparation skills. Do such qualities as mental focus and perseverance developed on the athletic fields influence study habits? It seems implausible to argue that sports develop student-athletes' cognitive abilities when authoritarian coaches make most of the important strategic and tactical decisions. This is not to say that sports participation doesn't provide some developmental benefits.

Athletes versus Nonathletes

School administrators set the priorities, determine the agenda, and direct the focus of the school's staff and students. The scheduled activities in a typical school reflect these priorities. The account of an event at a high school in Ohio exemplifies the disproportionate attention accorded athletes. In the school gymnasium, family, friends, faculty and students gathered for the "signing" ceremony of the school's star athlete. Teachers brought their classes; coaches brought teammates and athletes from other school teams; community members attended. All in all, half the gymnasium was filled with supporters. At the ceremony, the school principal referred to the college-bound athlete, as a "beast." Students threw confetti and released balloons, while media cameras took photos. At this high school, there was no comparable celebration for prestigious scholars who earned academic scholarships (Washington 2011, 36).

Pep rallies (as depicted in Chapter 5) are a similar institutionalized ritual. Typically they are held during the school day with classes canceled and students generally required to attend. Cheerleaders, pompon girls, and bands perform at these rallies. School pep rallies are scheduled to generate enthusiasm for school athletic teams. Academic pep rallies appear to be the rare exception, although a few principals have organized such events to motivate student achievement on state exams, most often at the junior high and middle-school levels.

Two contrasting theories have been proposed to explain the effects of sports on students' academic achievement. The developmental theory proposes that participation in sports has positive outcomes for students. Conversely, the zero-sum theory postulates that students squander their time and energy on sports rather than use it for academic pursuits. Those who adhere to the zero-sum theory point out schools and students have finite resources. When students', schools', and communities' resources , are diverted from the classroom to the athletic arena, academic achievement is undermined (Fejgin 1994, 211–12; K. Miller et al. 2005, 188).

Developmental theorists maintain that athletic participation contributes to better academic performance by developing skills, habits, and values transferrable to the classroom; integrating students into a network of adults and peers; providing tangible incentives to stay in school and get good grades; and increasing commitment to the school. Studies have reported that sports participation is associated with positive academic outcomes such as higher GPA, fewer disciplinary referrals, lower absenteeism and dropout rates, higher college aspirations, and stronger commitment to school. These findings imply that participation in sports adds to, not detracts from, academic pursuits (K. Miller et al. 2005, 179, 187–88).

Broh (2002, 86) postulates that athletes are more likely to talk with their teachers outside class than are nonathletes and that relations between athletes and teachers may act as sources of social control—that is, teachers monitor athletes and keep them in line. In some schools, athletes absorb a disproportionate share of resources. In addition, student-athletes' visibility and popularity with teachers may lead to leniency in grading and result in inflated grades. The positive effect of athletic participation on educational aspirations may be attributed to students' plans to use athletic prowess as capital in gaining access to college—often in collaboration with the teaching staff (Fejgin 1994, 224). Given this scenario, grade biases in favor of athletes can cross the line into unethical practices, as discussed above. Corrupt schemes for keeping college-bound athletes academically qualified have included doctoring grades and sending fraudulent transcripts to colleges that inflate the student-athlete's GPA (later restored to original); athletes' academic records are "lost"; athletes' grades are changed without supporting documentation, and athletes have even been allowed to graduate without meeting academic requirements (Winfrey 2010, 156).

Studies examining the effects of sports participation on students' academic achievement have drawn mixed conclusions. Researchers comparing athletes' and nonathletes' grades often fail to control for relevant external factors that might explain the differences in academic achievement. As noted, involvement in athletics is subject to strong selection effects; for instance, high school athletes disproportionately hail from socioeconomically advantaged backgrounds, a phenomenon exacerbated by schools charging participation fees. One of the more plausible explanations of differences between athletes and nonathletes is that superior students' self select into sports disproportionately, as they do into other extracurricular activities.

Most studies compare athletes, as a group, to nonathletes. In making these comparisons, researchers have examined several correlates of sport participation, notably grades, graduation rates, and dropout rates. Typically, the independent variable is broadly framed as participation in sport. Amidst the ongoing debate about the relationship between sports participation and academic performance, relatively little attention has been paid to how different dimensions of athletic involvement affect students' behavior. Most studies fail to determine if the benefits of participation vary by athletes' individual characteristics or whether the effects of participation on academics differ from sport to sport (Broh 2002, 86; Miller et al. 2005, 179).

Athletes versus Athletes

Athletes' gender is a major distinguishing factor. Gorman (2010) found significant differences in the GPAs and ACT scores of male and female athletes in favor of the women, and lesser differences between athletes and nonathletes. Other studies have found differences in GPA between female and male athletes as a group and gender differences between revenue sports (football, basketball) and nonrevenue sports. Taking race into account, data from the 1990s suggest that white, female nonrevenue sports participants tend to have the highest GPA's (Miracle and Rees 1992, 142).

Sitkowski (2008, 85, 89, 92–94) reported significant differences between males and females with respect to GPA. The girls' grade point averages were higher in general than the boys. Collectively, females who participated in sports performed better when compared to their non-athletic counterparts than did male athletes. There was a statistically significant difference in the seasonal performance of male athletes (sophomores and juniors) with respect to their GPA scores, but not female athletes. The specific sport that male athletes participated in had a significant impact on the difference in GPA scores. But this wasn't the case for female athletes. Male athletes in football and basketball experienced significant declines in their GPA scores postseason when compared to athletes in other sports. The results of this study concur with the general findings that male athletes experience statistically significant declines in GPA scores postseason, whereas female athletes do not.

High school girls are more likely to play sports strictly for enjoyment, love of the game and, if exceptionally talented, an opportunity for an athletic scholarship that may lead to a college degree. Unlike the boys, they are much less distracted by the dream of playing professional ball. The lack of professional sports opportunities actually motivates young women to focus more on their education. Moreover, female athletes aren't fawned over by sports fans and recruiters to the degree that male athletes are and thus are less likely to develop an exaggerated view of their talent (Powell 2008, 240–41).

Researchers have found ethnic/racial differences, as well as gender differences, in the connection between sports participation and academics. Longitudinal studies on African American and Hispanic high school athletes going back to the 1990s find little evidence that sports participation improves the grades or test scores of these subgroups. Other studies suggest that participating in high school sports was beneficial for long-term goal attainment only if it was coupled with participating in other, service-related activities—for example, student council. Data indicate that troubling graduation rates for black athletes are concentrated in football and basketball, the two main revenue-generating sports and the ones in which participation by blacks are the highest. Boys' basketball has had the worst graduation rates (Powell 2008, 77; Broh 2002, 87–88).

African Americans males appear to be strongly influenced by their immediate peer group as well as viewing college and professional athletes as role models. This focus may lead them to view sports as the only available opportunity to advance in life while negating their identification with academic pursuits. Black athletes are disproportionately represented on sports teams in many American high schools. Half of Kentucky's Scott County High School's boys' basketball team were African Americans, while of the sixteen hundred students on campus, less than 7 percent were black (O'Brien 2012, 95).

A significant number of black athletes are products of less than ideal circumstances, often raised by single mothers or grandmothers, living in poverty, with absentee fathers and with few positive role models outside of sports. The options for youngsters growing up under such conditions are limited (Powell 2008, xiv, 22). Black male high school students see sports as a ticket to college, and then on to a professional career. As sports columnist Shaun Powell (2008, 78) observes, "College is being used as a starting line by black athletes when in reality it's the finish line." Numbers from the Bureau of Labor Statistics confirm Powell's point. Fewer than fourteen thousand adults in the

United States make their living playing spectator sports. African American high school athletes would be better advised to direct their time and energy toward academic achievement.

Time Out

The time commitment of student-athletes is detrimental to academic achievement. In addition to the hours of practice, team meetings, weight training, and the time devoted to competition (often weekly), high school teams travel long distances to competitive events resulting in students getting home at very late hours, yet they're still expected to complete homework and other academic assignments. In basketball and other sports, games may be scheduled on school nights. The notion that student-athletes can do homework while on a long bus ride rings hollow: few students have the self-discipline to devote quality time to studies among spirited team members (Streich 2009; Conn 2012, 22).

While academic reformers have recommended that schools spend more time on academics, few educators on the local level have discussed cutting back on time devoted to athletics. Coaches may schedule before-school team meetings, practice sessions before and/or after school, and meetings even during school hours. The typical after-school practice sessions prevent student-athletes from seeking after-school academic help, although athletes may also have access to tutoring and other assistance that is not offered to other students. Excessive practice sessions not only impact student-athletes' study time but also their ability to facilitate and participate in other activities such as student clubs or community service projects. Student-athletes' time is consumed by "the *narrow* world of sports" (Levy 2015, 10; Streich 2009).

The American Academy of Pediatrics has urged middle schools and high schools to start no earlier than 8:30 a.m. to allow adolescents, who are biologically programmed to stay up later than adults, to get the recommended 8.5 hours of sleep. As of 2015, a survey by the Centers for Disease Control found that more than 80 percent of schools start before the recommended time, and estimates show that two-thirds of high school students fail to get adequate sleep. But proposals to start school later often run into opposition on the grounds that later dismissal times would make it difficult to schedule after-school sports activities. Once again, athletics trumps academics (Szabo 2015).

In the American high school, academic classes typically run 45 to 55 minutes, five days a week. A generous estimate of the time allotment would be around 250 minutes per week per subject. Athletic practice sessions in many high schools average two and a half hours a day, excepting game days when the time commitment is closer to four hours. Assuming some combination of four practices and two games per week or five practices and one game, athletics is given more than triple the time commitment that English or mathematics is allotted (Cotton 1996, 42). What would happen if students practiced math or writing for two hours every school day, as they do football or basketball, and then competed in math or writing contests on weekends on a dozen occasions during a semester? Does that sound excessive? In an ideal world, students would be accorded time to engage in both sports and academics.

Calculating the actual time costs of school sports programs is complicated; there's time off for pep rallies, homecoming week celebration, and other athletic ceremonies. Scheduling accommodations for sports can consume a significant portion of the school calendar. While these types of interludes affect all students, athletes may be pulled from classes for other reasons. A Kentucky basketball player with injured knees was removed from his first period class for a week and transported to physical therapy with the goal of getting him back in the starting lineup by the next game (O'Brien 2012, 152). Injured football players might spend three days in the trainer's office, thus missing their classes. Student-athletes are pulled out of classes to watch game films in the coach's office. Some high school students in Texas receive academic credit for "athletics classes" offered during the school day; that is, credit for watching game films or studying the playbook (Bissinger 1990, 49, 298; O'Brien 2012, 233–34).

In effect, high schools are exploiting these students. The prevailing system nurtures them for their athletic feats rather than academic excellence, and stresses academic eligibility rather than academic achievement. Schools thus limit student-athletes' opportunities for career exploration. Upon graduation, these students find themselves with limited career options and plans. The truth is, throwing, hitting, or kicking a ball are not job skills for 99.9% of high school graduates; but excelling in math and writing do contribute to getting a trade school certificate or a college degree, and ultimately a good job (Goldberg 1991, 332–40).

Another factor that affects the amount of time students devote to athletics is the length of the season. Playoff tournaments have been a key element in the expansion of schedules. For example, New York had no high school football playoff system before 1993 and seems to have added one primarily because other states did it. This change necessitated starting regular season games before Labor Day so that the playoffs could be over by early December (Svare 2004, 91; Jack Roberts 2007, 280). In some states, championship tournaments mean that football teams play as many as sixteen games in a season; in Texas, teams that make the championship game have a seventeen-week season. Postseason all-star games have proliferated as well and may require players to miss as much as a week of classes (Levy 2015, 155; Easterbrook 2013, 214–20). Regular season game creep has also lengthened the season for many sports. Kentucky's high school basketball teams played schedules of thirty-plus games by 2009, a 50 percent jump from the twenty-game schedules that prevailed during the 1960s (O'Brien 2012, 45).

Finally, offseason programs, which at one time were virtually unknown in high school sports, have now become common. Texas allows public high schools to hold winter football practices and spring scrimmages. Pennsylvania allows football practices to be held forty-nine weeks a year (Easterbrook 2013, 214–20). Under Ohio regulations, coaches and players cannot participate in any organized workout or practice for thirty days after the high school football season ends; after that time, however, players begin training four days a week—generally with a two-hour daily workout consisting of weightlifting, agility drills, and sprints. Beginning in July, practice sessions occur for two hours in the morning and two hours in the afternoon (Heffron 2009). In addition, coaches may find ways to circumvent restrictions on out-of-season practice— for example, with "voluntary" workouts and "optional" open gym and lifting/conditioning sessions.

So why have coaches instituted so many "offseason" activities? Because the program that puts in more hours usually wins. As Gray Levy (2015, 59) points out, the fate of a high school football coach is determined on ten Friday nights a year, but success on those nights is decided in large part by decisions made on the other 355 days.

Academic Eligibility

School districts and state athletic associations have developed policies and rules to ensure that student-athletes are enrolled in school, attending classes, making regular academic progress, and on track to graduate. These academic requirements are now among the defining principles of school-based sports. If these rules are put in place and function as intended, then interscholastic sports should motivate students to do better academically because they have to maintain eligibility to participate—what has been labeled "no pass, no play." Advocates of eligibility rules argue that there are values in the requirements of participation as well as the intrinsic values of participation.

Eligibility rules of various sorts have been part of high school sports since the 1920s. However, the implementation and enforcement of these rules often leave much to be desired. Renewed efforts to reform academic eligibility requirements for high school athletes were evident in the mid-1980s amid some strong resistance. One of the more prominent attempts at reform occurred in 1984 when the Texas legislature introduced a no pass, no play rule stating that athletes could not have any failing grades if they were to participate in a sporting activity. Initially, a large number of students became ineligible to compete, triggering strong opposition from coaches and parents (Bukowski 2010).

This law became the linchpin of a sweeping school reform effort. Many states followed Texas's lead. The initial rule was relatively ironclad: any athlete who scored below 70 (considered passing) in a course couldn't practice or play for six weeks. Other states subsequently adopted similar eligibility rules, some stricter than others. Several states benched students with bad grades for nine or ten weeks (Ayres 2007).

Texas became the showcase for the successes and the failures of academic eligibility policy and practice. While Texas educators and state politicians praised the rule, it quickly came under assault. Over the following years, lawmakers weakened the law several times. In 1995 the state legislature amended the rule to allow school districts to make sweeping changes. The revisions included a provision to cut the suspension from six weeks to three weeks and to let students practice while they boosted their grades. Following the changes, a principal could remove the suspension for students making less than 70 in "advanced" classes. School districts used this loophole to lower the standard for student-athletes (Ayres 2007).

Texas school districts later created no-pass, no-play exemptions for classes ranging from calculus to auto shop. Some districts exempted more than 100 classes, while other districts exempted no classes, which created an uneven playing field. No one at the state level had the power to deny such exemptions. Local school boards were allowed to exempt any courses labeled "advanced" or "honors." School districts could easily craft a schedule in which nearly all of an athlete's classes were exempt. The Austin Independent District exempted 166 courses, including cooking and hospitality (Ayres 2007).

In other states, no pass, no play led to grade manipulation. At one school district in North Carolina, the new superintendent discovered that coaches were consistently fielding ineligible athletes on teams that went on to compete in statewide tournaments. The coaches had pressured teachers to change students' grades and attendance records to cover up the infractions. Under North Carolina rules, students who exceed 13.5 days of absence in a semester weren't allowed to compete in sports the following semester. Some coaches knew they were playing students who'd missed more than 70 days of school. The North Carolina High School Athletic Association requested a statewide review of high school athletic records. Forty-eight schools reported using ineligible players in a wide array of sports. Several principals and coaches were fined, and two athletic directors lost their jobs. At an Oklahoma high school, more than forty student athletes in four sports, including at least seven starters on the football team, were found to be playing while ineligible for academic reasons, residency, or recruiting issues (Beem 2006, 1018; Baker 2013).

There were some positive developments. By the millennium, all state athletic associations had recommended a form of academic eligibility requirements for participation in interscholastic sports; however, some were rather limited. The requirements ranged from just being enrolled in a minimum number of courses to a combination of a minimum number of courses, no failing grades, a minimum grade point average, and an attendance policy. All states eventually required a minimum unit of courses in which high school students must be enrolled to participate in athletics. Some schools based eligibility on the number of F grades rather than GPA; other schools required students to have attendance rates of 80 percent or better to participate, along with academic criteria (Bukowski 2010).

Eligibility rules for participation in high school sports continue to vary from state to state. Indeed, many states allow school districts to set their own standards, with varying degrees of stringency. A 2001 survey found that in only four states did all high schools follow the guidelines set up for academic eligibility by the state association. In short, academic eligibility for student athletes in public high schools has assumed many variations and changed constantly over the past thirty years. There's a range of GPA standards among schools for athletes to remain eligible. On the low end, a student is eligible to play sport in some schools by passing four of seven courses with four Ds and three Fs. Other schools require no grade point standard for eligibility (Bukowski 2010).

Within this wide-open framework, three general approaches to eligibility have emerged: (1) maintaining a set grade point average, (2) passing a certain number of classes, and (3) making progress toward a diploma. Some states combine these approaches to provide more flexibility or offer alternatives to demonstrating eligibility. Several years ago, the NCAA upgraded its standards to specify the high school courses and GPA students must have to participate as freshmen in college. The National Federation of State High School Associations has recommended that states bench students for a full grading period if they don't pass four core courses, but the association lacks the authority to enforce the recommendation (Ayres 2007). In 2004, the National Association of State Boards of Education voted to require high school athletes to pass all their classes to be eligible to participate in sports. Previously, athletes were required to pass only four classes per semester (Beem 2006, 10–18).

The reaction from the athletic community continues. Some schools that incorporated a grade point average into their eligibility standards later removed this criterion because of opposition from coaches and parents. A number of athletic directors report that they would like to have even lower academic requirements than those already in place. ADs often defend low academic requirements by arguing that athletic programs should remain "student-friendly"—that is, all students, no matter what their grades, should have the right to participate. However, in schools that have strong academic requirements, administrators report that students have adjusted (Bukowski 2010).

Normally, there is no appeal process for athletes who have missed the academic eligibility standards, since participation is not a right and eligibility standards are in place for all member schools. (The courts have confirmed that participation in interscholastic sports is a privilege, not a right.) These are not decisions that can be made by the central administration or school boards (Hoch 2006). This practice stands in stark contrast to what occurred previously. To cite an example from the 1980s, athletes at Glen Ridge High School in New Jersey had to meet grade standards to play varsity sports. The school required at least a 1.75 GPA (C–). Athletes had to pass all but one of their major classes. They could repeat the course in summer school. Also, they could ask an appeals board to reverse the decision. The school principal had ultimate authority over the appeal. Some athletes would mount letter-writing campaigns to waive the requirement. One way or another, most athletes found a way to stay eligible (Lefkowitz 1998, 165). The fact that state associations and interscholastic sports leagues subsequently developed eligibility standards meant that local school administrators no longer would adjudicate appeals (Hoch 2006, 17).

Academic suspension from sports participation for an athlete varies among schools and states. Suspensions may range from one week to half a school year. Athletes found ineligible have different ways in which to gain back their eligibility—for example, weekly grade checks. Normally, students put on probation become eligible at the end of this time period if their grades meet the minimal requirements (Bukowski 2010).

The question is raised as to why athletes are subject to eligibility requirements while students involved in band, theater, yearbook and other extracurricular activities may not have to meet the same standards. This distinction isn't universal. A Los Angeles Unified School District rule reads, "To be eligible for participation in extracurricular activities students must maintain a C average in four subjects and have no failures." Likewise, the original Texas no-pass, no-play reform law covered band members and students in other extracurricular activities (Bukowski 2010; Ayres 2007). A segment of the public continues to believe that all students, regardless of grades, should be allowed to participate in all school programs (Humphrey 2002, 74).

Another academically questionable practice spawned by the pressure to produce winning teams is the increased number of athletes being "redshirted." Redshirting—like specializing in one sport—can be traced back to the 1980s. The term originally referred to colleges holding an athlete (typically a football player) out of competition for one year to extend his eligibility. These athletes wore red jerseys during practice sessions, hence the label. Academic redshirting refers to the practice of postponing a student's entry into school by a year or having the student repeat a grade to provide more time for the child's intellectual and social maturation. Parents are increasingly using this practice to provide children with a competitive advantage in sports (Farrey 2008, 294; Robbins 2006, 216).

The impression is that many redshirted students aren't being held back for academic reasons but to provide them with advantages on the athletic fields. It's become common to redshirt middle schoolers to endow them with a size and maturity advantage in high school. The practice is most common in football, where size is perceived as vital. This practice regularly occurs in sixth through eighth grades, when differences in male size and strength are considerable (Malina 2010, 365). In a number of states, high school students are eligible to play in as many as eight semesters. Age limits—typically the nineteenth birthday—for high school athletes set by state associations are the only limiting factor.

Research suggests that students are more likely to be harmed than helped if they are held back and schooled with students who are younger than they are. Grade retention is also a major factor in increasing the risk that a child will drop out of school. Despite growing criticism from educators, the practice of redshirting has increased for both academic and athletic purposes. While some school districts have attempted to discourage the practice of athletic redshirting, others have allowed it to promote competitive sports programs. O'Brien (2012, 182–85) reports an incident in Kentucky where parents of middle school basketball players attempted to redshirt their sons for athletic advantage. When the school principal disapproved, the parents took their case to the school board. The board overruled the principal.

◆ ◆ ◆

Alan Goldberg (1991) argues that school administrators, coaches, teachers, and parents have found ways to enable student-athletes to meet the impractical demands of interscholastic sports. These practices ultimately can be detrimental to student-athletes, who may not develop the skills necessary for adult life in a nonathletic world. As education activist John Gerdy (2000, 135–36) notes,

> The challenges we face in educating our children and maintaining our economic status as a world power are simply too great to invest in activities that are educationally counterproductive. The information-based, high-tech, global economy of the future requires all of us to be better educated. To effectively meet the challenges represented by these changes, we much critically assess our nation's educational priorities and outcomes.

In the final analysis, achievement is what counts, and school priorities determine whether students value and strive for sports or academic achievement. If the culture of the high school is balanced, sports and academic achievement are likely to coexist; otherwise, sports achievement may come at the expense of academic achievement. Too often, American high schools tend to validate sports achievement at the expense of academic achievement (Sitkowski 2008, 26).

There is little indication that a healthy equilibrium between interscholastic sports and academics can be realized under the current system of interscholastic sports, and radical reforms are necessary. Shifting to an intramural/sports club model would facilitate a balance between sports and academics. This approach would ameliorate the hypercompetitive environment that requires long hours of practice, training, and travel that invade the academic calendar and impinge on student-athletes' study time. This change, in turn, would reduce the need for no pass, no play rules and diminish the incentive for academic compromise. There is no reason to believe that joining a sports club that competes on weekends and holds practice sessions a couple of times a week would adversely affect students' grades. All students would be encouraged to participate in sports *and* to improve their academic performance.

PHYSICAL FITNESS—OR NOT?— OF THE STUDENT-ATHLETE

> I've played with IVs before, during and after games. I've played with a broken hand, a sprained ankle, a torn shoulder, a fractured tooth, a severed lip, and a knee the size of a softball.
> —Kobe Bryant

Health, Fitness, and Sports: A Mixed Bag

The image of the student-athlete usually connotes health and fitness, a lean, muscular young adult full of stamina and dexterity—in short, the picture of physical well-being. But what does this term imply? *Well-being* is defined in terms of human vitality and productivity, a life free from infection, degenerative conditions, and defective organs. Disease and degeneration have behavioral causes as well as effects: for example, overeating or eating unhealthy foods can lead to obesity and dental problems. Young adults in the United States and other developed nations increasingly suffer from a variety of ailments that stem at least in part from behaviors and choices. Schools— and specifically school-sponsored sports—can play an important role in teaching health-promoting behaviors, especially regular physical activity (Stillwell and Willgoose 1997, 3).

With 95 percent of American youth aged between five and seventeen enrolled in school and the average child spending thirteen hundred hours on a school campus each year, schools are one of the primary locations where children can learn to be healthy and stay physically fit. Schools are a logical setting for promoting physical activity among youth: schools exist in all communities, attendance is mandatory, and they have the requisite staff, equipment, and facilities (at least when adequate funding is provided). In favorable school environments, students have opportunities to reduce their current and future risk for developing ailments associated with a sedentary lifestyle (Samuelson et al. 2010, 811; Kanters et al. 2013, 113–14).

Regular physical activity confers multiple physical and mental health benefits and plays a vital role in efforts to combat obesity. Well-planned activities develop and maintain physical fitness, which has two facets. Skill-related fitness refers to the ability to perform well in sports and games—such qualities as agility, speed, strength, balance, and coordination. More important is health-related fitness—the ability to perform routine daily activities and enjoy a physically active life. This capacity depends on cardiorespiratory endurance, muscle endurance, and flexibility, which also enhance athletic performance. Cardiorespiratory endurance is considered most beneficial to overall health. Ultimately, enjoyable physical activities enhance students' feelings of well-being (Byl 2004, 22).

The US Department of Health and Human Services recommends that children and adolescents get at least sixty minutes of daily moderate to vigorous aerobic activity and that they participate in muscle-strengthening physical activities at least three days a week. Aerobic exercises such as running and swimming produce an increased rate of breathing, promote the circulation of oxygen through the bloodstream, and thus develop cardiorespiratory endurance. Most students don't reach the minimum activity guidelines. Moreover, physical activity levels tend to decline during adolescence, suggesting that school efforts to promote physical activity during this period are critical (Colabianchi, Johnston, and O'Malley 2012, 1; Lowry et al. 2013, 1). Factors that contribute to students' daily physical activity include available recreational facilities, minutes of physical education per week, and support for biking and walking to school.

Too many adolescents have become couch potatoes, and as few as one in seven high school students engages in at least sixty minutes of daily physical activity. A quarter of high school students spend three or more hours per day watching television, on the computer, or playing video games, far more than the two hours per day of screen time recommended by the Healthy People 2020 physical activity objectives. Studies have found a disproportionately high prevalence of sedentary behaviors among African American and Hispanic students. Youth are more likely to spend time in low-intensity activities such as hanging out with friends or going to the movies than to engage in physical exercise. Among the factors that determine adolescent participation in sports and other forms of exercise are proximity to and cost of accessing facilities, perceived competence and skill, and friends' behaviors (Erwin 2008; Lowry et al. 2013, 1–4).

Youngsters from low socioeconomic backgrounds depend more on school programs to provide physical activity than do affluent children, who can afford to join private sports clubs. Consequently, when participation in after-school sports programs is limited to a few students, the populations most in need of these activities may be affected (Bocarro et al. 2014, S68). The most influential physical activity interventions for adolescents are those that guarantee safe, attractive, and convenient locations and offer both structured and nonstructured programs that educate and motivate individuals to use available facilities (Erwin 2008, 61). Schools are a natural source of such facilities, and experts recommend that youngsters engage in half of their daily physical activity at school (Samuelson et al. 2010, 811; Edwards, Kanters, and Bocarro 2011, 597).

So what is the best way for schools to offer all students physical activity as part of a well-rounded educational experience? Fitness and recreational skills can be taught in physical education classes. In addition, intramural sports provide opportunities for students to be physically active beyond the classroom. Although interscholastic sports offer another venue for promoting healthy activity, the prevailing focus on elite competition appears to be badly out of step with the nation's health needs and young people's well-being (Gerdy 2000, 129, 2014, 191; Kanters et al. 2013, 113–14). At one Florida high school known for its athletic teams, only 20 percent of the twenty-five hundred students played on the school's seventeen athletic teams, while most students failed the state fitness test (Miracle and Rees 1994, 214–15; Farrey 2008, 325).

A 2007 study showed that although most middle schools offered activity programs for students, girls were less likely than boys to participate. In addition, major obstacles to physical activity among students included a lack of district support and funding, a dearth of indoor facilities, poor staff development, and lack of equipment. About two-thirds of the schools offered alternative transportation home for students who remained after school for programs, but only a quarter of the schools accommodated after-school free play (Young et al. 2007).

After-school sports offer an accessible and safe way for adolescents to engage in exercise, but the choice of activity also matters. Track and field, soccer, basketball, and flag football provide higher levels of uninterrupted activity than do golf, tackle football, baseball, and softball. Sports that promote aerobic capacity, muscle endurance, and flexibility should be emphasized (Gatz, Messner, and Ball-Rokeach 2002, 33; Skinner 2013, 927; Bocarro et al. 2014, S65, S68).

Moreover, involvement in sports teams does not necessarily translate into physical fitness. In adult-organized sports, athletes are often inactive for a significant amount of time during these practices. One study reported that no more than 46 percent of athletes were engaged in moderately vigorous physical activity during softball, baseball, soccer, and basketball practices

(Bocarro et al. 2014, S66). Coaches often schedule "light" practices on the days immediately before and after games, meaning that the amount of exercise is deliberately limited so that players conserve their energy. And bench warmers generally don't participate much, if at all, in games (Stanec and Lay 2008).

These findings are backed up by another study that monitored two hundred athletes between the ages of eleven and fourteen during soccer, baseball, and fast-pitch softball practices. Only 10 percent of the were achieving the recommended level of exercise, with girls active for about eleven minutes less than boys and softball and baseball players active fourteen minutes less than soccer players. Just 2 percent of softball players achieved the recommended standard (Leek et al. 2011).

Though coaches may also require players to perform calisthenics and run laps, such drills are often used as punishment, and they are generally not considered fun. They do nothing to promote fitness as an enjoyable activity, which is an important part of creating lifelong wellness habits (Miracle and Rees 1994, 216).

Schools should promote lifetime health and fitness behaviors for both immediate and long-term benefits. The extracurriculum should emphasize recreational sports that most students can continue to enjoy as adults—swimming, tennis, golf, slow-pitch softball, recreational basketball, and volleyball. Sports participation during adolescence is a general predictor of sports participation and engagement in fitness activities during young adulthood, but young people who participate in recreational athletics are more likely to continue those pursuits as adults then are young people who participate in organized competitive sports (Erwin 2008, 62–63).

Eating Disorders and Obesity

High school athletes have not been immune to the issues with body weight, including both anorexia and obesity, that have plagued US society as a whole. Eating disorders have long been a problem for athletes in aesthetic women's sports such as gymnastics and figure skating. A lingering "thin to win" mentality abetted by a natural competitiveness can lead to anorexia nervosa and/or bulimia, with serious consequences, among them heart arrhythmia, irreversible bone loss, and dehydration. Eating disorders have led to the deaths of some young athletes (see J. Ryan 1995). Wrestlers, who must fit into particular weight classes, have resorted to extreme measures (laxatives, rubber sweatsuits, induced vomiting) to "make weight," resulting in stricter weight-cutting rules for the sport (D. Putnam 1999, 36–38).

The National Eating Disorder Information Center also recognizes *anorexia athletica*, or exercise addiction. For some athletes, compulsive exercise offers a way to experience power and a sense of self-worth. These athletes who are obsessed with their physical condition and body weight rarely, if ever, take a rest day for fear of losing control. They may exercise to the point of exhaustion or until they are waylaid by overuse injuries. The excess calorie expenditure may cause the athlete's body mass index to drop below normal. Coaches should be aware of this phenomena and counsel young athletes who appear to be overdoing it (Steidinger 2014, 99).

High school athletes appear to be particularly vulnerable to eating and exercise disorders, since the absence of the extensive support network available to college and Olympic athletes may allow the problem to go unnoticed. Coaches and athletic trainers should emphasize the importance of healthy eating habits and should screen underweight athletes, particularly females, for eating disorders (Yard and Comstock 2011, 189).

Young athletes also aren't immune to the US obesity epidemic. According to a 2011 survey, one-third of the nation's seven million high school athletes are overweight or obese (Yard and Comstock 2011, 182). The proliferation of three-hundred-pound college and professional football players has led high school football players and their coaches to equate larger body size with physical domination ("High School Athletes" 2015) (see chapter 10).

More than 50 percent of injured high school football players are overweight or obese. Obese athletes sustain a disproportionate number of knee injuries and fractures and are at higher risk of heat stress. Football players are more likely than other athletes to be overweight or obese, with excess body weight also common in wrestling, baseball, and boys' basketball. Female soccer players were least likely to be overweight or obese. In football and baseball/softball, obesity is linked to playing position: defensive tackles and offensive interior linemen are most likely to be obese, followed by first basemen (Yard and Comstock 2011, 182–84). These findings imply that the perceived ideal weight for a sport or position may not be the ideal weight for wellness.

Fast food consumption may contribute to the weight problem, as overscheduled teen athletes lack the time to eat healthy meals and/or games and practices interfere with mealtimes. Teams often stop for fast food on the way home from out-of-town games or to celebrate a win, and a cheeseburger and fries can easily exceed the calories expended during the game—and is high in fat. After-game meals are another ritual that contributes to the prevalence of overweight athletes. Coaches or parents transport team members to a fast food outlet to celebrate a win. A bit of caloric arithmetic underscores the problem: a teenager may burn around 200–300 calories an hour during competition in an active team sport like basketball or soccer; fewer calories while playing baseball or softball. The typical fast food meal more than compensates for this caloric expenditure. For example, a McDonalds Big Mac with cheese contains 700 calories and more than 40 percent of the recommend daily fat allowance. An order of fries adds another 340 calories.

Since around 1980, the number of overweight adolescents has quadrupled, and ten years into the twenty-first century, nearly 40 percent of US high school students were obese or overweight (Lowry et al. 2013, 3). As a result, today's young people have a shorter life expectancy than their parents, an unprecedented occurrence. Current projections show that by 2030, half of the American population will be obese (Reed 2015, 92, 94). Given these statistics, one can only wonder why a school would put up with the following event. A Texas town sponsors a "gallon challenge" as a high school homecoming tradition. The event takes place at a local supermarket parking lot after the game. Male students guzzle a gallon of milk and run a race. Whoever finishes first without throwing up is the winner (Levy 2015, 72).

Youth obesity increases the risk for such adult health problems as heart disease, cancer, type 2 diabetes, and bone and joint problems. Lifestyles that include healthy eating and regular physical activity can reduce obesity and thus lower these risks. School sports should be part of the solution, not part of the problem.

Habits acquired during adolescence have long-term consequences: according to one study, for example, girls who play sports have a 7 percent lower risk of obesity when they are in their late thirties and early forties (National Women's Law Center 2012).

Unnecessary Roughness: Sports-Related Injuries

School-sponsored sports should be high in fitness benefits while exposing students to a low risk of serious injury. While the health benefits of physical activity are irrefutable, various sports bring various risks. During the 2005–6 school year, athletes competing in football, soccer, basketball, wrestling, volleyball, baseball, and softball sustained an estimated 1.4 million injuries (Yard, Collins, and Comstock 2009, 645). However, the actual number is almost certainly higher: some athletes do not seek treatment for injuries, some coaches or trainers may administer first aid but not report injuries, and some physicians may not report injuries as sports-related. Some sports are riskier than others: for example, catastrophic injuries (defined as those resulting in "permanent severe functional disability" [Smith 2013]) are nonexistent among high school tennis players, while football (see chapter 10) and wrestling have the highest percentages of sports-related injuries (Streich 2009). While some injuries are unavoidable, schools must do everything they can to ensure athletes' safety.

Most if not all schools require athletes to undergo a physical exam prior to trying out for a team. A qualified medical professional must not only examine the student but also ask a series of medical history questions. Some states have developed standardized physical exam forms (Goldenbach 2006).

Nevertheless, these "sports physicals" may fall short of adequately assessing a student's fitness to participate. Exams may be conducted in as little as five minutes and may involve only a cursory physical assessment. The emphasis on questions regarding medical history requires students and their parents to be completely honest. Thirty-six states allow chiropractors to conduct exams; in some districts, school nurses provide them. There are no national standards, and only about 1 percent of students are denied clearance (Goldenbach 2006; Humphrey 2002, 70). One of the most important areas where the exams may fall short is heart ailments. In some cases, examining physicians failed to diagnose heart irregularities that were later implicated in the deaths of student-athletes (Goldenbach 2006).

Today, most schools require some sort of accident insurance coverage for student-athletes, but such was not the case until relatively recently. In some instances, the state athletic association provides insurance, while private insurance plans are used elsewhere (Humphrey 2002, 71; Jordon 2006).

The Michigan High School Athletic Association, for example, provides participants at all member schools and all registered officials with catastrophic insurance for medical bills. Coverage is provided for all students in grades 7 through 12 accidentally injured while engaged in interscholastic athletic activities under the jurisdiction of the MHSAA. This coverage is offered at no cost to the eligible athletes of member schools or to registered officials. MHSAA is the policyholder and pays the premium for this layer of accident coverage. It will pay up to $500,000 in medical expenses per claim, after a deductible of $25,000 has been met.

Whether or not state athletic associations require athletes to demonstrate that they have injury insurance, school districts may require that students show evidence of insurance coverage prior to participating in athletic program. While it is considered prudent for schools to ensure that athletes are covered by private injury insurance, it raises issues in school districts with indigent families who can't afford insurance. Districts may choose to provide supplemental policies to offset the deductibles that parents' or guardians' primary insurance may incur. Supplemental insurance can also serve as a primary policy if the parents don't have insurance. There are districts where a significant proportion of students appear *not* to be covered by private health insurance plans. In some instances, booster clubs purchase policies covering student-athletes (Doleschal 2006, 320; Corbett Smith 2013).

Catastrophic coverage for high school students is designed to provide for the tremendous costs resulting from a serious mishap such as brain or spinal cord injury suffered in football or resulting from falls in cheerleading. Disability benefits, in-home custodial care, and mobility equipment are among the items paid for from these policies, with maximum benefits ranging from $1 million to $7.5 million. As noted, parents and guardians are responsible to meet the deductible (on average, $25,000) before the policy kicks in. The most commonplace sports injuries like broken bones and ACL tears don't approach the amount of the deductible unless there are complications (Corbett Smith 2013).

When athletes do suffer catastrophic injuries, the costs for care can be staggering. A 2011 National Spinal Cord Injury Statistical Center estimate reported that for those who suffer partial or total loss of use of all the limbs, the first-year cost for care was in excess of $1 million, with each subsequent year costing $180,000. According to the National Center for Catastrophic Sport Injury Research, 468 non-fatal injuries, where "permanent severe functional disability" was the result, occurred from direct participation in high school sports from 1982 to 2011 (Smith 2013). The costs of catastrophic injuries can easily reach beyond the affected family's means; they are absorbed by society at large.

The North Carolina High School Athletic Injury Study conducted at the turn of this century estimated that school sports injuries cost the state ten million dollars a year in medical expenses. Most high school sports injuries are relatively minor and transient, and the mean medical cost was about seven hundred dollars per injury. However, the study also concluded that although rare (an average of about fifteen per year between 1982 and 2011), catastrophic injuries constitute a public health problem, with significant economic costs to society (Knowles et al. 2007; Corbett Smith 2013).

At the same time, catastrophic insurance policies are affordable, since these policies are rarely called on to pay benefits. These plans are far less expensive than other policies the schools might provide. An average school district with one high school and one junior high may pay under $2000 annually to carry catastrophic injury insurance on students—about the cost of a charter bus transporting the football team across the state to an away game (Smith 2013). Following a catastrophic injury to a Chicago high school football player in 2013, the state of Illinois implemented legislation known as "Rocky's Law" that required both public and private school districts to purchase catastrophic injury insurance to cover up to $3 million over a five-year period if a student suffers an injury while playing sports (Bowean 2013). The Illinois High School Association catastrophic insurance plan costs districts approximately $3.33 per student. It's likely that insurance premiums that cover tackle football are going to increase rapidly in the near future due to the increasing diagnosis of concussions in high school athletes (Smith 2013).

Several states have recently moved to require catastrophic care insurance for student-athletes. The Arkansas Activities Association provides a $1.5 million policy to its schools. Florida's high school athletic association demands that its schools carry at least a $1 million catastrophic plan; it also requires all participants to be covered through their family's medical insurance or purchase a school-offered plan for base medical coverage. However, a few states remain reluctant to require such coverage. As of 2013, insurance coverage was not mandatory for schools in Texas nor officially recommended by the University Interscholastic League (UIL), the state's public school extracurricular governing body. The UIL and the Texas Legislature relegated the issue as a local decision for school districts. Consequently, Texas has a level of uninsured students one and a half to two times the national average. An earlier 2004 survey of school superintendents found that 202 of the 1000 plus school districts still didn't carry catastrophic insurance on students participating in extracurricular activities (Smith 2013).

A 2013 study by the Institute of Medicine and the National Research Council found that young athletes (especially males) face a culture of resistance to reporting serious injuries, including concussions. Adolescent athletes are often taught to sacrifice their bodies for the team and subtly or not-so-subtly encouraged to play while hurt (Gerdy 2014, 185, 195).

Schools can combat this tough-guy culture by encouraging coaches to focus on student-athlete well-being rather than winning and having medical personnel attend games. Medical personnel are present at about three-quarters of public secondary school sports contests. For higher-risk sports such as football, a physician is usually present. For lower-risk sports, medical care is often provided by athletic trainers (Svokos 2014).

Certified athletic trainers hold four-year degrees (or in many cases master's degrees) and have training in injury prevention, physiology, nutrition, and first aid. The great majority of states require athletic trainers to be licensed. Their main responsibilities include (1) implementing programs to prevent injury and illness, (2) applying protective and injury-prevention devices such as tape and braces, (3) recognizing and evaluating injuries, (4) providing first aid and emergency care, and (5) keeping records and writing reports. According to the American Academy of Pediatrics, soccer players at high schools without athletic trainers had recurrent injury rates more than five times higher than their counterparts at schools with trainers; for basketball players, the rate was almost three times higher at schools without trainers. In addition, injured athletes at schools without athletic trainers experience longer recovery times than their counterparts at schools with trainers (Svokos 2014; Yard, Collins, and Comstock 2009, 651).

But many high school athletes do not have access to an athletic trainer. According to one estimate, only about 40 percent of high schools have athletic trainers on staff (Reed 2015, 43), and those trainers cannot attend all of the school's athletic events. Only Hawaii has athletic trainers in all schools, while one-third of Arkansas schools have trainers, as do a quarter of Oklahoma's schools (Svokos 2014).

Injuries to athletes fall into two general categories: repetitive microtrauma or overuse injuries and acute macrotrauma injuries—contusions, bone fractures, and concussions. Minor injuries are often treated by coaches or trainers and don't require a visit to the doctor. Acute injuries such as fractures require a physician's attention. Most young athletes with sports-related injuries who are seen in doctors' offices and clinics suffer from overuse injuries. Minor overuse injuries like tendinitis might limit but not prevent sports participation. Severe injuries, whether repetitive or acute, are defined as those requiring hospital care. These injuries may cause prolonged disability. Acute injuries occur at a specific time; overuse injuries occur over time and often lack a specific causal event.

Athletic injuries commonly involve the ankle, knee, or shoulder. Sprains are the most frequent injury, followed by strains and bruises. Different sports are more likely to produce different sorts of injuries: for example, most football injuries are acute, while cross-country runners usually suffer overuse injuries. Athletes and their parents tend to believe that injuries are a part of playing sports, particularly in the case of acute fractures resulting from accidents. Half of all injuries to high school athletes are sustained following contact with another person. Other frequent injury mechanisms are contact with the playing surface and noncontact mechanisms (e.g., rotation around a planted foot) (Knowles et al. 2007, 418; Yard and Comstock 2011, 185; Malina and Clark 2003, 94–97).

Mismatches in size heighten risk of injury to smaller athletes. Lighter athletes sustained a larger proportion of fractures than did athletes of normal weight. Smaller athletes may have decreased bone mass, which can increase the risk of fracture. Underweight athletes also may have decreased muscle or adipose tissue, both of which may provide them with less cushion to absorb the force of collisions (Yard and Comstock 2011, 189). Such mismatches are a particular concern for middle schools, whose students vary widely in maturation level.

In contrast to acute and accidental injuries, overuse injuries are preventable. Sports medicine practitioners estimate that as many as 70 percent of the injuries they treat are caused by overuse and cite the trend toward having young athletes focus on a single sport as responsible for the escalating rate of overuse injuries, which occur in a wide variety of youth sports (Joffe 2008, 1–2). Teen baseball pitchers are ruining their arms; teen soccer players are wearing out their knees and ankles. Physicians recommend that young athletes train and compete no more than twelve hours a week and that competition not run year-round.

College coaches have commented on the dramatic increase in overuse injuries. They're observing extraordinary wear and tear on the bodies of recruited athletes, particularly those who have been steered into a single sport at an early age. Baseball coaches have witnessed a growing number of teen athletes who have ruined their pitching arms. Soccer players tend to injure their knees and ankles. One high school soccer player estimated that she had been on soccer fields between 200 and 250 times a year over the previous six years of her life. She complained that her ankles seemed to be permanently sprained, so she played in braces. She also had shin splints that hurt all the time. Overuse injuries can compromise normal development and lead to permanent disability (Sokolove 2008, 239; Malina 2010, 367–69).

One of the more troubling forms of overuse injury is the tearing of the anterior cruciate ligament (ACL) in the knee. Most ACL tears occur after persistent body-to-body contact or when an athlete is landing from a jump. This injury tends to occur disproportionately in basketball, volleyball, and soccer, which involve jumping and pivoting. Sports trainers tend to view ACL tears as resulting not from fatigue but from repetition over time (Sokolove 2008, 3, 92, 181–85). Postpubescent girls appear to be more susceptible than boys to ACL tears (Sokolove 2008, 6–7, 34–35, 104).

In recent years, the issue of concussions has garnered enormous concern. Unlike bones, joints, and muscles, the brain is the seat of intelligence and behavior (Reed 2015, 51). A concussion is defined as "a traumatically induced physiological disruption of brain function that can be caused either by a direct blow to the head or by indirect impulsive forces transmitted to the head" (Johnson 2012, 180). Football players' skulls can sustain hits equivalent to the impact of a car crash at twenty-five miles per hour. A severe impact or abrupt change in head speed can push the brain through the surrounding fluid so that it crashes into the cranium. The brain isn't bruised; there's no bleeding, swelling, scratching, or abrading; and the brain has no pain receptors, so it can be difficult to tell when a concussion has occurred(Lehrer 2012).

Concussions are diagnosed based on external symptoms, although postconcussion symptoms may or may not appear. Only 5 percent of concussed athletes lose consciousness. The most common symptom is a headache. Other frequent symptoms reported at the time of the injury include dizziness, blurring, disorientation, confusion, disequilibrium, nausea, and amnesia. Three days after the concussion, the common persisting symptoms are headaches, neck pain, sleepiness, and irritability. There is no typical postconcussion scenario in interscholastic sports. Researchers at the University of Illinois found that youngsters who had sustained a single sports-related concussion still had impaired brain function two years later. High schools with athletic trainers report more concussions, which likely reflects better reporting rather than higher rates of injury (Nowinski 2007, 28, 36, 65; Svokos 2016, 14).

A study conducted in the 1990s found that concussions accounted for 5.5 percent of all high-school-sports-related injuries, a number that rose to about 9 percent by 2007. Again, the increase may reflect better awareness of and diagnosis of concussions. Between 2005 and 2006, more than five hundred thousand patients between the ages of eight and nineteen made concussion-related emergency room visits, about half of them sports-related. Only motor vehicle crashes cause more traumatic brain injuries among young adults (Gessel, Fields, and Collins 2007, 495, 500–501; Halstead and Walter 2010, 597–99).

Data from Minnesota for the 2013–14 academic year corroborate the link between concussions and sports, as 43 percent of concussions treated in the state's hospitals resulted from participation in sports and recreational activities. Certified athletic trainers at thirty-six public high schools in the Twin Cities metropolitan area reported that 1 percent of all athletes sustaining concussions, which would translate to an estimated three thousand sports-related concussions among high school athletes statewide (Dugan et al. 2014, 43).

The national attention on sports concussions has focused mostly on professional athletes, particularly in football and ice hockey, but concussions constitute a substantial risk for high school athletes as well. The conventional wisdom has been that collegiate athletes had higher *rates* of concussion but that concussions represented a greater *proportion* of injuries among high school athletes. Some studies, however, have reported that rates of concussions are higher among high school athletes than among their college counterparts, apparently because of more playing time, lower-quality protective equipment, and lower skill levels. Size disparities among adolescent athletes represent a unique risk factor for concussion, and it is well established that children and adolescents are more susceptible anatomically to concussion than are adults and take longer to recover (Gessel, Fields, and Collins 2007, 495, 502; Johnson 2012).

The consequences of concussions appear to be particularly severe for the adolescent brain. According to one study, high school athletes who suffered two or more concussions reported much higher rates of headaches, dizziness, and sleeping issues. Scientists describe these symptoms as neural precursors—that is, warning signs of serious trauma. One study reported that adolescent athletes with multiple concussions were seven to eight times more likely to experience a major drop in memory performance and experience persistent deficits in processing complex visual stimuli. These cognitive deficiencies have a significant impact: athletes with two or more brain injuries demonstrate statistically significant lower grade point averages than students who have no history of concussions (Lehrer 2012).

Although concussions are generally considered a transient injury, growing evidence indicates that such trauma can result in subtle, persistent cognitive and neurological deficits lasting up to three years, though such deficits may not be clinically observable. Football players appear to be especially vulnerable to concussion and thus at risk of neurocognitive deficits lasting a year or more, with serious effects on academic and athletic performance. Concussions can result in continuing discrepancies in attention and concentration, reaction time, processing speed, and so-called executive (frontal lobe) function—that is, memory and reasoning, communication, expression, and understanding. They also can lead to personality changes (Johnson 2012; Dugan et al. 2014, 43).

An estimated 136,000 concussions were reported among high school athletes participating in nine sports during the 2005–6 academic year. Full-contact sports and partial-contact sports (e.g., soccer and basketball) have the highest competition-related rates of concussion. A 2010 study of high school athletes found concussions to be a significant issue in football, hockey, boys' and girls' lacrosse, wrestling, boys' basketball, and girls' and boys' soccer. According to a 2016 study, the number of school-aged soccer players seeking emergency room treatment for concussions increased by a factor of sixteen over the preceding twenty-five years. The majority of concussions resulted from contact with another player. Heading the ball is also a concern; some schools now require female soccer players to wear protective headbands, although there is no conclusive evidence regarding their effectiveness (Gessel, Fields, and Collins 2007, 500–502; Reed 2015, 51; Schmidle 2017, 41).

Repeat concussions are also a concern. Of the nearly 740,000 sports-related concussions estimated to have occurred in high schools from 2005 to 2010, 13 percent were recurrent concussions. Young athletes suffering recurrent concussions are particularly at risk for second-impact syndrome

(SIS)—catastrophic swelling of the brain as a result of a second concussion before the brain has fully healed from an earlier concussion. Though SIS is rare, it is fatal in about half of cases, and survivors are typically left with severe impairments (Johnson 2012).

High school girls have higher rates of both initial and recurrent concussions than do boys playing the same sports. In addition, concussions represent a greater proportion of total injuries for girls than for boys. Some observers suggest that these discrepancies result from females' smaller ratios of head to ball size (in soccer), weaker necks, or less mass in the head and neck. Other factors affecting both male and female athletes may include the lack of protective equipment and an increased emphasis on physical play (Gessel, Fields, and Collins 2007, 495, 501; Castile and Collins 2012, 603, 609; Bogage 2017).

Gender culture may also play a role in differences in concussion rates between male and female athletes. Society has traditionally been more protective of females, and coaches, trainers, and parents may consequently err on the side of caution when a female athletes has a head injury. Conversely, boys suffering from head injuries may not report their symptoms for fear of being removed from competition. One study found that only 47 percent of high school football players who believed they had suffered concussions reported their injuries (Gessel, Fields, and Collins 2007, 501).

Moreover, mounting evidence indicates that routine *subconcussive* hits can do as much harm to the brain as spectacular concussive hits. A study of high school football players found neurocognitive and neurophysiological deficits in athletes without clinically observable signs of concussion. These deficits might be explained by undetected/unreported concussions or as the effect of repetitive subconcussive impacts, both of which are implicated in chronic traumatic encephalopathy (CTE), a degenerative brain disease caused by repeated head trauma (Johnson 2012; Easterbrook 2013, 157).

Victims of CTE suffer from memory loss, mood disorders such as depression, early dementia, disinhibition and erratic behavior, and amyotrophic lateral sclerosis (Lou Gehrig's disease). They are at risk for suicide. CTE can only be definitively diagnosed via autopsy and has been documented in the brain of an eighteen-year-old multisport athlete with a history of football-related concussions (Johnson 2012; Lehrer 2012).

Because concussions are diagnosed based on symptoms, it is important to have trained professionals conduct preseason baseline testing of athletes. The tests record an athlete's balance and brain function; if a concussion is suspected the tests can be repeated and the results compared.

The current standard of treatment for sports-related concussions is physical and cognitive rest until the athlete is asymptomatic, with a stepwise approach to rehabilitation prior to return to play. However, the applicability of this approach to high school athletes isn't entirely clear. The uncertainly is due to the baseline not being an entirely reliable measure of recovery in adolescents. The baseline can be expected to change rapidly during normal periods of cognitive maturation. A teen athlete who has returned to a previously measured baseline may still lag behind. Repeated baseline testing, although time-consuming, is a potential solution to this problem (Johnson 2012).

How long it takes a brain to recover from a concussion is impossible to predict. Most concussed subjects require at least ten days to recover, with younger athletes generally requiring longer. While most athletes with concussions recover fully within a short period, a small percentage experience postconcussion syndrome, in which symptoms last longer than three months. Full recovery in these athletes can be confounded by many factors, including their concussion history. Further, concussions can have a secondary impact as a consequence of a massive loss of neurons. Because adolescent brains are still developing, the loss of these cells can alter the trajectory of brain growth (McKeon et al. 2013, 841; Lehrer 2012).

One study found that between 85 and 90 percent of high school athletes with concussions recovered symptomatically within one to two weeks, and most returned to play within seven to nine days (McKeon et al. 2013, 836–40). In a 2009 survey of some 1,300 concussion incidents reported by high school trainers, more than 40 percent of athletes returned to the field too soon in violation of guidelines. The same survey found that 16 percent of football players who lost consciousness after being hit returned to the field the same day. Most medical experts recommend that adolescent athletes should never return to play on the day of injury, and only return subsequently when clinically symptom free (Johnson 2012).

All states as well as the District of Columbia have enacted sports concussion laws establishing mandatory protocols regarding issues such as removal-from-action and return-to-play (RTP) procedures, although significant variations exist (L. Green 2014). More research is needed to determine whether current RTPs are adequate to prevent future concussions and promote recovery from cognitive deficits in student-athletes. Further, RTP guidelines do not prevent sports-related concussions or address the chronic damage caused by subconcussive brain trauma. Emphasizing RTPs as the solution to the concussion problem in school sports like tackle football risks neglecting genuine reforms that would prevent concussions across school sports (Johnson 2012).

◆ ◆ ◆

Injuries, including concussions, can never be completely eliminated from interscholastic sports—or from life. Accidents happen. In sports as elsewhere, it is necessary to determine *acceptable* levels of risk. Schools are obliged to provide a secure environment and safe activities for students, which means that school sports must be evaluated in terms of the benefits they provide and the risks they entail. Students should be encouraged to participate in activities that contribute to physical fitness. Thus, despite the risk of injuries, soccer and basketball, for example, promote aerobic fitness and thus are appropriate school-endorsed activities. However, heading in soccer is a growing source of concern.

Ideally, schools should establish athletic health care teams to ensure that appropriate medical care is provided for all sports participants. Team members could include athletic trainers, consulting physicians, school nurses, physical therapists, EMS personnel, and other allied health care professionals from the community. All coaches should be trained in first aid and cardiopulmonary resuscitation, and the necessary equipment should be on hand at all times. In addition, athletic trainers and other professionals should be available to treat injuries at all practices and games (Almquist et al. 2008, 420–21, 423).

Finally, moderating the competitive atmosphere of school sports under an intramural/sports club model would alleviate the pressure on student-athletes and coaches to hide injuries. The school district should employ a sufficient number of athletic trainers, or contract such services, to provide diagnosis and treatment of injured athletes. Likewise, health educators should monitor all students to see that they maintain a healthy body weight. Finally, school districts should be required to provide accident insurance for student-athletes that doesn't shift unreasonable costs to their families.

CHARACTER VERSUS BAD BEHAVIOR

> One man practicing sportsmanship is better than fifty preaching it.
> —Knute Rockne

Do Sports Build Character?

The belief that competing in athletics makes the participants better people can be traced to the ideals of muscular Christianity, a movement that came into fashion during the Victorian era. In the private boarding schools of Britain and the United States, the sons of the elite were expected to acquire manliness and other character traits through a combination of the psychological pressures and physical discomforts of competitive sports such as rugby, cricket, and cross-country running. Experiences in athletic activities were thought to teach other social skills, including sportsmanship, fair play, leadership, teamwork, perseverance, and self-control. This ethic carried to the rising middle class and the public school system (Rees and Howell 1990).

Thus, sports have been assigned to teach more than physical skills and fitness habits. The athletic experience is believed to instill positive values and habits in the participants. Young athletes ostensibly receive moral guidance from their coaches and learn the lessons of life by competing. Conventional wisdom holds that sports teach valuable lessons that carry over into other walks of life and thus benefit the individual and society as a whole. Participation in sports is viewed as a stepping-stone to success, especially for poor and minority youth. The value of sports participation has remained an unquestioned belief through much of this nation's history (Gatz, Messner, and Ball-Rokeach 2002, x, 4, 9).

Justifications for school sports are based in large part on these assumed character-building benefits. Educators believe that sports participation has a positive effect on educational attainment and that interscholastic sports provide opportunities for student-athletes to succeed within a stratified system of rewards (Rees and Howell 1990). Many school administrators defend interscholastic sports: in the words of one Tennessee principal, "If I could wave a magic wand, I'd have more athletic opportunities for students, not less.... I've seen truancy issues completely turned around once students begin playing sports.... When students have a sense of belonging, when they feel tied to the school, they feel more part of the process" (Ripley 2013a). Other administrators argue that sports can serve as a lure for students who otherwise might not care about school.

And indeed, under the right circumstances, school-based sports place the participant at the center of a social network that reinforces commitment to the school and mandates conformity to conventional expectations. Most schools have a code of conduct to which students must adhere if they want to participate in interscholastic sports. Violation of school and team norms can result in suspension or even expulsion from the team; misconduct thus becomes a criterion for exclusion. But schools and local communities send a mixed message to young athletes when uncivil behavior is tolerated either on or off the court, a problem that is especially acute among male athletes (Humphrey 2002, 74; K. Miller et al. 2005, 189; Kreager 2007, 720).

Despite the conventional wisdom, social scientists are less than convinced that sports build character. Child psychologists point out that character is pretty much established by the time youngsters complete elementary school, suggesting that interscholastic sports are more likely to reveal or at best reinforce character. And scholars have found scant evidence to support the assertion that sports consistently shape character in a positive way. Most of the evidence is anecdotal and is typically promoted by individuals with vested interests in sports. Critics of the competitive excesses in organized sports have pointed out that sports may teach antisocial as well as prosocial behavior (Rees and Howell 1990). Philosopher Michael Novak (Umphlett 1985, 47) suggests that the "virtues" taught by sports are like those involved in artistic excellence; they are of a nonmoral nature and suggest more about the uses of craft and the limits of will than about character per se.

In and of themselves, sports arguably have no innate moral content. Rather, the environment in which the athletic experience occurs shapes behavior. Sports teams are social groups with specific structures and governance; they reflect both common and individual interests, shared and divergent goals. They have a mode of leadership, a hierarchy, and a method of decision making. The operation of a team can provide social experiences that influence the character of team members positively or negatively. To believe that every student-athlete acquires traits such as honesty and self- discipline through athletic participation is misguided (Gerdy 2002, 45, 210; Shields and Bredemeier 2011, 26).

Moreover, students with certain character traits self-select into sports. Studies have found innate differences between students who try out for sports teams and those who don't. These differences may account for the apparent behavioral correlates of sports participation. Research shows that students who try out, make the team, and continue their athletic involvement tend to have better-educated parents, more self-confidence, and higher aspirations for college than students who do not try out, get cut, or quit. Participation in sports is associated with greater civic engagement—but association is not causation. Civic inclinations may stem from personal traits that also motivate a student to join a school team (K. Miller et al. 2006, 3; R. Ward 2008, 563; Gardner, Roth, and Brooks-Gunn 2011, 33; Lopez 2006).

Dichotomous measures comparing students who do and do not participate in sports fail to take into account the specific experiences of individuals. Athletes aren't a homogenous group and marked variations in behavior occur among sports as well as between male and female athletes. And of course, each athlete is an individual, shaped by both nature and nurture at home. Football players engage in more problematic behaviors than athletes in most other sports, and female athletes tend to be better behaved. But as women's sports have grown in popularity and competitiveness, some female athletes are mirroring the questionable behaviors of male athletes (Gerdy 2002, 50).

The cherished ideal of *sportsmanship* implies a set of positive behaviors. For example, athletes have been known to make "honor calls," pointing out errors made in their favor. But honor calls rarely occur at higher levels of competition, where bad calls are considered an unavoidable part of the game and official replays are increasingly common (Delaney 2010, 27).

Those who remain sympathetic to the proposition that sports build character argue that athletes are generally good sports and cite examples of good sportsmanship. But one survey of forty-two hundred high school athletes found that more than one-third of the boys surveyed believed that "it's more important to win than be considered a good sport," nearly half of those surveyed said that it is acceptable for a football player to intentionally injure an opponent, and one-quarter condoned illegally altering a hockey stick. Significant numbers of respondents declared that fooling a referee or deliberately breaking rules would be acceptable as long as they didn't get caught. Overall, boys were far more likely to support unsportsmanlike tactics than girls (Buchanan 2006). Another study found that high school athletes scored lower on moral development and cognitive moral reasoning than did their nonathlete peers. Athletes' moral reasoning declined steadily from ninth grade through high school (Sage 1998, 270; Gerdy 2002, 43).

When high school coaches follow the win-at-all-costs model and the local community lives and dies with the high school team, athletes learn that winning is paramount and fair play secondary. When coaches can lose their jobs for not winning, moral principles are more likely to take a backseat to self-interest, and the character-development potential of sports is compromised. Impressionable young athletes develop an "end justifies the means" mentality. In the current atmosphere, therefore, high school sports often suspend moral obligation and encourage unethical behavior for strategic reasons, a mind-set that is reinforced by the culture of college and professional sports (Miracle and Rees 1994, 96–97; Gatz, Messner, and Ball-Rokeach 2002, 38).

Sports scholars have adopted the label *gamesmanship* to identify a separate set of values embraced by athletes during competition. The term refers to gaining a strategic advantage by morally questionable means, while sportsmanship implies adherence to both the letter and spirit of the rules of the game. For the gamesman, personal interaction in sports is perceived as a special situation in which normal moral rules are suspended. This game reasoning can justify both cheating and aggressive acts toward opponents (Rees and Howell 1990, 303–15; J. Lee and Lee 2009, 201).

The social behavior expected of an adolescent athlete resembles in many ways that expected of a young child or an irresponsible adult. The athlete is not supposed to appreciate and internalize the reasons for following rules but functions under a system of penalties that forces unquestioning compliance with instructions. Athletes are rewarded lavishly for good behavior (i.e., winning) and punished inconsistently for misbehavior. The character development of athletes would be enhanced by providing them with opportunities to make appropriate moral choices in game settings. But winning has become too important to allow the players any meaningful role in decision making. Student-athletes become dependent on external sources for self-esteem. Rewards are contingent on athletic prowess and superior performance. This system does little to enhance self-discipline or an internal locus of control (Goldberg 1991).

School sports are directed and choreographed by adults, a system that promotes an authoritarian environment and creates groupthink among participants. Sports encourage the subordination of self to group, group to authority, and authority to the goal—of winning. Personal independence is viewed as problematic, particularly in sports that promote sacrifice of the individual for the good of the team, resulting in an overemphasis on perceived goals and norms that can lead athletes to engage in behavior that is personally harmful, such as playing while injured and taking performance-enhancing drugs. This pattern of behavior has been rationalized as "positive deviance" (Miracle and Rees 1994, 118; Gerdy 2014, 130–31).

Social scientists have identified a number of personal-development problems that can accompany sports participation. The short-term rewards in competitive settings invite overidentification with the role of athlete and may thus delay the development of other facets of the adolescent personality. Students invested in an "athlete" identity may not seek an identity outside of sports, hindering athletes' maturation. When this happens, failure to perform to expectations leaves many athletes disillusioned and socially isolated and the "wide world of sports" becomes the "narrow world of sports" (Goldberg 1991; Culbertson 2005, 67–78).

From this viewpoint, Gray Levy's (2015, 50) statement about a high school football season in Texas, intended to be positive, is instead sobering: "For the past five months, thousands of hours have been dedicated, and the [coaches and athletes] involved have spent more time with each other than their families." When interscholastic sports constrict relationships with others and encourage a one-dimensional view of self, they can produce negative developmental outcomes. And when sports discourage athletes from participating in family events or other student activities, converting the positive values of participation into the context of the larger community becomes difficult. The increasing time investment necessary for success in school sports detracts from the time available to develop skills and behaviors necessary for a more broadly based identity formation and personal competence (Goldberg 1991; Gatz, Messner, and Ball-Rokeach 2002, 25–26).

Team travel provides a classic instance of constricted experience that is often painted as broadening. The typical high school overnight road trip itinerary includes bus to lodgings, unpack, bus to gym or field, practice, back to hotel, dinner, sleep, breakfast, pregame workout, back to hotel, to game, to bus, and back home. Meaningful educational or cultural outings are rarely included (Gerdy 2002, 79–80).

Student-athletes may consequently fail to learn appropriate life lessons. The notion that school athletic programs must prepare students to be as competitive as possible as they pursue their future livelihoods is becoming outdated because of rapidly developing global perspectives and contemporary business philosophies that emphasize reducing cutthroat competition. Creativity has become a valuable skill in a more complex world, but many interscholastic coaches stifle creativity among their athletes, even in the aesthetic sports. Improvisation by athletes in the competitive arena is often reprimanded (Glover 1999; Gerdy 2014, 130–31).

Major school sports create a climate of dominance and entitlement. Young athletes are imbued with celebrity status, creating a sense of privilege in elite athletic programs that can foster prejudice, intolerance, and discrimination. Derek Kreager (2007, 706) has observed that rather than building socially competent young men and women, the culture of modern-day athletics is marred by homophobia, sexism, and even racism. Within the context of competitive sports, middle-class white males have the most to gain, while disadvantaged minority and female athletes are marginalized. Why do male athletes hold dysfunctional values and engage in antisocial behaviors? Professor Kadence Otto (J. Lee and Lee 2009, 201) blames the values and norms associated with sports, notably the public's infatuation with athletes, the single-sex environment with the resulting sexism, and an absence of regulation of athletes' conduct in school and community settings.

Educators need to take a step back and reassess the broad co-curricular experiences of students. Gerdy (2000, 132) cautions, "To think that one can develop characteristics such as perseverance, teamwork, communication skills, and discipline only through athletic participation is woefully misguided. One does not need to get a bloody nose (or risk a concussion) to learn about perseverance. Mastering a musical instrument, for example, takes an incredible amount of perseverance, discipline, and hard work." But music is rarely touted as "building character."

Interscholastic sports seems to be ground zero for concern regarding student behavior problems in the extracurriculum. There is no reason to believe that educators can't design sports experiences that promote positive character development and eliminate the problems that surface in elitist, highly competitive settings.

Hypermasculinity

The Victorian conviction that boys participating in organized sports would acquire the trait of manliness took on religious connotations, with the "muscular Christian" expected to use his strength to protect the weak and advance righteous causes (see Higgs 1983). In the context of contact sports, the concept of manliness has morphed into a perverse form of masculinity, with repercussions that are antipodal to Victorian ideals.

Masculinity refers to a set of attributes generally associated with boys and men that include muscularity, strength, robustness, and ruggedness. Psychologists describe the positive facets of masculinity as males using their unique resources to confront life's challenges. *Affirmative masculinity* includes engaging in vigorous physical activities, banding together to achieve a common purpose, caring for and protecting family and friends, and behaving courageously in the face of danger (Grenville-Cleave 2010).

But masculinity can also have a negative side. *Hypermasculinity* describes an excessive emphasis on masculine traits and behavior, an extreme form of masculinity that few if any males can actually embody. The perceived expectations can create tensions within males who aspire to achieve such masculinity (Pringle and Hickey 2010, 115–17).

Hypermasculinity creates an adversarial physicality and a facade of toughness that compels males to control their emotions, especially fear and response to pain. Any display of emotionality generates feelings of disgust. Becoming a "real man" means suppressing one's own cries of distress as well as being callous to cries of distress in others. This feminine emotion is transformed into the manly emotion of anger. Big boys don't cry; they have temper tantrums, make others cry, and then show contempt for those who do. Thus, manliness incorporates a cool contempt for inferiors and an arrogant distancing from them (Mosher and Tompkins 1988).

Masculine practices extend beyond male bodies and are manifested in relation to spaces, objects, and other beings. Hypermasculinity subordinates and marginalizes others. Manly males pay considerable attention to asserting dominance and jockeying for position. They aggressively seek individual success and exclude the weak from their group. The most aggressive and dominant men are generally the leaders and seen as central to the group's success. Conversely, males who express gentleness rather than assertive traits are characterized as effeminate; social aspersions are cast on their manhood and heterosexuality (Grasmuck 2005, 198).

The masculinizing process begins during the developmental years. An unwritten "boy code" offers a set of behaviors and rules of conduct along with a vocabulary that society inculcates into young males. The code stipulates (1) be stoic, stable, and independent; never show weakness; (2) give 'em hell—engage in bravado and daring behavior, take risks; (3) act like a big wheel—always wear a mask of coolness, push yourself excessively; (4) no sissy stuff—never express feelings such as warmth or empathy in a way that might be interpreted as feminine (Pollack 1998, xxv, 23).

Although gender is typically considered an individual attribute—something one has or enacts—individuals don't simply import their gendered selves into neutral settings. Schools and families are the primary institutions for social development and identity formation of young males. Adolescence is a turbulent time psychologically, biologically, and socially for both males and females. School-sponsored sports can play a significant role in forming identity, including gender identity. Some social institutions, such as contact sports, are gendered (Grindstaff and West 2005, 11; Pascoe 2007, 16–18).

Social scientists tend to view male sports as central to the construction of "masculine hegemony" (i.e., dominant influence over others). This ideal is embodied in the claim that organized athletics socialize young men into business, politics, and war. Male hegemony is constructed through sports. This bond extends to spectating, which reproduces traditional schemes of masculinity, as in the macho behavior of Europe's "football hooligans." The various manifestations of sports offer a celebration of masculinity (Grindstaff and West 2005, 3; Wann et al. 2001, 204).

Historically, athletics has been one of the most masculine and sex-segregated social institutions. Through much of this nation's history, organized sports bolstered the ideology of male superiority in the face of converse social developments. Despite recent gains by women, sports remains largely organized by and for men. At its core, masculine sports continue to be linked to physical power and socially sanctioned aggression, most evident in football, men's basketball, ice hockey, and wrestling. The male establishment downplays "feminine sports" with aesthetic elements such as gymnastics and figure skating (Grindstaff and West 2005, 11–12).

Four norms comprise the male-oriented sports ethic: athletes make sacrifices for the game; athletes strive for distinction; athletes accept risks and play through pain; and athletes accept no limits. While the attributes of masculinity learned in sports—how to get back up after being knocked down, how to express oneself forcefully, how to mask pain—aren't inherently pernicious, their potential for misappropriation traverses a fine line. Often the first lesson that sports teach young boys (redolent of the boy code) is that of repression and denial, a guise that will ultimately fragment their gendered reality. Male athletes learn to attend only to those bodily signals that identify them as masculine, and over time they come to know only those signals of identity. Masculine sports can force boys into a cookie-cutter mold, inflexible and rigid, hard, aggressive, closed (Finley and Finley 2007, 199; Hickey 2008, 148). The effect of this subculture on young athletes is inimical to the development of prosocial personality traits.

Sports where use of the body as a weapon and brutal bodily contact are necessary for success create conditions where violence becomes an acceptable means of performing masculinity and maintaining masculine identity. Accordingly, these sports encompass enduring symbols of masculinity that promote violence, and male athletes come to perceive violence legitimate within the norms of a sport. Contact sports celebrate toughness and endurance, advocate competitiveness and shame in losing, and bond maleness with a taste for violence and confrontation (Finley and Finley 2007, 200; Kreager 2007, 709). A coach on a football team at a Catholic high school in Florida praised one player and added, "Next time, put him on his butt and rub your balls in his face" (Schmidle 2017, 44).

The hypermasculine culture of sports valorizes administering and receiving physical pain. Players are sometimes referred to as animals and studs and idolized by other players. Casts, bandages, and stitches can become badges of honor, while those who play hurt can be venerated. This ethic extends to the dialogue of sports: football players and their coaches extoll the virtues of "taking a lick" or "knocking somebody on his ass." Expressions of physical or emotional pain are treated as signs of weakness that could undermine team success. In parallel fashion, demonstrations of the ability to ignore physical and emotional pain are rewarded. Those who can ignore their own pain find it easier to ignore the feelings of others (Foley 1990, 127; Gatz, Messner, and Ball-Rokeach 2002, 244).

To some extent, the relationship between sports and aggression may be explained by selection effects. A prior history of fighting and violent behavior by athletes attenuates the direct effects of sports such as football and wrestling on precipitating violence. Aggressive boys are more likely to play contact sports, and coaches are likely to choose aggressive kids for more competitive teams. However, selection doesn't explain all of the ensuing violence among athletes in these sports (Kreager 2007, 719).

By rewarding physical aggression on the field with success and prestige, contact sports both elevate athletes above their peers and increase off-the-field violence toward perceived outsiders and "weaker" students. Masculinized sports become socially sanctioned stepping-stones toward privilege and power, sites where coaches, peers, parents, and the media encourage masculine identities founded on physical aggression and domination (Kreager 2007, 706). The hypermasculine culture of sports thus carries beyond the field of play and influences athletes' relationships with fellow students and the larger community.

The code of hypermasculinity bonds young men into social groups that distinguish between the strong and the weak in accordance with success in the athletic arena. During informal rites of passage, boys are judged by male peers and either accepted or rejected. These occasions may include fight scenes, danger scenes, and/or callous sex scenes. These ritualized events celebrate machismo with a vicarious audience of supporters and result in the formation of a new identity. Following victory in an adversarial contest, men are allowed to smile at and touch one another with affection. Within the macho group, a member can boast, ridicule, and tease as long as he demonstrates submission to the leader. Such overtly homosocial behavior is coupled with strong elements of misogyny and homophobia (Pringle and Hickey 2010, 119).

The aggression model in sports carries over to disdain for nonathletes, who are derided as weak and effeminate and thus subject to victimization. Male athletes feel compelled to repeatedly repudiate the specter of failed masculinity. Homophobic speech and gender epithets maintain the boundaries of privilege. Masculine identity is shored up by assertions of heterosexuality and homophobic taunts (Kreager 2007, 709–10; Tonso 2002; Pascoe 2007, 5, 58).

Sporting events serve as venues for harassment of gay students. Male nonathletes may join in the harassment of vulnerable males as a way to shore up feelings of masculinity. During the "biggest football game" of the school year, boys in the crowd targeted a group of gay students with water balloons. When one gay student tried to sit in the bleachers to watch the halftime show, which he had choreographed, harassment—including being called a "fucking fag"—forced him to leave (Pascoe 2007, 67–68).

Male band members have often been singled out for taking on a "feminine" role as boosters rather than as athletes. Band members have also been called geeks or nerds and been harassed by students during football games. They have been shunned by high-status athletes and even by cheerleaders. Such harassment sends the clear message that some students belong in lower-status locations. Football players, conversely, have been considered "real men" (Tonso 2002).

Influenced by the culture of hypermasculinity, some male athletes may fail to treat girls as intellectual or social equals and instead view them as appendages or trophies that can enhance a masculine image. As a special, distinct, and often protected class of adolescents in high school, these young men may believe that their status entitles them to do and say whatever they want to and about women (Lefkowitz 1998, 279).

Some male athletes and their peers engage in sexist discussions of girls' bodies and sexual experiences. Female bodies serve as the crux of heterosexual performance, bolstering the boys' claims of heterosexuality. High school boys often share stories that aren't about sexual intimacy or girls' attractiveness but rather serve as proof of the male capacity to exercise control over female bodies. Sexual exploits are part of the hypermasculine image (Pascoe 2007, 103–4).

A holdover from the era when many schools sponsored few girls' interscholastic sports is the annual powder-puff football game scheduled at many high schools. This ritualized touch football game with girls as football players is typically held sometime before the final boys' football game. The girls seem earnest about playing the game, while the males treat the occasion as burlesque. The football athletes dress up as female cheerleaders and parody sideline cheerleading (Foley 1990, 118). Many women have come to view these games as condescending and sexist. Some schools have discontinued the annual powder-puff game.

Male athletes may tend to segregate themselves in the hallways, in the school yard, and in the school cafeteria; studies have shown that sexual abuse is more prevalent in cultures where the two sexes are isolated (Lefkowitz 1998, 280; Pascoe 2007, 73). Several high-profile rape cases involving athletes underline the relationship between male sports and sexual exploitation. Although these models of hypermasculinity have begun to lose their cultural relevance as US society has become more gender-neutral, the conventional narrative of masculinity continues to maintain a hold on young males that exceeds correspondence to their lived experience (Grasmuck 2005, 198).

Hypercompetitiveness

Philosopher George Santayana (1994, 491) observed that America "is a perpetual football match, a brave struggle with no further purpose." The competitive ethic is promoted on the individual, community, state, and national levels in all areas of American life. When the US Department of Education launched a four-billion-dollar program to spur innovation and reform in states and local school districts, the program was called Race to the Top. Part of the American Recovery and Reinvestment Act of 2009, Race to the Top was announced by Secretary of Education Arne Duncan, a former professional basketball player. The campaign to improve the nation's schools was framed not as a cooperative venture but as a competitive race. Jumping on the competition bandwagon, Georgia chief executive Sonny Perdue initiated the Governor's Cup Program, which awarded thirty-pound trophies and two-thousand-dollar checks to the five high schools in the state with the most improved SAT scores. And in response, some schools reportedly cheated by recording the SAT scores of only their best-prepared students (Barak 2004, 19).

Academic competition may be entrenched in the nation's schools, but the competitive mind-set reigns unchallenged in the athletic arena. The social context of competition is crucial, determining how young athletes interpret and evaluate the outcome of their efforts. Social scientists are concerned that the singular focus on winning can have a detrimental impact on the development of students with an interest in sports. Games are competitive by nature; however, schools might encourage student-athletes to focus on improving their personal level of achievement and developing social and physical skills.

Coaches could instill in their athletes a realistic mind-set—You win some and you lose some. Instead, schools and local communities fixate on promoting unfailing winners. Too often, the game's intrinsic values are subordinated to winning, the results more important than the competitors' experiences (Sage 1998, 15–18; Eitzen 1995).

Competition in a sports setting can play out on the individual level or within groups. Athletes can engage in personal competition, attempting to improve on their earlier performances. Athletes can compete against nature, as in rock climbing. In swimming, golf, and running, competitors perform parallel to opponents, not directly against them. In tennis and wrestling, the competition is interactive: success is directly related to an opponent's actions. Team sports combine intragroup cooperation (teamwork) and competition (vying for a position on the team) along with intergroup competition (beating the other team).

Psychologists point to the distinction between structural competition and intentional competition. Structural competition means an activity is characterized by mutually exclusive goal attainment, which usually involves the comparison of individuals or teams so that only one will be judged the best. Intentional competition is an attitude—that is, competitiveness. Intentional competition has drawbacks. Constantly trying to outperform others ultimately fails to allay the self-doubts that give rise to this behavior, in large part because all competitors eventually lose. Fierce competitors find their goals constantly receding; no single victory is satisfying for long. Because winning doesn't ultimately satisfy, competitors continue to compete, unable to quit when they're ahead or even when they've won and certainly not when they're behind or after they've lost. Beating others at sports seems to contribute less to self-esteem than to reinforcing the need to continue beating other people (Kohn 1992, 3–4, 108–9, 111–12).

Unbridled competition reduces human interaction to a situation where one person's gain is another's loss. As such, competition can become both selfish and egoistic. In most sports, zero-sum competition prevails—the winner takes all. In its extreme forms, such as single-elimination tournaments, competition maximizes the number of losers, producing a negative-sum game. The most negative forms of competition are those that increase the differences among competitors and sustain a spiral of winning and losing, leading to big winners and repetitive losers (Rosenau 2003, 6, 9). In contrast, positive-sum conditions prevail when performance is measured against past results and the outcome is tied to individual effort.

The modern Olympic Games acknowledge first through third place, with the gold-, silver-, and bronze-medal winners sharing the victory stand in celebration. However, too many interscholastic coaches promote the "Winning is the only thing" mind-set. American sports have remained the embodiment of hypercompetitiveness.

But this ethos does not emanate from the athletes themselves. A study of Minnesota soccer players between ages twelve and seventeen found that only one-fifth of girls and two-fifths of boys responded affirmatively to the statement "I get upset when my team loses" (Steidinger 2014, 32). Many students cite the social connections created within sports as mattering more than winning or even personal success (Tufte 2012, 3).

Coaches and parents are another matter, however. The most zealous among them will do almost anything to win, including cheating. Schools try to manipulate their classification so that they compete against smaller, weaker schools. They hire individuals with connections to the school to officiate games, regardless of potential bias. They provide visiting teams with substandard locker rooms to create a competitive disadvantage (Carnovale 2012, 5, 8, 19).

Winning alone often isn't enough: coaches feel a need to crush the opposition. A Laramie, Wyoming, girls junior high school basketball team won a game by a score of 81–1, employing a full-court press the entire game. One season, a Catholic high school in Nevada boasted an average margin of victory of 40 points, including a 70–0 win. A Texas high school football team won games by scores of 84–0, 80–0, 77–0, 76–0, 70–0, and 56–0, with the coach keeping his starters on the field through the fourth quarter to run up the score (Eitzen 1995; Easterbrook 2013, 21, 213).

Intense competitiveness can escalate the desire for status, power, and dominance. Carried to an extreme, it can generate interpersonal hostility, generalized violence, deception, cheating, and fraud. When competition becomes a source of prejudice or bias, it often creates unhealthy rivalry, which can lead to aggressive and ruthless behavior (Rosenau 2003, 39, 50–51). Psychiatrists believe that athletes' aggression is in part a response to the increased pressure under which they compete. As individual athletes face increasing pressure to avoid screwing up, they may displace their feelings onto others and exhibit aggressive behavior (Adler 1999).

Many educators champion the benefits of exposing teenagers to competitive sports as a way of preparing them for life. In truth, the professed values of competition are determined by how the experiences are organized and structured: they can be either beneficial or harmful. Competition is good when it maximizes the acquisition of skills and knowledge, promotes social skills, and enhances self-image, bad if it detracts from these goals and promotes undesirable behaviors such as poor sportsmanship, ruthless aggression, and unhealthy rivalries. Moreover, a singular focus on competitiveness isn't necessary for people to perform well. Schools are tasked with preparing students for the world of work. In the developed world, competitiveness no longer seems to be a relevant job skill. Sociologists and economists agree that cooperation keeps the ecology of the modern business world healthy. Even entrepreneurs have to work with others to make the system function. Students can learn how to cooperate as well as compete in appropriately structured sports settings.

Hazing

Hazing has been observed in a range of settings including colleges and schools. The American practice of hazing was transported from Europe—most notably, English prep schools, where older boys practiced "fagging," or making younger boys perform disagreeable tasks. Hazing practices had become problematic in American schools by the early twentieth century, with a high school student killed in a hazing incident in 1905 (Nuwer 2004, 172).

Hazing in secondary schools remains largely a masculine practice, though female hazing may be on the rise, particularly among gymnasts and cheerleaders. Hazing occurs in various school organizations such as student clubs, marching bands, and sports teams, which account for about half of all high school hazing victims. Athletes are both perpetrators and victims of hazing. In one study from the early 2000s, nearly half of college athletes reported they were hazed in high school or middle school. At Many hazing incidents go unreported, and many victims are reluctant to identify their ordeal as hazing (Nuwer 2004, xv; Finley and Finley 2006, 198–99; J. Lee and Lee 2009, 172).

Hazing is perpetuated in schools and other settings that emphasize conformity to group norms. Students who haze may act on indirect cues from administrators, teachers, and coaches whose actions, attitudes, and words imply that the only social choices are assimilation into the group or isolation from it. Schools can thus function as sites where negative social values and behaviors are learned and practiced. The code of secrecy that is part of male locker room culture makes it a prominent location for initiation rituals that include hazing. Coaches and other school staff too often condone or ignore hazing practices until an incident is formally brought to the attention of a larger public audience. Hazing within athletic settings is not taken seriously but often depicted as boys just being boys and as part of playing sports (Howard and Kennedy 2006, 347–49).

Formally defined, hazing constitutes "any activity expected of someone joining a group that humiliates, degrades, abuses, or endangers, regardless of the person's willingness to participate." Components of hazing include power, acceptance, and exploitation. Alcohol consumption is often a contributing factor in hazing activities (J. Lee and Lee 2009, 173–76). Hazing typically comprises silly, potentially risky, or degrading acts that full-status members require low-status or probationary members to perform. Initiates engage in the embarrassing or dangerous activities to prove their loyalty to the group thus gain full admission. Hazers rationalize the practice as beneficial or harmless and excuse their actions by calling them part of a tradition. Sports teams justify hazing as building camaraderie (Nuwer 2004, xiv–xvi).

Students often compromise their principles to be part of a team, a form of groupthink. Members of the group suspend their good judgment and participate in hazing because of pressure to belong. In school settings, hazing is commonly an initiation ritual enacted among peers without the supervision of an authority who might otherwise direct or curtail the event. In some cases, initiates engage in the process willingly. While the act of hazing can be interpreted as an endeavor to include the initiate in the group, it is simultaneously an expression of coercive power (Howard and Kennedy 2006, 348; J. Lee and Lee 2009, 174).

Hazing can constitute a form of bullying, an expression of domination over smaller or weaker individuals specifically designed to intimidate or injure the bullied subject. Male hazing often includes distinct themes of misogyny and homophobia. Hazing practices frequently are overtly sexual. High school hazings have included acts of sodomy and coerced sexual simulations, paddling, coating bodies with foul or vile substances along with forced drinking and eating repulsive substances. As such, hazing can be viewed as part of a larger culture of sexism and violence (Howard and Kennedy 2006, 360; Nuwer 2004, xiv–xvi).

Social scientists argue that as long as school sports continue to be authoritarian, promote groupthink, and condone violence, they may promote a climate conducive to hazing. Sports hazing incidents run the gamut from mildly embarrassing to dangerous and degrading. In one comparatively benign incident, members of a high school football team forced newcomers to disrobe and climb into a sleeping bag together. More seriously, in 1997, the older members of a high school wrestling team were accused of sodomizing younger wrestlers with a mop handle. In another incident, teammates accosted a freshman football player in a locker room, pulling down his shorts and underwear and sexually assaulting him. In 1998, four high school football players pled guilty to misdemeanor hazing for forcing a soda bottle into a rookie's anus. Eight members of a Connecticut high school wrestling team were arrested in connection with an incident in which they hogtied their victims with athletic tape, stuffed them inside a locker, threw them against a wall, and repeatedly sodomized them with a plastic knife (Nuwer 2004, 176–77).

In 2003, a group of varsity football players from a Long Island high school sodomized three freshman players with broomsticks, pinecones, and golf balls on at least three occasions, with one incident so vicious it caused a witness to vomit. In addition, the initiates were sprayed with shaving cream, had powder and gel put in their eyes and hair, and had the hair ripped off their legs and buttocks with duct tape. A black player on the team was subject to racial harassment. One victim required surgery to treat his injuries (Finley and Finley 2006, 203–4).

In the wake of this incident, the team's head coach apologized but denied any prior knowledge about what was going on. After it appeared that similar incidents had occurred in the past, the school board voted to cancel the football season because so many players were aware of the attacks and had done nothing to intervene or inform the coaches, a violation of the district's code of conduct. The three assailants were suspended from school and were eventually charged with more than ten first- and second-degree felonies, though they pled guilty to lesser charges and received sentences ranging from military-style boot camp to probation (Finley and Finley 2006, 203–4).

As in this case, coaches and administrators often claim to be unaware of hazing, but they can nevertheless be held responsible for hazing incidents. In 2007, a high school coach in the Baltimore area was fired after a hazing incident, and other high school coaches have been indicted after failing to stop hazing. In addition, courts generally have allowed hazing victims to initiate legal proceedings against school districts. Nearly all states have passed some form of legislation addressing hazing. Nevertheless, despite the growth in antihazing programs and proliferation of state laws against the practice, forty university students died as a result of hazing incidents between 2007 and 2017, with most of the deaths caused by alcohol poisoning (Nuwer 2004, 226, 229; Howard and Kennedy 2006, 360; J. Lee and Lee 2009, 172–73, 178; "Hazing Deaths" 2017).

Degrading, abusive, and dangerous hazing practices must be eliminated. Doing so would not only reduce physical and emotional abuse of students by other students but would also help to end the wider acceptance of violence, sexism and alcohol abuse associated with interscholastic sports (Nuwer 2004, xx).

Drug Use

Does participation in sports encourage drug use or deter this behavior? The answer is complex. A considerable number of high school students, including athletes, use both legal and illegal drugs. Based on a study of some 2000 high school seniors, Bryan Denham (2011, 362) reported that athletes in baseball, football, and weightlifting consume alcohol more frequently than do other students. Baseball players and weightlifters reported significantly more use of marijuana. Among female students, participants in every sport reported both drinking alcohol and smoking marijuana more frequently than their nonparticipant counterparts.

Studies dating back to the mid-1990s found that nearly 70 percent of high school athletes had consumed alcohol in the previous twelve months, and more than one in three had smoked marijuana during that time. Patterns of drug use varied by race and gender. Adolescent athletes also tended to engage in binge drinking more frequently than their peers, thereby increasing the risk that they would engage in unprotected sex or drunk driving (Denham 2011, 363). Illegal drug use can lead to more serious consequences. One of the top high school basketball players in Kentucky, with a promised college athletic scholarship, was confronted by the school principal smelling of marijuana. The principal found a packet of crack cocaine in his socks. Instead of attending college, he served time in jail (O'Brien 2012, 148). Such incidents, of course, aren't limited to student-athletes.

Several studies from the early 2000s indicate that athletes and nonathletes differ in their drug use. High school athletes drink alcohol more frequently and in greater quantities, started using alcohol earlier, and engaged in alcohol-related risk behaviors more frequently than did students who had never been athletes. Athletes also had more friends who used alcohol. This pattern was evident by middle school. Athletes in grades 7–9 were more likely to report alcohol use but less likely to use cocaine and psychedelics than their classmates. A study of more than sixteen thousand high school students found that athletes were less likely to smoke tobacco but more likely to chew tobacco than their nonathlete counterparts. Peer influence clearly plays a role in drug use (Pandina et al. 2005, 119–20; Gardner, Roth, and Brooks-Gunn 2011, 21).

Adolescent athletes are more likely to use creatine, a performance-enhancing drug, than nonathletes, and data indicate increasing consumption of performance-enhancing drugs by adolescents. Use of synthetic human growth hormone (HGH) among high school students more than doubled from 5 to 11 percent according to a 2014 survey by the Partnership for Drug-Free Kids. Synthetic human growth hormone is only available legally with a prescription. (Some teens may be consuming substances that they think contain synthetic HGH but in reality do not.) The Partnership attributes the increase in the use of these drugs to the demands of athletic performance and pressure to do well to receive college athletic scholarships (Pannoni 2014).

A study by Tonya Dodge and James Jaccard (2006, 372) found not only that high school sports participation was associated with an increased likelihood of use of legal performance-enhancing supplements but also that the use of such supplements was positively related to anabolic steroid use. The data also suggest that exposure to the sports environment during early adolescence may increase the likelihood of using performance-enhancing drugs. In addition, boys appeared more likely than girls to use legal performance-enhancing substances, probably because adolescent male athletes are more likely to be immersed in a social environment that condones or supports the use of drugs to improve physical performance.

Performance-enhancing drugs can have serious side effects. Individuals who use anabolic steroids without a prescription and without medical supervision are at increased risk for a range of health problems, including heart disease and reproductive disorders, and are more likely than nonusers to experience mood disturbances, including aggression and depression (Dodge and Jaccard 2006, 367). The benefits to young athletes of taking supplements rarely outweigh the risks, and, indeed, there is no consensus that many of these supplements actually enhance performance (see Winfrey 2010, 132).

High school athletes have not been immune to the epidemic of opioid abuse that is sweeping the United States. When physicians prescribe opioid painkillers for concussed athletes, they may become addicted. Fifteen-year-old high school football player John Haskell was prescribed Vicodin, a drug with high addiction potential, following his fourth concussion. Haskell developed a dependence on pain pills and then became addicted to heroin. He remained addicted for three years before breaking the habit. Critics have questioned physicians who prescribe opioids for concussion symptoms in such cases, but we might also question parents who allow teenagers to continue playing tackle football following multiple concussions (Hager and Nadi 2016).

By the early 1990s, many school districts began to consider drug testing as a way to curb student drug use. Such plans raised objections regarding student privacy rights, but the US Supreme Court has declared the practice constitutional. Nevertheless, cost has limited the use of drug testing for high school athletes, and some states, including Florida, have discontinued drug testing programs because of lack of funding (Taylor 1997; Palka 2009; "Jury Is Out" 2014).

Despite the burden on school budgets, several states had enacted legislation by 2005 requiring interscholastic athletes to submit to drug testing. In a nationally representative sample of school districts with high schools, 14 percent were conducting random drug testing. Almost all districts randomly tested athletes, and 65 percent tested other students engaged in extracurricular activities. About a quarter of schools randomly tested all students, exceeding the current sanction of the US Supreme Court (Ringwalt et al. 2008, 826–28). By 2014, about 20 percent of high schools had implemented student drug testing policies, but not all students are checked routinely for performance-enhancing drugs. A typical drug panel tests for marijuana, amphetamines, opioids, cocaine, and PCP (Pannoni 2014).

In 2006, New Jersey became the first state to implement statewide drug testing of high school athletes that included testing for steroids. The state athletic association randomly tested five hundred athletes who qualified for state championship tournaments in football, wrestling, and a half dozen other sports (J. Lee and Lee 2009, 31). Texas also implemented steroid testing, screening 3 percent of students involved in athletics at 30 percent of the state's high schools after nine student-athletes at Heritage High School in Frisco admitted to injecting muscle-building anabolic steroids during the 2004–5 school year. Athletes at other Texas schools, including football powerhouse Southlake Carroll Senior High, were also implicated (Scelfo and Johnson 2005).

The effectiveness of drug testing remains open to debate. The National Center for Education Evaluation has concluded that drug testing leads at best to modest decreases in student drug use (https://ies.ed.gove/ncee). During the 2007–8 school year, Texas tested more than ten thousand high school athletes and caught only two taking unauthorized substances. Four tests came back unresolved, and three students refused to be tested. One athlete left a testing area without cause or approval, and eighteen others missed the mandatory testing without an excused absence. Conversely, however, an Oregon study found that athletes at a high school with random drug testing reported drug use at a rate only about one-fourth of that in a neighboring school with no testing. Moreover, student-athletes subject to random drug tests were one-third as likely than their nontested peers to use performance-enhancing substances, including steroids (Gehring 2003, 10).

Previous studies on the frequency and efficacy of drug testing—mostly in workplace environments—indicate that those tested may engage in "compensating behavior." Applied to schools, increasing the burden of being an athlete by imposing drug testing could reduce athletic participation. Competing in school athletics is strictly voluntary and is likely influenced by the perceived costs and benefits. Testing invades students' privacy and makes habitual drug use difficult or impossible. Such increased cost of athletic participation may lead marginal athletes (who may be drug users) to drop out of sports. Freed from the athletic training and testing regimen, these former athletes may revert to the drug use patterns of their nonathlete peers, who may have higher rates of drug usage (Taylor 1997, 351–64).

Clearly, the recreational drug problem is not due to sports participation per se. Running and jumping, throwing and catching a ball doesn't induce one to use drugs. Arguably, such activities may have the contrary effect by inducing a natural high. While recreational drugs are a growing problem, the most serious issue regarding young athletes remains the use of performance-enhancing drugs with potentially serious side effects. Again, such drug use may be attributed in part to the intense demands placed on young athletes to perform. This includes high school coaches, fans, and college scouts. Schools and parents need to shield young athletes in highly competitive sports from unreasonable pressure. Schools would be well advised to promote effective drug education in health education classes and/or orientation sessions for athletes.

The drug culture encompasses both recreational drugs and prescription drugs, poorly regulated and readily available through legal and illegal channels. The nation's drug problem isn't limited to schools. But the schools play an important role in developing attitudes and behaviors regarding prudent drug use. They need to take this responsibility seriously. Interscholastic sports are tainted with a distinct drug problem, the illegal use of performance-enhancing substances by athletes. To alleviate this plight, schools might begin by reducing the intense pressure to perform in the athletic arena.

Athlete Misbehavior

Sports scholars and journalists point to a host of social problems in and around interscholastic athletics. Prominent among these is the behavior of athletes, particularly male athletes. Sports participation is associated with various forms of antisocial behavior that extends from preadolescence into early adulthood and beyond. Of particular concern are contact sports that have cultivated a culture of physical aggression. Values and attitudes acquired on the playing fields influence conduct beyond the arena and can lead to deviant behavior (Gerdy 2002, 59).

Sociologists describe deviance as an action or behavior that violates social norms, including formally enacted rules. This meaning extends to the rules and norms of sports. In the athletic context, deviance can take on two forms, negative (failing to measure up to behavioral expectations) and positive (going beyond the norms or rules of the sport). Use of illegal performance-enhancing drugs has be interpreted an example of the latter (Finley and

Finley 2007, 199). Sports psychologists employ the term *bracketed morality* to refer to the suspension of the level of ethical morality obligatory in everyday life. Situation-specific morality in the context of sports may breach the boundaries of the arena. Deviant behavior may carry over into other settings (K. Miller et al. 2007).

Deviant behavior seems most prevalent among athletes in a few particular sports. Thus, it makes sense to view participants in various sports as distinct subgroups, sharing some characteristics with other athletes but possessing a nexus of traits that are characteristic of their sport. For example, football players' behavior tends to differ significantly from that of golfers or tennis players. One study found that girls' participation in interscholastic soccer had a strong positive relationship with problem behavior similar to that for boys who participate in football, while girls' participation in individual sports correlated negatively with problem behavior (Kreager 2007, 710; Sokol-Katz et al. 2006, 187–88).

Demonstrating a direct cause-and-effect relationship between participation in school sports and deviant behavior is difficult, in part as a consequence of selection bias. Students who are attracted to particular sports may be more likely to possess aggressive traits that increase the likelihood of their sports participation as well as a tendency toward individual violence (Kreager 2007, 711–12). One study found that athletes were more likely than nonathletes to describe their upbringing as abusive and their school experiences as physically confrontational. Thus, self-selection into sports may be a significant factor in the discrepancies in behavior between athletes and nonathletes (J. Lee and Lee 2009, 202). But sports may reinforce these behavioral tendencies.

Sports participation appears to influence deviant behaviors, particularly when violence is intrinsic to the sport. Many observers believe that sports do more to glorify violence and aggressive behavior than to promote civility (Gerdy 2002, 59). Sports violence can be divided into four categories (Gatz, Messner, and Ball-Rokeach 2002, 207–10): brutal (but legal) body contact in the course of the game; violent acts that are prohibited by the rules but occur routinely (elbowing in basketball); quasi-criminal violence (sucker punches); and criminal violence (physical assault). Athletes in the context of sports can hit someone with a stick (ice hockey), run into people with tremendous force (football), or pound someone insensible with their fists (boxing) with relative impunity. These behaviors would be considered deviant outside the arena (Miracle and Rees 1994, 110).

Athletes in contact sports are trained and conditioned to employ a form of violence but are supposed to turn off the violent behavior when the game ends. Some athletes have difficulty decompressing and reorienting, while others have little trouble. Research links aggressive contact sports to violence off the playing field and substantiates the unique effects of playing tackle football. The most prominent boys' sports in the nation's secondary schools are football, basketball, and baseball. Basketball and baseball are less contact-oriented than football. Wrestling is positively associated with serious fighting among males (Sokol-Katz et al. 2006, 188–89; Kreager 2007, 711, 719).

Peers play a significant role in augmenting the behavioral consequences of sports participation. Friends influence attitudes and behaviors both positively and negatively. Much adolescent behavior is learned through observing and imitating peers. Youth who spend more time socializing with their peers, particularly when unsupervised, engage in more problem behaviors. The evidence suggests that affiliating with deviant peers increases youths' risk for delinquency, and participation in certain sports appears to increase youths' exposure to risky peers. Embeddedness in exclusive teammate networks is an important intervening link in fomenting violence and substantially increases the risk for serious fighting. Male athletes often follow a code of silence that encourages them to look the other way when teammates commit physical and sexual assault. Football players are frequently positioned at the center of a school's peer culture, where they accrue social benefits that do not suggest that they reject most conventional norms; nevertheless, they exhibit inflated rates of violence (Finley and Finley 2007, 199; Kreager 2007, 711; Gardner, Roth, and Brooks-Gunn 2011, 21–22).

Aggression is necessary for success in some sports, but it is not clear how participation in high school sports affects the development of aggression. Some educators and coaches maintain that participation in contact sports has a cathartic effect on aggressive behavior (Rees and Howell 1990). But the preponderance of evidence suggests that sports like ice hockey and football don't constitute a safety valve; rather, participants in these sports were found to become *more* aggressive over the course of a season, likely as a result of modeling (Kohn 1992, 144).

Football and ice hockey aren't the only sports in which violence has occurred during games. Physical aggression has become more common in high school soccer. During just three weeks of competition in 2014, 51 players and coaches were ejected from high school soccer games. Over the previous season, 107 athletes and 12 coaches were ejected from games. Fourteen of these ejections resulted from rule violations, while the others were for unacceptable behavior on the field. One boy was beaten so badly during a soccer game that his eye swelled shut, and he was later diagnosed with a concussion. A fight during another game landed one boy in the hospital and his attacker in jail.

The Utah High School Athletics Association put the sport of soccer on probation *twice* in an attempt to deal with the violence problem (Donaldson 2014).

Violence remains a particular problem in high school football. Some of the brutality borders on criminal behavior. During a 1996 game in Albuquerque, New Mexico, one player was found to have deliberately sharpened the edge of the buckle on his helmet, causing deep cuts on their arms of several opposing players, including one wound that required twelve stitches. The attacker was dismissed from the team and placed on probation (D. Putnam 1999, 46–47).

In 2015, players on one Texas high school team became enraged after officials nullified two touchdowns and then ejected a key player. One of his teammates hit an official from behind, knocking him to the ground, where another player speared the man with his helmet. Coaches had apparently encouraged the players to launch the attack. The defensive backs coach admitted to commenting in reference to the injured game official, allegedly away from his players, "That mother****** needs to pay the price" (Rodriguez 2015).

The athletic arena tolerates coaching practices that promote abuse and wouldn't be allowed in classrooms or tolerated in other school settings. The National Association of Sports Officials now provides assault insurance to umpires and referees at all levels of play (Gerdy 2002, 49, 79).

Sports violence has enjoyed relative immunity from criminal sanction in the United States, although there have been exceptions. In 2001, a high school soccer player was convicted of felony assault with a deadly weapon for kicking an opponent in the head during a game (J. Lee and Lee 2009, 90). In 1999, a San Antonio High School basketball player received a five-year prison term after elbowing an opponent in the face, breaking his nose and causing a concussion. The assailant claimed that his coach had encouraged aggressive play and had commented following the assault, "It's about time we drew some blood" (Teitelbaum 2005, 218–19).

Generally, however, interscholastic athletes are legally classified as minors, meaning that they are too young for criminal prosecution and that their offenses are defined as juvenile delinquency. There is a widely held perception that organized sports provide help to minimize juvenile delinquency and social rebellion, but it is not clear that this belief reflects reality (Pruter 2013, 320).

The claim that participation in athletics deters crime, delinquency, and deviance dates back more than a century to the Progressive era. As the nation rapidly urbanized, the adult establishment became concerned about use of free time by youth. Organized sports appeared to be a good way to fill time and teach civic virtues (Hartmann and Massoglia 2007).

While some research shows a positive correlation between sports participation and deterrence, other studies have concluded that participation has little effect on delinquency. Athletes in certain team sports exhibit more delinquent behavior than nonathletes, and the privileged status of athletes in contemporary culture can lead them to consider themselves above the law (Gardner, Roth, and Brooks-Gunn 2011, 20–21).

Deterrence theory has two dimensions: (1) sports fill leisure time with wholesome activities, and (2) the positive values and behaviors learned in sports carry over into the participants' behavior outside the arena. There is some logic to the argument that involvement in sports keeps kids off the street and out of trouble (Gatz, Messner, and Ball-Rokeach 2002, 21–22). Juvenile crime peaks during the hours at the end of the school day, leading to interest in increasing adolescents' options for supervised and constructive after-school activities, particularly in high-crime areas. By structuring adolescents' time, these activities limit opportunities for delinquent behavior (Gardner, Roth, and Brooks-Gunn 2011, 19; K. Miller et al. 2005, 2007).

The first aspect of deterrence theory doesn't specifically require involvement in sports—any organized activity under adult supervision would suffice. The second aspect, however, posits the distinct character of the athletic experience as a deterrent to delinquent behavior. Sports are seen as a particularly effective way to keep students under control by promoting a conformist, authoritarian orientation. If delinquency is viewed as a result of weak social controls exerted on youth by family or other institutions, then the strict regimen of athletics and the discipline imposed by coaches may provide the necessary antidote (Griffin 1998, 72; Miracle and Rees 1994, 104–5).

One way to assess whether positive values and behaviors learned in sports carry over into participants' behavior outside the arena is to compare the behaviors of athletes and nonathletes. Few studies comparing these two groups distinguish between nonathletes who participate in other extracurricular activities and those who participate in no organized activities. Because some evidence indicates that youth who participate in organized activities of any type demonstrate less risky behavior than youth who do not, this is a weakness of the research design. Studies that divide youth into these three distinct groups find that sports participants demonstrate more delinquency than youth who participate in other organized activities, but they engage in no more delinquent behaviors than youth who participate in no organized activities (Gardner, Roth, and Brooks-Gunn 2011, 20).

Another limitation in the research on sports and delinquency is the use of measures that fail to distinguish between violent and nonviolent delinquency. One study found that the odds of nonviolent delinquency were roughly 39 percent lower among boys who participated in nonathletic activities versus boys who participated in sports. Athletes and boys who participated in no organized activities had the same rates of nonviolent delinquency (Gardner, Roth, and Brooks-Gunn 2011, 20). Rebellious youth are unlikely to find such conventional activities as school sports appealing, and submitting to these types of constraints may have caused their initial rebellion. Several studies have found that delinquent adolescents were more likely to voluntarily self-select out of sports (Miracle and Rees 1994, 106; K. Miller et al. 2005)

Social scientists look for specific elements in school sports culture that explain the troubling relationship between athletic participation and deviant behavior. Athletes' status can make behaviors such as drug use, drunkenness, and promiscuity appear excusable in the eyes of their peers. Some high school students view these behaviors as consistent with the jock image (Miracle and Rees 1994, 109, 117). Athletes' sense of privilege can also reach beyond the school community if they receive substantial media attention and are placed on a pedestal. Their status may make them feel as if they are immune from taking personal responsibility for their actions. In addition, studies show that athletes are less likely than nonathletes to be convicted of crimes. When athletes aren't punished for misbehavior, this reinforces the notion that they are above the law (J. Lee and Lee 2009, 204–5; Glennie and Stearns 2012, 533).

Evidence shows that when athletes from the major sports misbehave, authorities at times look the other way, exempting athletes from normal sanctions for behaviors such as tardiness, unexcused absences, rudeness, and school pranks as well as for more serious transgressions (Miracle and Rees 1994, 166). For example, in 2006, an eighteen-year-old star football player was discovered in a school restroom with a naked underage girl. School officials apparently never reported the incident to the police. The girl's mother pursued the matter, and the athlete was charged two days before the state championship game. Contrary to policy, he was nevertheless allowed to play, resulting in a scandal that caused the firing of the coach and school principal (Sailer 2007, 27).

Accusations of sexual misbehavior against high school athletes are not uncommon, and it is highly likely that additional incidents go unreported. In several notorious cases, both school authorities and the surrounding community have prioritized the school's reputation and the team's performance over female students' safety. After an August 2012 incident in which two football players from Ohio's Steubenville High School raped a sixteen-year-old girl, photos of and rumors regarding the incident circulated widely in the community. The Ohio attorney general ultimately charged the school superintendent and four other adults for failing to report the rape (Macur 2013).

A similar incident occurred at New Jersey's Glen Ridge High School in 1989 (Lefkowitz 1998).

In other instances, of course, authorities do respond appropriately to sexual misbehavior by athletes. In 2015, school administrators and coaches in Cañon City, Colorado discovered that the high school football team was at the center of sexting ring that included at least one hundred students, including some middle school students, who had traded naked photos of themselves on electronic devices. Separate community meetings were held for parents of football players and parents of other students to address the scandal. Because of the large number of football players involved, officials forced the team to forfeit its final game of the season (Cloos and Turkewitz 2015).

Male athletes are at much greater risk for delinquency and particularly for serious delinquency than are female athletes. As a masculinizing force, sports may reinforce tendencies toward aggression and domination that appear much less salient for female athletes. Given that sports are less consistent with traditional female gender roles, participation doesn't appear to afford girls the same elevated social status or opportunities for unstructured group activities that it affords male athletes. The research generally suggests no significant association between girls' sports participation and nonviolent or violent delinquency (Gardner, Roth, and Brooks-Gunn 2011, 23, 31–32).

But school sports culture is changing, and C. J. Pascoe (2007, 120–23) has documented behavior among girls on a high school basketball team that resembles the actions of male athletes:

> "The Basketball Girls" were instantly recognizable because their attire set them apart from other female students. They wore long hair, typically slicked back into tightly held ponytails ... They dressed in baggy hip-hop clothes generally indistinguishable from boys' hip-hop clothing ... immaculately clean athletic shoes unlaced with socks rolled up under the tongues so that they stuck out, and large jewelry. They spat, walked in a limping "gangsta" style, wore boys' clothing, ditched class, and listened to loud hip-hop music.... They performed special handshakes.... They continually shoved each other and wrestled on the top bleachers.... One could almost always hear them coming because of their hollers, screams, and laughter....
>
> The Basketball Girls got into food fights at lunchtime in the cafeteria. Their proclivity to fights brought them into conflict with the school's disciplinary rules.

In short, these girls appropriated the culture and style of male sports to express their independence and agency. Their sports participation seemed to provide them with a different sense of their bodies than other teenage girls had. The basketball girls' bodies weren't objects to be ogled but were active and powerful. And the behavior that Pascoe describes does not involve violence or qualify as juvenile delinquency.

◆ ◆ ◆

Despite anecdotal evidence of misbehavior by athletes and of authorities' failure to respond appropriately to such events, there is no question that the overwhelming majority of student-athletes do not engage in antisocial violence. At the same time, it is not clear that organized sports deter delinquency, as the conventional wisdom has long held. Rather, some sports sociologists have hypothesized that sports may socialize participants toward delinquency (K. Miller et al. 2007; Gardner, Roth, and Brooks-Gunn 2011, 188). And still other studies have concluded that violent juvenile offending is rooted more in individual characteristics than in normative contexts (Gardner, Roth, and Brooks-Gunn 2011, 32).

What is not open to debate is the fact that schools need to set rules for proper behavior both on and off the field of play and then enforce those rules. Athletes should not enjoy privileged status and be permitted to flout those rules. Removing school sports from the limelight and reducing the hypercompetitive environment should go a long way toward improving the behavior of athletes. Schools should stress the principles of sportsmanship, including the need to avoid cheating via the use of performance-enhancing drugs and the need to treat others with respect. Educators should actively work to counteract the culture of hypermasculinity, teaching students that boys and men can and should exhibit vulnerability, express their feelings, acknowledge pain, and empathize with the suffering of others. Sports can only build character if they promote appropriate attitudes and behaviors among athletes. In the words of legendary sportswriter Grantland Rice, it is "not that you won or lost—but how you played the game."

THE CORRUPTING INFLUENCE OF OUTSIDE INTERESTS

> Sports have become the great national lottery to many of our youth.
> —**Tom McMillen**, NBA, Rhodes Scholar

National Recognition

Traditionally, interscholastic sports competition operated within the boundaries of individual states. There were state championship tournaments in several sports, and the top football and basketball teams were ranked statewide. More recently, however, high school sports have followed the pattern of college programs, with interstate competition, national rankings, and all-star games that draw athletes from across the states. Much of the impetus for national recognition has come from external actors, notably the print and electronic media, as well as commercial enterprises that exploit school sports for marketing purposes.

In 1982, *USA Today* began publishing national rankings of high school football teams, and the newspaper later added Top 20 rankings in an array of interscholastic sports (Beem 2006). The Internet has facilitated the growth of such rankings, with numerous websites offering news, videos, and discussions about high school sports. One CBS-owned website, MaxPreps.com, for example, ranks high school teams in boys' and girls' basketball, football, baseball, and volleyball, with the goal of covering every team, every game, and every player. MaxPreps.com and some other websites rank athletes as well. The enterprise claims to have formed a partnership with nearly forty thousand varsity coaches throughout the United States (B. Cook 2014). The inherent subjectivity of these national rankings seems obvious to sophisticated sports fans, but high schools and athletes cherish the attention.

Commercial enterprises such as Wendy's (the Wendy's High School Heisman) and Gatorade (Gatorade Player of the Year) have instituted award programs that provide national recognition for high school athletes based on athletic achievement, academic excellence, and exemplary character.

Another college tradition that has extended to the high school level is all-star games. The US Army All-American Bowl is touted as the premier high school football all-star game. The game, held annually in San Antonio, Texas, brings together ninety of the nation's top high school football players and is televised by NBC Network. The bowl's dozen sponsors include Gatorade. Held in early January in California, the Semper Fidelis All-American Bowl is televised by Fox Sports (Cam Smith 2015). Similarly, the Under Armour High School All-America Game, also held in early January, takes place in St. Petersburg, Florida, and is broadcast by ESPN. In basketball, McDonald's hosts all-star games for American and Canadian boys and girls, showcasing athletic talent, creating a television audience, promoting the sponsor, and facilitating college recruitment (Yanity and Edmondson 2011, 417).

Wary educators caution that the forging of links with external groups on the national level—as well as alumni and booster groups on the local level—renders athletics administrators and coaches more accountable to these interests and can reinforce the incompatibility of high school academics and athletic programs. The growing influence of external actors on impressionable student-athletes is a related worry. In both instances, the role of commercial interests is of particular concern.

Commercialism

Commercialism impacts sports from the professional leagues to the high school level and youth sports. Commercial enterprises appreciate the potential revenues available in marketing sports. Sports have become increasingly linked to the consumption of goods and services. Fans are being transformed into consumers. American sports culture has become one vast infomercial, an exercise in crass commercialism (Gioia 2008). As one cynic put it, "The purpose of televised football is to sell cheap beer."

One explanation for the commercialization of interscholastic sports is readily apparent: high school administrators seek nontraditional sources of income. In 2006, for example, two-thirds of secondary schools reported a reduction in their budgets, forcing administrators to turn to corporate sponsorship to fund athletics. High schools report soliciting corporate sponsorships that include naming rights and facility signage as well as game program advertisements. Apologists for the practice argue that sponsorships ease the financial burden on parents, who otherwise would be required to pay even higher participation fees (Pierce and Bussell 2011, 43, 46; Fuller 2013).

Corporate sponsorships of high school sports were evident by the early 1990s, when the Georgia High School Association initiated contracts with Coca-Cola Bottling and Rawlings Sporting Goods, which provided high school programs with cash contributions and equipment in return for official product recognition at statewide events. At that time, similar arrangements existed between corporate sponsors and state athletic associations in California, Texas, Utah, and Oregon (Goldman 1991). In the ensuing two-plus decades, corporate sponsorships of high school programs have increased, and in 2011, 57 percent of high schools solicited sponsorships. In 2012, the California Interscholastic Federation announced the approval of corporate title sponsorships for all regional and state championships. They sought to obtain sponsorship by a single commercial firm for all events at five hundred thousand dollars annually (J. Peterson and Pierce 2014, 8).

School representatives, including the athletic director, principal, coaches and in some cases even booster clubs, can sell the rights to corporate sponsorship, or they can be outsourced to a third party. By 2011, 10 percent of high school athletic departments used sports marketing firms. Under most public school district policies, athletic directors cannot unilaterally make decisions regarding corporate sponsorships; rather, the superintendent and the board of education must be involved. In private and parochial schools, where sponsorships are quite common, athletic directors have more leeway to make decisions on their own (Pierce and Bussell 2011, 48, 58; Fuller 2013).

Schools in the American South are more inclined to pursue sponsorships than those in other regions, and large high schools are more likely to sell sponsorships than are smaller schools. The more athletes who participate in interscholastic sports and the more sports offered, the larger the athletic budget—and the incentive to seek out new funding sources. Typically, sponsorship revenue generated at the schools with higher participation rates makes up a smaller percent of the budget. Most high school athletic departments generate no more than five thousand dollars from their largest corporate sponsor, less than 5 percent of their total budget (J. Peterson and Pierce 2014, 8; Pierce and Bussell 2011, 57–58).

The top industry segments involved in sponsoring high school sports include food and beverages, along with sports apparel and sneakers. Many schools around the country are known is "Coke schools" or "Pepsi schools." The most frequent sponsors in Texas high school football stadiums are Coca-Cola, Dr. Pepper, and Gatorade, and the state honors a Gatorade Football

Player of the Year (J. Peterson and Pierce 2014, 9; Levy 2015, 103). One survey found that food and beverage companies focusing their investments toward on-site sponsorship accounted for nearly 40 percent of all signage (Pierce and Bussell 2011, 45).

School districts have sold corporate naming rights for their football stadiums to raise money and broaden their fan base. Naming rights for athletic facilities and events typically draw the greatest amount of money from commercial sponsors. Midland, Texas, secured $1.2 million from Grande Communications, a San Marcos–based telecommunications company, for the fifteen-thousand seat football stadium used by all of the city's high schools (Pierce and Bussell 2011, 45; Roan 2006). A number of high schools in Indiana contracted with local businesses for stadium naming rights following a series of drastic tax cuts by the state. A Chevrolet dealership in Noblesville, for example, pledged $120,000 over ten years for the naming rights to the local high school stadium (Neddenriep 2016).

High school football programs rely heavily on commercial signage for revenue. To this end, large-screen LED video boards and scoreboards have proliferated at stadiums. A Minnesota high school installed a 264-square-foot video board at their football facility at a cost of $350,000, with primary sponsorships ranging from fifteen hundred to ten thousand dollars per year (J. Peterson and Pierce 2014, 8). Game programs are another long-standing source of advertising revenue.

Businesses sponsor high school athletic programs to enhance their image by demonstrating their willingness to support local schools. At rural schools, local companies are twice as likely as national companies to sponsor sports like football (Pierce and Bussell 2011, 45; J. Peterson and Pierce 2014, 9). One survey found that consumers expressed significant interest in patronizing companies that support local high school sports programs. Home Team Marketing (www.hometeammarketing.com) has developed a nationwide network with about three thousand member high schools to facilitate marketing and sponsorships for sports programs. Marketers can purchase local, regional, or national campaigns for exposure at thousands of high school events, and participants have included Ace Hardware, Allstate, AT&T, Grand Home Furnishings, the National Guard, and the US Army (R. Miller and Washington 2014, 323–24).

Sports apparel companies have played a prominent role in commercialism in high school sports. Teenagers constitute a major market for basketball sneakers and athletic gear endorsed by big-name athletes. The companies appreciate that high school athletes are sartorial role models, especially for boys. Marketing originally focused on professional and college sports, but they have expanded their campaigns to the high school level (Powell 2008, xv).

Nike, Adidas, Under Armour, and other sporting goods companies offer high school athletic teams money and free or discounted equipment—shoes, workout gear, travel bags—in exchange for exposure. In 2006, a Nike spokesman acknowledged that the company sponsored nearly two dozen high schools and paid them as much as twenty thousand dollars to wear Nike products (Drape 2006). A few schools have signed similar contracts with local sporting goods companies (Kleps 2014).

The manufacturers of sneakers and athletic gear have pursued a marketing strategy that places head coaches in the pivotal role, signing them to contracts that allow the companies to distribute free gear at commercial basketball camps. Several dozen basketball coaches had promotional deals with sneaker companies by the early 1990s, and the number has grown exponentially (Kleps 2014; Svare 2004, 80; Goldman 1991). The practice provides the companies with continuous built-in advertising.

Critics of commercial sponsorships voice concerns about the exploitation of schools and their athletic programs by businesses corporations and view commercialism as undermining the wholesome character of these programs. And as of 2011, half of high school athletic directors did not use corporate sponsorships: in some cases, the schools prohibited such sponsorships, while in others, the officials expressed personal concerns (Pierce and Bussell 2011, 59). At the same time that activists have been working to get junk food and soft drink vending machines out of schools in the interest of promoting healthy eating habits, school stadiums, gyms, and locker rooms are plastered with the corporate logos of these products. Corporate sponsorships, in tandem with national media attention, represent a continuing challenge for public school administrators.

Mass Media

Sports and the mass media enjoy a symbiotic relationship. On one hand, the popularity of sports results to no small extent from the enormous amount of attention provided by the electronic and print media. On the other hand, the media enjoy huge benefits in audience and advertising based on their extensive coverage of sports. The relationship is on an upward spiral. Media attention generates interest in sports, and increased interest in sports warrants further media attention (Yanity and Edmondson 2011, 407).

There are two forms of media, news and entertainment, and the former often merges into the latter. Much of sports journalism is cheerleading rather than true reporting. In late 2002, for example, television brought superstar interscholastic basketball phenomenon LeBron James and his private parochial high school in Akron, Ohio, to the national stage and cast him as the leading man and his teammates and their opponents as supporting actors in a successful national television event. A telecast of one of his high school games generated ESPN2's third-highest rating for an amateur basketball game to that date. High school athletics have become the latest entrée on the television sports menu, served up to help satisfy sports fans' voracious appetite (Braig 2004, 346; Almond 2014a, 159–60).

Content-starved television networks show all kinds of sporting events every day of the week at all hours of the day and night. This pervasive offering of a commercialized and professionalized version of sports has affected college sports and more recently interscholastic sports. High school sports and the mass media have become fast friends. Virtually every local newscast will include scores, interviews, and commentary on teams. Radio networks sponsor coaches' shows, and local call-in radio shows focus on high school basketball and football. "Media days" feature local athletes and coaches. These ventures to make high school sports newsworthy exemplify the pervasive influence of the electronic media (Jack Roberts 2007, 279; Tufte 2012, 8; Levy 2015, 133, 136). Local television stations are increasing high school sports programming within their markets. In 2014, one of the most popular programs on WFSB, the CBS affiliate in Hartford, Connecticut, was *Friday Night Football*. Memphis's WMC aired a *Game of the Week*, while WNYW in New York City included game-of-the-week highlights during its ten o'clock newscasts and KUTV in Salt Lake City presented the *High School Touchdown Report* (R. Miller and Washington 2014, 323).

On the national level, Fox Sports and ESPN were routinely televising selected high school football games by the early 2000s. A few Indiana high school basketball games were televised nationally beginning in 2004 (Drape 2006), and by 2012, television trucks with satellite dishes awaited the return of a basketball team after a Kentucky state tournament game (O'Brien 2012, 11). In 2013, ESPN broadcast twenty-six high school football games, while Fox Sports 1 aired another seven. The participating schools received no compensation from the networks other than having their travel expenses paid—and received publicity (Brennan 2013). Two Ohio high schools moved a football game to Sunday to allow ESPN to televise the game live to a national audience. ESPN now routinely shows regular-season high school football games, and the number of nationally televised postseason all-star games has tripled, with the telecasts often including scenes of players announcing their official college choices (Heffron 2009, 80–83; Yanity and Edmondson 2011, 417).

The broadcasting of high school sports carries back to 1989 when a cable network signed a five-year agreement with the National Federation of State

High School Associations (NFHS), which sought an additional source of income. The deal included rights to televise a weekly package of high school sporting events, mainly football and basketball (Goldman 1991). In 2013, the NFHS Network entered into a joint venture with PlayON! Sports. In conjunction with state high school associations, the digital-content network broadcast twenty-eight thousand sporting events over its first year, attracting millions of viewers via paid subscriptions. The NFHS also created school broadcast programs, which allow schools to generate their own broadcasts and solicit commercial sponsorships, enabling high schools, as the network president commented, to join the "big leagues" (Haddix 2014).

The Internet has provided a limitless market for sports promoters and fans. A flurry of companies poured tens of millions of dollars into purchasing or developing online properties devoted to high school sports. By 2014, HighSchoolPlaybook.com, operated by Hearst-Argyle Television, was in seven of Hearst-Argyle's twenty-six local TV markets. MaxPreps, owned by CBS, provided information on eighty thousand high school football games and more than five hundred thousand basketball games each year. Rivals.com, owned by Yahoo!, had a network of more than 150 high school and college sports websites. Takkle partnered with Alloy Media to operate a social networking website for high school athletes. Varsity Networks, "a high schools sports media and Internet service company," was developing online communities built around individual high school sports teams (R. Miller and Washington 2014, 323).

TexasHSFootball.com was founded in April 2001 and became the state's leading high school sports network, used primarily by high school football fans and players, along with coaches from all fifty states. In 2014, it became part of the Sports Marketing Experts Network, which specializes in the creation, development, and execution of innovative marketing programs. Content from TexasHSFootball.com has been featured in many media outlets, including *USA Today*, ESPN, and Fox Sports ("Sports Marketing Experts" 2014).

The Internet is laden with blogs and fan forums for high school football teams, and YouTube and other sites offer endless game videos. Under the guise of sports journalism, "fan journalists" publish countless articles on websites devoted to the college recruiting process. In addition, recruiting websites employ large numbers of sports media professionals who appear less concerned with formal journalism than with making contact with undecided recruits. Coverage of the recruitment of high school athletes has exploded into a multimillion-dollar industry (Yanity and Edmondson 2011, 403, 417).

The print media have covered high school sports for at least a century, with sports pages expanding into sports sections as coverage increased. Medium-sized and smaller newspapers generally devote more coverage to local sports than do large newspapers, which focus more on college and professional sports. Local newspapers devote a disproportionate amount of coverage to boys' sports (J. P. Green, Holtzapple, and McKinley 2016).

A number of national magazines cover high school sports. *Sports Illustrated* devotes an entire section to high school players, chronicling the lives of these talented teenagers and stroking their egos. Some star athletes are profiled before they're old enough to drive. LeBron James, for example, was on the cover of *Sports Illustrated* as a high school sophomore. Some magazines are devoted solely devoted to high school sports. *High School Sports Magazine*, founded in 1997, covers high school sports in Texas. As of 2005, *VYPE High School Sports Magazine*, headquartered in Tulsa, Oklahoma, distributed more than two hundred thousand high-gloss monthly magazines in fourteen markets, primarily in the central states. The magazine provides in-depth coverage of high school sports, highlighting local athletes and schools (Gehring 2004b; Frantz 2008). These and other magazines are also available on the Internet.

All this media attention can have an detrimental effect on student-athletes. The mass media can build up young athletes to heroic proportions and imbue them with laudable virtues when in reality they have few concrete accomplishments. The mass media can distort viewers' perspective, leading fans to believe that a sporting activity must be televised to be important. Thus, the state championship game seems more significant than the intramural tournament at the local high school, a distorted standard for judging sports participation (Gerdy 2002, 122–23).

The excess media attention has provoked some resistance. As far back as 1990, some state high school athletic associations argued that the NFSH should end live national telecasts of high school football, basketball, and ice hockey on the grounds that the promotion and entertainment values of the telecasts would inevitably overtake educational goals. The forty-eight state delegates in attendance rejected the proposal by a four-to-one margin. Major national education groups, including the American Association of School Administrators and the National School Boards Association, also have opposed telecasts of high school athletic contests (Goldman 1991). But over the last two decades, the mass media's presence has become more pervasive, and it is difficult to visualize this trend abating in the near term.

Recruiting

Two forms of recruiting occur in interscholastic sports. Colleges recruit high school seniors, usually with inducements such as athletic grants or scholarships. In addition, secondary schools—typically private schools—attempt to entice talented athletes to leave their present school and transfer to the recruiting school.

Colleges began recruiting high school athletes by the late 1890s, with the advent of student-directed athletic clubs. Its purpose, then as now, was to gain an advantage in accruing outstanding athletes. As the pressure to win at the college level increased, so did recruiting efforts—and abuses (Klungseth 2005). College recruiting remained problematic throughout the twentieth century, leading various governing bodies to develop policies and rules that sought to control recruiting excesses. Founded in 1906, the Intercollegiate Athletic Association of the United States later became the NCAA and instituted major reforms after World War II.

The NCAA continues to regulate the recruiting of athletes by college coaches and their agents, publishing the *Guide for the College Bound Student-Athlete* (NCAA Eligibility Center 2017–18). The NFHS provides guidance to high school athletic directors and coaches, along with parents of athletes, regarding the college recruiting process. Even though recruiting is basically a college-initiated process, high school coaches must take the initiative to control it in their schools and guide athletes. The NCAA stresses that high school coaches should have basic knowledge of the rules regarding (1) limits on telephone calls and contacts, (2) their role as representatives of athletes' interests, (3) offers and inducements, (4) official visits, and (5) national letters of intent. NCAA rules extend down to the sophomore year of high school (Klungseth 2005). The complex and frequently changing rules cover such things as when coaches may initiate contact with students, when students may initiate contact with coaches, when colleges may pay for recruits to visit campus, how many campus visits a recruit can make, and contacts via various social media platforms (Winfrey 2010, 176, 194; Yen 2011, 599–600; NCAA Eligibility Center 2017–18).

When student-athletes sign national letters of intent during their senior year, they are committed to attending a school, and the school is obligated to provide a scholarship or grant. Other colleges must cease recruiting high school student-athletes who have signed letters of intent (Yen 2011, 598–99). In some cases, students ask for a release from the letter of intent, and the college may decide whether to grant that release.

The college coaching community has developed ways to evaluate prospects. One is the sports combine, a brief training camp during which players going through a series of physical and psychological tests for the benefit of coaches and scouts. Sports combines such as Nike Basketball Camps provide student-athletes with the opportunity to display their abilities and gain exposure—they don't purport to be instructional camps where players are taught skills. Schuman's National Underclassmen Combine, is a three-day event that allows high school football players to showcase their skills and college coaches to do some one-stop shopping (Winfrey 2010, 187).

Gregg Easterbrook (2013, 222–25) argues that many parents with unrealistic hopes of college scholarships waste their time and money sending their children to these events. Similarly, college coaches earn revenue by conducting "prospect camps," where high-schoolers' come to show off their skills to a particular school. Attendance at such camps does not necessarily translate into a better chance of being recruited (Easterbrook 2013, 205–6).

Recruiting in football and boys' basketball garners the most public attention. This media circus escalated in the 1980s, when wannabe college recruiters and self-appointed scouts began marketing their expertise to college football and basketball coaches. Because college coaches cannot be aware of every high school prospect in the nation, scouts who can identify talented athletes offer a valuable service. National football scouting services provide information about high school athletes to fans as well as to coaches. For example, *SuperPrep*, a California-based sports magazine founded in 1985, provides recruiting information on high school football players and has become a major actor on the national recruiting scene (Yanity and Edmondson 2011, 404).

Launched in 1997, Rivals.com (originally RivalsNet) has become the leading Internet-based scouting service, with 225,000 subscribers and twelve million viewers per month by 2007. These services continue to prosper. Subscribers can access the latest recruiting news and participate in various message boards dedicated to schools covered by the network. Other recruiting services include Scout.com and ESPN and CBS Sports (Yanity and Edmondson 2011, 404; O'Brien 2012, 108–9; Cam Smith 2015).

The National Collegiate Scouting Association (NCSA), founded in 2000, connects middle and high school student-athletes with college coaches. The NCSA's coaches, scouts and former college athletes assist current high-schoolers in developing recruiting profiles—for a fee. Athletes can create public web pages to display their athletic and academic profiles. Takkle.com, a partner of the NCSA, operates a social network for high school student-athletes, who create profiles that include stats and videos (Winfrey 2010, 167).

The number of scouting and recruiting networks has proliferated over the second decade of the twenty-first century. Started in 2010, 47Sports.com is a network of websites focusing mainly on football and basketball recruiting. In 2013, the company signed a long-term agreement to become the official online selection partner of the US Army All-American Bowl. Another social-networking platform, BeRecruited.com, allows student-athletes to connect and interact with college coaches. EdgeTalent.com and TopJock.net promote talented high school players to colleges, charging students or their parents for the service (Cam Smith 2015; G. Cook 2003, 15).

Most college coaches begin the recruiting process online, watching videos of high school athletes. High school football coaches enter player data into computer scouting programs. High school athletes create their own recruiting pages on Facebook and Twitter. Some athletes' families hire professional recruiters or recruiting companies (Levy 2015, 35; Winfrey 2010, 192).

Despite the hoopla surrounding recruiting, the fact remains that according to the NCAA, only about 5 percent of students who play high school sports will compete at the college level, and some of those who do continue don't receive scholarships (see table 1). Only 2 percent of prep players receive recruiting offers from colleges. The number of college athletic scholarships remained largely flat from the late 1990s until 2013, although the total dollar amount has increased (Braig 2004, 353; Conn 2012; Easterbrook 2013, 220).

Table 1. Estimated Number of Participants by Sport, 2013

	High School Seniors	NCAA Freshmen
Men's Basketball	154,000	5,000
Women's Basketball	124,000	4,600
Football	310,000	20,000
Baseball	136,000	9,000
Men's Ice Hockey	10,000	1,100
Men's Soccer	117,000	6,700

Source: NCAA Research 2013

As the executive director of the NFHS has noted, young athletes are bombarded with messages encouraging them to believe that they can become professional athletes, and they may view intercollegiate sports as a step in that direction (Gehring 2004a, 1–4). However, the chance of a given athlete making it to the pros are literally one in a thousand. The five major men's team sports—football, basketball, baseball, ice hockey, and soccer—recruit fewer than two thousand athletes each year, and only one of every two thousand high school football players will reach the NFL (Easterbrook 2013, 217).

Players occasionally go directly from high school to professional sports leagues, without stopping in college. The NBA requires draftees to be nineteen years old and one year removed from high school. The NFL requires draftees to have been out of high school for three years, although athletes may petition to enter the draft early. MLB drafts athletes who have graduated from high school if they have not attended college or junior college, and most MLB draftees spend several years playing in the Minor Leagues, where the average salary is roughly thirty thousand dollars. To be eligible for the National Hockey League draft, players must be at least eighteen. As in baseball, NHL teams have minor-league affiliates to develop young players (Gehring 2004a, 1–4).

Educators worry that the emphasis on college recruiting and professional player drafts sends the wrong message to student-athletes by devaluing education. Given the odds, athletes would be better advised to focus on academics. As former NBA player Tom McMillen (1992, 22) comments, "A youngster gambling his future on a pro contract is like a worker buying a single Irish Sweepstakes ticket and then quitting his job in anticipation of his winnings."

The NCAA has implemented policies that promote the importance of academics. Proposition 48, enacted in 1986, stipulated minimum high school grades and standardized test scores for participation in the college draft. Those standards were upgraded in 2016 to require completion of core courses by high school student-athletes. But despite attempts to ensure that academic standards are being met, plenty of evidence indicates that athletic recruiting compromises academics.

Recruited athletes are as much as four times more likely to gain admission to colleges than other applicants with similar academic credentials (Conn 2012). Echoing this finding, William Bowen and Sarah A. Levin (2005, 120) note that at the most academically selective colleges, recruited athletes are nearly four times more likely to be admitted than other applicants of similar academic caliber and are significantly more likely to be in the bottom third of their high school class.

Recruited high school athletes with subpar standardized test scores (SAT and ACT) or GPAs often attend prep schools for a year or so to qualify for college admission. Many of these schools operate with little or no oversight from accreditation agencies, state departments of education, or school districts. In some cases, schools have allowed students simultaneously to take courses that normally are sequential, such as Algebra 1 and 2; in others, students take abnormally large numbers of classes (Trotter 2006). According to sportswriter Frank Deford (2006), some prep schools are essentially basketball or football teams attached to a perfunctory classroom. In some cases, it's not even perfunctory: University High School, an unaccredited correspondence program based in Miami, had no classes or teachers (Trotter 2006).

At the collegiate level, schools continually exploit loopholes and at times flout the rules in search of a competitive advantage. The NCAA has issued a lofty statement of principle that the recruiting process should shield student-athletes from undue pressures that may interfere with their scholastic or athletic interests but has found it rather difficult to govern in a manner fully consistent with such statements (Yen 2011, 594–95, 600–601).

To be fair, the NCAA has made some progress in taming the excesses of the recruiting process. When basketball player Tom McMillen was being recruited in the 1970s, before the NCAA instituted reforms, sixty colleges were pursuing him by the end of his freshman year. That number grew to three hundred by the end of his junior year, and a University of Kentucky booster had a private jet fly McMillen and his coach to the Lexington campus, where they were greeted by three thousand fans (D. Putnam 1999, 1–2). Such a scenario is less likely under current rules.

The collective attention that highly recruited athletes receive from colleges and their high schools—exacerbated by the electronic and print media—reaches a frenzy every February, when the nation's high school football players send their national letters of intent to the college coaches for whom they have chosen to play. This annual ritual generates a great deal of fan interest. On signing day in 2007, Rivals.com reported 74.5 million page views (Yanity and Edmondson 2011, 405). Rivals.com currently has 150,000 subscribers (https://n.rivals.com).

High schools hold rallies and invite television networks to watch and cheer as athletes announce where they will be playing. A Kentucky high school basketball player convened a press conference at Memphis's famous Peabody Hotel to announce his choice of college, with two hundred people in attendance and television cameras rolling and microphones in his face. The nation's top-ranked high school football player and the most targeted recruit of college football coaches in 2006 arrived at the College Football Hall of Fame in a white Hummer limousine. Surrounded by fifteen family members and friends, he announced to the throng of reporters his intention to play college football for Notre Dame. Commented one sportswriter, "The recruiting process has given these kids a sense of entitlement that goes beyond rational thought (Yanity and Edmondson 2011, 405; O'Brien 2012, 113–14; Tufte 2012, 105).

While college recruiting has remained a constant on the American scene, recruiting at the high school level has escalated in recent years in tandem with the growth and commercialization of prep sports. Public high schools generally do not recruit athletes since students must reside within the district

(Tufte 2012, 29), and school boards establish policies regarding athletes who transfer from one school to another without changing residence.

Private schools operate under different rules, however. State associations have traditionally focused on preventing schools from recruiting students from other schools for athletic purposes. Most state high school athletic associations bar students from changing schools to gain athletic advantage, imposing penalties such as requiring athletes who change schools to sit out a year. But rules meant to limit or prevent athletics-related transfers are often difficult to enforce (Braig 2004, 343; B. Cook 2014). A 2002 survey found that public schools were concerned about private schools' ability and willingness to engage in intercommunity recruiting (Braig 2004, 362). In some cases, public school teachers coach at private schools, creating an inherent conflict of interest regarding recruiting (Carnovale 2012, ix).

Parents of athletes shop for schools with the most competitive sports programs. One Florida athlete changed schools four times in four years (G. Cook 2003, 13). Derek Sparks, who went on to play running back at Washington State University, attended four different California high schools in the late 1980s and was offered a car and money in exchange for transferring (Gerdy 2000, 81).

States have enacted open-enrollment legislation that has expanded the possibilities for students, including athletes, to change schools. Some states allow students to transfer to schools only within their district, while others permit interdistrict open enrollment. Such policies apply to all students and permit students to choose schools based on a variety of factors such as academic programs but can lead to athletic recruiting. High school coaches may make contact with student-athletes enrolled at other high schools; increasingly, however, coaches also scout middle school athletes and attempt to persuade promising athletes to enroll (Deford 2006).

In 2017, the California Interscholastic Federation, the state's governing body for high school athletics, revised its transfer bylaws to allow students to switch schools for sports-motivated reasons, although athletes who transfer without moving into the new district must sit out, generally for half a season (Wieberg 2004; Sabedra 2017). Courts in some other states have also allowed parents to transfer their children for athletic reasons, meaning that we may be seeing the beginning of free agency in high school sports (B. Cook 2014).

There are cases where coaches have sought to evade transfer restrictions by helping athletes' families relocate. One Michigan public high school allegedly recruited a running back from a neighboring high school and moved the player's family into a rental home owned by a local booster and freshman football coach. A neighboring parochial school also allegedly recruited a running back at a public high school by having a real estate agent offer his family a place to live at a reduced rent (Kolker 2015). According to Keith O'Brien (2012, 62, 71–73), high school basketball in Kentucky was rife with recruiting-related problems, with parents, coaches, athletes, and boosters frequently breaking the rules.

Recruiting of athletes now crosses district lines, state lines, and even international borders (Goldman 1991). Too often, recruiting occurs without appropriate consideration of what is in the students' best interests, not only athletically but also academically and socially (Braig 2004, 357).

Sports in Private and Nontraditional Schools

The growth of nontraditional schools and the greater allowance for student and parent choice of schools have provided private schools with the means to create athletic dynasties. Catholic high schools have been prominent among athletic powerhouses. In many states such as Ohio, high school football is dominated by Catholic schools. The dominance of Catholic schools is evident from coast to coast. De La Salle in Concord, California, won 151 straight games from 1992 to 2005. St. Thomas Aquinas High School in Fort Lauderdale, Florida, a football powerhouse, draws talented players from across the country (B. Cook 2013; Sailer 2007, 27; Schmidle 2017, 42). Similar patterns of dominance are apparent in interscholastic basketball in a number of states.

Private, parochial, charter, and magnet schools consolidate athletic talent by drawing student-athletes from just about anywhere. Recruiting by these schools is widespread in one guise or another. Private schools not only have no zoning boundaries but may not be required to follow no pass, no play rules. As a result of these advantages, private schools win a disproportionate number of state athletics championships when they compete against public schools. State athletic associations have consequently sought to level the playing field (Epstein 2009). While state high school athletic associations seek to discourage the transfer of high school students for athletic reasons, parents, coaches, and administrators find ingenious ways to bypass these rules. Moreover, some schools have been lax about confirming student residency (Svare 2004, 81–82).

A number of states have private schools compete separately from public school athletic leagues. Maryland has separate associations and tournaments for public and private schools (Patsko 2014). Texas has a private school football championship separate from the public school University Interscholastic League championship, though private schools can petition to compete against the public schools. Louisiana now holds separate public and "select" football playoffs. Private schools in some states have taken the initiative to organize their own athletic associations. The Texas Association of Private and Parochial Schools has 220 members, 218 of which are Christian or secular private schools (B. Cook 2013; Levy 2015, 7, 164).

The Mississippi High School Activities Association (MHSAA) is the state's largest governing body for high school athletics, with both private and public members. In 2013, administrators attempted unsuccessfully to bar private schools from the association. In 2015, the MHSAA banned out-of-state students from participating in athletics at private and parochial schools, prompting three private Catholic high schools to withdraw from the organization and join the Mississippi Association of Independent Schools (Patsko 2014; Cronin and Whitaker 2015).

A dispute between the Tennessee Secondary School Athletic Association (TSSAA) and a football powerhouse, Brentwood Academy near Nashville, ended up in court when the private school challenged the association's rule barring schools from contacting prospective students about sports programs. Brentwood, like many other public and private schools in Tennessee, sends brochures and otherwise advertises its sports programs. The dispute ultimately reached the US Supreme Court, which ruled in favor of the TSSAA, which had the backing of the NCAA, the National School Boards Association, and the NFHS. Writing for the Court, Justice John Paul Stevens opined, "Hard-sell tactics directed at middle school students could lead to exploitation, distort competition between high school teams and foster an environment in which athletics are prized more highly than academics" (Sherman 2007).

State athletic associations continue to explore ways to equalize competition to counteract the apparent advantages of (mostly) private schools that solicit athletic transfers vis-à-vis (largely) public schools that don't. New York's state athletic association slotted nonpublic schools into competitive divisions based both on enrollment and past success (Svare 2004, 81; Patsko 2014). New York, like most states, equalizes competition by dividing schools into classes/divisions for state tournaments based on school enrollment.

Several state associations, facing similar problems, have come up with multipliers for "nonboundaried" schools (making one private student count as, say, 1.5 public students), and/or "tradition factors" (schools that win a lot move up a class) in an effort to even out competition. Private schools are thus classified with much larger public schools (B. Cook 2013; Epstein 2009, 2–3).

At least a half dozen states have employed some form of multiplier, while other state associations have discussed or are considering the policy. Private schools have challenged the multiplier rule in the courts. But as in the

Brentwood Academy case, courts have generally ruled that state athletic associations have the authority to enact regulations designed to equalize high school athletic competitions. Georgia's state athletic association voted to end its 1.5 multiplier in 2008, and private schools formed their an independent league, which has attracted about two-thirds of the state's private schools; the remainder compete against public schools (Epstein 2009, 15, 21; Patsko 2014).

In addition to traditional private schools, recent years have seen the creation of private sports-oriented schools with professional coaches and trainers. IMG Academy, a boarding school in Bradenton, Florida, enrolls about one thousand students between ages ten to eighteen who train throughout the traditional school year. A typical day at IMG begins with breakfast from 6:30 to 7:30 a.m., followed by three eighty-minute classes, forty minutes of tutoring and preparation for standardized tests, lunch, athletic training and conditioning from 1:30 to 5:30 p.m., dinner, an hour of optional tutoring, and a mandatory ninety-minute study hall before a 10:30 p.m. curfew (Alsever 2006; Longman 2015).

Conventional schools increasingly are being challenged by this "professional" model as top high school players pursue college athletic scholarships. IMG claims that more than 85 percent of its graduates receive college scholarships. The for-profit school is applying a business model that has long been profitable for tennis and has expanded to other sports like soccer and basketball. The full cost of tuition and boarding for a year of football at IMG Academy was $70,800 in 2015. The school advertises that need-based financial assistance is available (Longman 2015).

IMG is trying to enhance its academy brand primarily with football. The Academy's football team is stocked with some of the nation's top senior recruits. A recent roster included players from 21 states. The school offers high-performance training, college prep courses, coaches with NFL experience, facilities that resemble a small college program, and a chance to play a national schedule and on national television (ESPN) against some of the country's highest-rated teams. As an independent school, IMG is ineligible to play for a Florida state championship (Longman 2015; Alsever 2006).

Another major development in American education is the charter school movement, which now includes some seven thousand schools in more than forty states ("Charter Schools" 2012). The "charter" is essentially a contract between the school and its authorizing agency that provides freedom from some regulations that apply to public schools. Charter schools are public schools of choice, meaning that parents choose them for their children. States may allow charter schools to draw students from a wider area than traditional public schools.

As of 2012, most states hadn't specifically addressed matters such as eligibility and access to interscholastic sports for students in charter schools, but changes are occurring. South Carolina has allowed charter school students to participate at other district schools when activities are not offered at the charter school. Washington state's charter school law likewise allows students access to district school programs, including athletics. Transfer rules remain complicated in the midst of school-choice laws that encourage families to place students in other schools if they feel that current schools are not meeting children's needs ("Charter Schools" 2012).

Some charter schools have developed interscholastic sports programs that follow the complex public school rules governing eligibility of athletes, school classifications, and recruiting. Tight restrictions apply as to how charter school coaches can recruit athletes, and failure to comply can result in significant punishments, as when a Florida charter school was fined heavily for violations of Florida High School Athletic Association rules ("Charter Schools" 2012).

Charter schools in some states have formed their own athletic associations. The Arizona Charter Athletic Association (ACAA) has 139 member schools competing in baseball, basketball, flag football, football, soccer, softball, track and field, cross country, volleyball, and ultimate Frisbee. The association provides the infrastructure to support Friday night football and state championships. The ACAA takes a less strict approach to student transfers than the Arizona Interscholastic Association, which governs traditional public schools, allowing students who switch schools to compete immediately instead of sitting out for a year ("Charter Schools" 2012).

About sixty of Texas's charter schools have joined the UIL, with a total of roughly fourteen hundred members. The UIL has revised its rules to keep the playing field as level as possible and prevent students from jumping to new schools simply to participate in varsity sports. Charter school students must meet the same varsity eligibility standards as other public school students. For the purposes of sports, the attendance zone for charter schools in Texas is defined as the traditional school district in which the charter school is located ("Charter Schools" 2012).

School districts and state athletic associations are also dealing with the issue of homeschooled students who seek to participate in interscholastic athletics. In 2014, the United States had approximately 1.7 million homeschooled students, most of them high-schoolers (Sieck 2015). There is wide disagreement regarding whether the voluntary decision to homeschool should bring with it a forfeiture of the opportunity for involvement in public school athletics. The question remains controversial. Parents who lobby for participation by their homeschooled children in athletics may ultimately have to submit to some form of oversight by education agencies (Joshua Roberts 2009, 195).

Currently, more than twenty states give homeschoolers the right to some type of access to classes and sports programs in public schools. In states that do not specifically mandate equal access, individual school districts or high school athletic associations may have the authority to determine whether homeschoolers can participate in public school activities. In 2013, thirty state activities associations allowed homeschooled students to play sports at the local public school. In the vast majority of these states, home schooled students had to play for the high school district in which they reside (Joshua Roberts 2009, 201; HSLDA 2017). Some states required students to be enrolled part-time, while other states allowed school districts to set their own policies. Nearly all of these states required homeschooled students to meet the same academic requirements as full-time enrolled students (Sieck 2015).

State and local regulations prevail. Whereas the right to an education has been deemed fundamental, that right has not been extended to include participation in interscholastic athletics. Participation in school sports is uniformly considered to be a privilege in the United States. The courts have routinely struck down constitutional claims, stating that a district's refusal to allow part-time access does not violate any constitutional rights and that school districts have the right to set eligibility requirements for participation in their own activities (Joshua Roberts 2009, 197; HSLDA 2017). School administrators express financial, academic, and ethical reasons for refusing to allow nonenrolled students to represent the school in athletic competition (Joshua Roberts 2009, 196). As Joshua Roberts (2009, 198–99, 201) has noted, "The principal justification offered in denying homeschoolers participation is the state's interest in promoting academics over athletics. The state's interest is implemented by making a student's athletic eligibility contingent upon achieving certain academic standards. Officials claim to be unable to satisfactorily monitor the classroom activities, grades, and attendance of homeschooled students." Educators express concern that parents of students with poor academic performance might withdraw those students from public school and begin homeschooling to maintain their athletic eligibility. Some school administrators also contend that allowing homeschooled students to participate in public school athletics will undermine loyalty and school spirit.

Both private schools and public schools might be commended for allowing homeschooled students to participate in extracurricular sports programs if their objective is to involve more adolescents in healthy competition, with the accompanying social and health benefits. But this often isn't the intent. Schools are primarily interested in recruiting outstanding athletes who can make teams more competitive—that is, they are focused on what the homeschooled student-athlete can do for the school, not what the school can provide the student.

❖ ❖ ❖

Outside interests have corrupted school sports. The mass media and other commercial enterprises appropriate interscholastic sports, coaches, and athletes to further their own agendas: though some businesses and professionals purchase advertising rights out of a sincere desire to support the local high school, in many cases, companies are interested in enhancing their bottom lines and see interscholastic sports as providing a means for doing so.

In the current fiscal environment, the public sector, including education, is underfunded. As a result, schools have needed to solicit private funding. But schools must defy the conventional wisdom and look their gift horses in the mouth, carefully examining the trade-offs that come with the money. On the other side of the equation, expenses for interscholastic sports programs at some large high schools have become disproportionate and need to be scaled back. An intramural/sports club model would go a long way toward achieving this goal.

The aggressive recruiting of athletes by colleges and private high schools subordinates academic achievement to athletic performance. Student-athletes—the overwhelming majority of whom will never pursue a career in sports—are ill served by these practices. Young people need to be educated in a way that prepares them for a more viable career. The focus should be on academic scholarships not athletic scholarships. Local school boards should relegate the collegiate/professional farm club system to community-based clubs and teams, allowing schools to devote their energies to educating all students without the distraction of external actors who have their own agendas.

10

THE CASE AGAINST TACKLE FOOTBALL

> Football: A sport that bears the same relation to education that bullfighting does to agriculture.
> —Elbert Hubbard

Hazardous to Your Health

What if schools set out to invent an appropriate sport for students and came up with tackle football? Sports columnist Christine Brennan (2015) invites us to envision

> that first parents' meeting in high schools across the country. How exactly would administrators break the news that the sport is based on hitting people? That their children would be involved in dozens of collisions every game, some including their heads? That one of the major goals of the sport is to run into someone, tackle him and slam him to the ground? That there certainly would be injuries, serious injuries, injuries that would prevent some kids from ever playing a sport again, or even living a normal life? Also, that there could be deaths.

The Economist ("Schools and Hard Knocks" 2016, 14) similarly frames the issue:

> Imagine being asked to take part in an activity that gives you somewhere between a 1-in-5 and a 1-in-20 chance of a serious head injury over a four-month period [that] could lead to weeks of impaired mental performance and headaches, and, especially if the blows are repeated, the danger of longer-term mental-health problems. Now imagine that your child is the one taking the risk.

Of course, this isn't how tackle football became a school activity. High schools adopted the game following the lead of colleges despite its notorious record of injuries and occasional fatalities. Today, football is one of the most popular sports in high schools across the nation—if not the most popular sport. About one million students—roughly one in eight American boys—play tackle football in its various forms. In 2014, the National Federation of State High School Associations (NFHS) reported that fewer than eighteen hundred girls played football, typically at the position of kicker. Girls who play tackle football rarely compete beyond their mid-teens (Belson 2015). The longer boys play, the greater their chances of serious injury.

Football injuries have caught the public eye, with significant consequences. Between 2009 and 2017, the number of US boys under age seventeen who played football had fallen by 19 percent (Schmidle 2017, 41). According to the NFHS, participation in high school football dropped by twenty thousand from 2007 to 2012. A number of state high school associations reported declines in participation: Michigan, for example, reported a drop of more than 10 percent. In contrast, only fourteen states saw participation rates rise. In Alabama, in the heart of the football-crazy South, the number of players rose by less than six hundred during those five years. The overall decline in participation can be attributed in part to fear of concussions, as parents are now better informed on the short- and long-term effects of head trauma and may discourage or prevent their children from playing (Van Milligan 2014, 41; Sentell 2014).

Tackle football has been defined as a heavy-contact and now more frequently a collision sport: highly physical contact is a necessary and acceptable component. Coaches are convinced that a football team is unlikely to succeed without physically dominating opposing players through tackles, blocks, and other forms of brutal body contact. In contrast, the rules of most other team sports (ice hockey excepted) prohibit play that is physically violent and allow body contact only when it is incidental to the normal course of the competition.

The physical risks inherent in the game have been the focus of much of the recent criticism, but there are other issues and concerns that bring into question the continuing promotion of interscholastic football. Previous chapters discussed several concerns, including overextended school budgets, athletes' behavioral problems, health problems, and obesity. With the exception of budget issues, these concerns will be revisited in the specific context of football. The discussion begins with the pervasiveness of football injuries.

According to the National Center for Catastrophic Sports Injury Research, football accounts for more than two-thirds of high school sports injuries that paralyze or otherwise severely disable athletes. The chances that a player will get a concussion while playing high school football are approximately three times higher than while playing the second-most-dangerous sport, girls' soccer. The injury rate for high school football is about four per one thousand athlete exposures (one incident of helmet-to-helmet contact would constitute one exposure). Running backs sustain more injuries than players at any other position, followed by defensive backs, linebackers, and wide receivers. As a group, defensive players are nearly five times more likely to suffer catastrophic injury. The leading injury mechanism is player-to-player contact, followed by player-surface contact. Injuries most commonly occur when players are being tackled or are tackling another player, especially with the head down. Likewise, blocking techniques are responsible for an inordinate number of injuries. Cut blocks (diving into the legs of linebackers) beyond the line of scrimmage are illegal in forty-eight states (Badgeley et al. 2013, 160; Lehrer 2012; Levy 2015, 16). Head injuries remain a major concern. Says Terry O'Neil, the founder of Practice Like Pros, a group that advocates safer football techniques, "After all the many excellent rule changes in the last few years, we don't expect any future rule changes to alter the game drastically. Game day will always be dangerous" (Belson 2015).

Most football injuries, including head injuries, occur during practice, largely because athletes spend much more time practicing than competing. Measures to minimize injury should include reducing practice time and full-contact drills and running tackling drills at reduced speed (Johnson 2012). High school coaches have reduced contact in practice, but most serious injuries occur in games. There is no simple formula to reduce injuries. One fourteen-year-old from Odessa, Texas, broke his right femur during a kickoff practice in seventh grade, requiring extensive surgery. The leg subsequently stopped growing and additional surgeries had to be performed to equalize the length of his legs. Another Texas football player broke his leg during practice in the seventh grade, tore the ligaments in his thumb the following year, shattered the bones in his arm in the ninth grade, and then suffered a herniated disk later in high school after a trainer ignored the boy's complaints about severe pain and sent him back into a game (Bissinger 1990, 48–49, 245–46).

One of the major factors that contributes to football injuries is the wide range of physical development among adolescent players. The potential for injury associated with size mismatches is a particular concern in sports that feature heavy body contact. Interscholastic football sets an age limit (typically eighteen), but weight divisions are uncommon. The strength and impact force disparities between large and small players are significant, as larger athletes can have double the body mass and strength of the smaller players. This disparity is a particular concern in middle schools, where the early maturers dominate late maturers. High school football players are still maturing physically and suffer about three times as many catastrophic injuries (e.g., neck fractures) as do college players (Malina and Beunen 1996, 204; Brady 2014).

The longer youngsters play football, the more likely they are to sustain serious, enduring injuries. Accumulated football injuries often prevent former players from participating in physical recreation during their adult years. As many as 80 percent of professional football players suffer from permanent physical disabilities. Lower extremity injuries are the leading cause of disability in retired pro players (see Domb et al. 2014).

Researchers have found that football injuries often go underreported. According to a 2014 study, players reported on average only one out of twenty-seven incidents in which they saw stars, became dizzy, or got a headache (Schmidle 2017, 41). Coaches do not always obtain training in recognizing and treating athletic injuries, and even those who are trained to respond to player injuries may not be inclined to act on this knowledge. Moreover, football coaches have subtle and not-so-subtle ways of discouraging players from reporting injuries, including one coach who required injured players to stand on the sidelines during practice wearing pink jerseys (Nowinski 2007, 131–32). Moreover, safety standards and procedures vary widely among states.

Parents' mind-set can be just as crucial. As H. G. Bissinger (1990, 43–44) put it, "Any parent who has let their child play football ... and claimed never to have understood the risks involved [is] either kidding himself or an idiot." Some parents are willing to accommodate—even encourage—the risks of injury. Bissinger cites an eighth-grade football player who broke his arm during the first defensive series of a game: "rather than come out, he managed to set it in the defensive huddle and played both ways the entire first half. By that time the arm had swelled up considerably to the point that the forearm pads he wore had to be cut off"; only then he was taken to the hospital. The boy's father praised his son's courage for continuing to play injured (43–44).

All sports contain risks. Many sports injuries are minor or temporary. Bruises, pulled muscles, injured tendons or ligaments, lacerations, and minor fractures occur occasionally, if not routinely, in baseball, basketball and track and field. Most such injuries result only in temporary disability. Risks of catastrophic injuries that cause long-term or permanent disability are of greater concern. The American Medical Association defines a catastrophic injury as a severe injury to the spine, spinal cord, or brain, including skull or spinal fractures. The National Center for Catastrophic Sports Injury Research reported that between 1982 and 2009, 97 percent of catastrophic injuries sustained in all high school fall sports occurred in football (Lake 2010, 130).

Since the early 1930s, more than seven hundred young males have died as a result of injuries or infirmities directly related to playing high school football. No other team sport comes close to this number of fatalities (Lake 2010, 130). The number of football-related deaths is lower today than at its peak of 1968, when twenty-six high school players died. Since the late 1990s, an average of five football-related deaths have occurred each year among high school players. In 2014, for example, five players died of causes directly related to football (e.g., head and spine injuries), and another six players died of indirect causes, including heart and heat issues. By the end of October 2015, seven football fatalities had occurred during the high school season (Brennan 2015; Rios 2015). New concerns about player safety arose in late September 2015, when a high school quarterback in New Jersey collapsed on the field after a hit and died soon after as a consequence of a lacerated spleen (Belson 2015).

Football players may be at risk due to heat-related issues, since many coaches still aren't adequately trained to recognize—or are disregarding—the risks. The National Center for Catastrophic Sports Injury Research reported that fourteen high school football players died from heatstroke from 1995 to 2000. In 2001, five high school football players died of heatstroke. The center's director, Fred Mueller, believes that such heat-related deaths could be prevented if coaches refrained from having teams practicing in dangerous heat (Gehring 2001b). Gray Levy (2015, 14, 68) notes that during summer practice sessions in Texas, players run up to fifty forty-yard sprints. Some players are required to run up hills on practice fields. He observed one team that practiced for nearly two hours in the heat before retiring to an air-conditioned weight room for a follow-up training session.

Among the catastrophic injuries associated with playing tackle football, none is more worrisome than head trauma caused by concussive and subconcussive hits. *Concussion* denotes low-velocity impacts that cause brain shaking and result in functional or structural injury to the brain. Concussions are caused by two types of forces, linear (e.g., an auto crash where the driver's head snaps forward violently) and rotational (e.g., a crunching tackle of a running back from the side), in which the head is whipped to one side. Rotational force can be much worse than linear force—one reason why blind-side hits have been outlawed (Hannel, Gartman, and Karpel 2014, 44; Cantu and Hyman 2012, 4–5).

Studies estimate that the typical high school football player sustains about five hundred head impacts in a season. The only practical way that concussions can be diagnosed is through symptoms. Almost half of players in one survey reported having suffered symptoms of a concussion; the average player reported three to four incidents per season. About one in five football players reported suffering a headache during or after their most recent game. Nine out of ten football players suffered at least one game-related headache (a common symptom of concussion) during the season (Easterbrook 2013, 161–62; Nowinski 2007, 5–6).

Concussions represent the third-most-common injury among high school players. In football, head trauma isn't an accidental occurrence, like getting hit with a line drive in baseball—it is part of the game. Some two-thirds of football-related concussions come from tackling or being tackled. Concussions are more likely to occur when players reach full speed—that is, on passing plays and kickoffs. No aspect of the game is more dangerous than kickoffs. Special-teams players are particularly vulnerable to concussions. For this reason, Pop Warner and some other youth football leagues have eliminated kickoffs for children under age eleven. Concussions also occur during practices. Some coaches employ drills that are clearly inappropriate: for example, the Oklahoma or bull-in-the-ring drill has two players repeatedly charge head-on at each other in a narrow corridor until one of them hits the ground. Younger players are at an increased risk for traumatic brain injuries with amplified severity and prolonged recovery. The increase in size, strength, and speed among today's high school athletes may contribute to the rising incidence of football concussions. High school offensive linemen weighing 240 pounds are now common (Easterbrook 2013, 153, 158, 161–62; Hannel, Gartman, and Karpel 2014, 47; Badgeley et al. 2013, 168).

The chances of getting a concussion while playing high school football are approximately three times higher than in the second-most-hazardous interscholastic sport. The Brain Injury Research Institute reports that 20 percent of high school football players sustain brain injuries each season. The only two other sports with risks of brain trauma equivalent to those in tackle football are boxing and mixed martial arts: most schools wouldn't consider sponsoring these activities (Lehrer 2012; Reed 2015, 50).

In 2010, between forty thousand and sixty-five thousand concussions were reported among high school football players, although the actual incidence is likely much higher, since many concussed athletes fail to report symptoms. Two years later, approximately twenty-three thousand football-related nonfatal traumatic brain injuries resulted in emergency room visits in the United States; athletes under eighteen years old accounted for nearly 90 percent of those injuries (Gregory 2010; Johnson 2012).

The major short-term danger for athletes who have suffered a concussion is second-impact syndrome, which can cause brain swelling and result in massive loss of neurons. High school players suffer repeated high-velocity hits. Their brains aren't fully mature and are thus more susceptible to second-impact syndrome. Even a slight loss of cells can alter the trajectory of adolescent brain development. Some 95 percent of second-impact syndrome deaths are in athletes under age eighteen. Following the diagnosis of a concussion, follow-up testing for symptoms and avoidance of further impact are the primary remedies. Regrettably, many concussed athletes continue to play. Coaches have been known to send concussed players back into the game (Nowinski 2007, 5–6; Badgeley 2013, 168; Brady 2014; Hannel et al. 2014, 44).

Concerns regarding subconcussive blows (jolts to the head that don't meet the diagnosis for concussion) are growing. Such hits may not result in the dizziness, nausea, and/or headaches that are the classic symptoms of concussion, but undetected damage to the brain may be occurring. Researchers have found that over the long term, routine subconcussive hits do as much harm to the brain as spectacular concussive hits. After several hundred subconcussive hits, damage to the white matter can be detected; cognitive issues can ultimately result (Easterbrook 2013, 157) The typical high school football player experiences more than 750 subconcussive impacts per season during games and practices. Interior linemen sustain a disproportionate number of subconcussive blows. The rules against helmet-to-helmet contact do little to diminish these incidents (Hannel, Gartman, and Karpel 2014, 45).

The longer a person's playing career, the more likely the risk of brain damage. Former NFL linebacker Bill Romanowski (Almond 2014a, 50) was diagnosed with twenty concussions over his football career, which began in the ninth grade. A 2011 study found that former football players who sustained two or more concussions during their youth showed higher ratings of concussion-related symptoms such as cognitive impairment (Easterbrook 2013, 162). A study commissioned by the NFL found that former players between the ages of thirty and forty-nine were diagnosed with severe memory-related diseases at approximately nineteen times the rate of the general population (Lehrer 2012). Reports are surfacing of high school football players turning down college athletic scholarships because of heightened awareness of concussion risks.

In recent years, much attention has focused on the epidemic of chronic traumatic encephalopathy (CTE) in veteran football players (see chapter 7). Researchers have found a significant correlation between the pathological stage of CTE and the number of years spent playing football (Toporek 2012b). CTE used to be referred to as *dementia pugilistica*, or being punch-drunk, and was first noticed among boxers in the early twentieth century. CTE causes progressive debilitation and can resemble Parkinson's disease (Hannel, Gartman, and Karpel 2014, 44–47).

CTE generally can be diagnosed only after death by examining the brain. Neuropathologist Bennet Omalu examined the brains of several deceased NFL players and became one of the first researchers to publish findings regarding the disease among football players. By 2017, the disease had been detected in 110 deceased NFL players (J. Ward, Williams, and Manchester

2017). Omalu (2015) makes a strong case against allowing children and adolescents to play tackle football. With brains that aren't fully developed, young people are at the greatest risk for trauma-induced depression, memory loss, suicidal thoughts, loss of intelligence, and dementia later in life.

Research confirms that repetitive blows to the head in high-impact contact sports such as football and ice hockey place athletes at risk of permanent brain damage. The risk of impairment is heightened by the fact that the brain, unlike most other organs, lacks the capacity to heal itself following injuries. There is not yet enough scientific data to identify a causal relationship between playing high school football and CTE, but the topical data are disconcerting (Toporek 2012b; Omalu 2015).

Coaches and players have assumed that football helmets protect the head from concussions. But although helmets do a creditable job of protecting the exterior of the head and preventing skull fractures, they do not protect against concussions since the brain still collides with the inside of the head (Gregory 2010). Unlike some bicycle helmets, football helmets do not crack or shatter on severe impact, meaning that the hard-shell helmet transfers the force of impact to the brain. To make matters worse, aggressive players have come to prefer tight-fitting helmets so that they can use their heads as a weapon (Nowinski 2007, 106–8).

Sporting goods companies market a never-ending line of "new" and "better-performing" equipment. Aggressively marketed advances in protective head gear may be delivering a false sense of security. In 2011, Jeffrey Kutcher, chair of the American Academy of Neurology's sports section, told a US Senate committee that all of the current concussion-prevention products being sold were largely useless: "The simple truth is that no current helmet, mouth guard, headband, or other piece of equipment can significantly prevent concussions from occurring." Despite "improvements" in football gear and helmet technology, the rate of concussions among high school football players has not significantly decreased over the last few decades (Lehrer 2012). A 2012 study found that state-of-the art football helmets tested in a biomechanics laboratory were no better than vintage leather helmets from the early 1900s in reducing the risk of internal head injuries during routine game-like hits (Bartsch et al. 2012).

No substantive rule changes regarding safety equipment in high school football appear to have had any significant impact on injury rates or patterns. Football gear may actually increase injuries by inducing more aggressive players to feel invincible. When hard football helmets were introduced, players were coached to make initial contact with the head when blocking or tackling. When face masks were added, players were instructed to hit opponents in the sternum with the face masks. These developments led to spearing, which, in turn, led to an increase in cervical spine injuries. Moreover, protruding face masks can increase the risk of rotational concussions. The dangers of spearing have been recognized, and the practice has been banned, but the rules are not consistently enforced (Badgeley et al. 2013, 168; Nowinski 2007, 102–3).

Should public schools, whose mission is specifically to develop students' brains, be sponsoring an activity that poses a significant threat to those brains? An increasing body of research makes the case that football is too dangerous for the human brain, especially young, still-developing brains. Critics have suggested that concussion-prone sports should be declared hazardous to the health, like smoking. In fact, many football helmets have a small warning label behind the ear hole, comparable to the label on cigarette packs: "Contact in football may result in concussion/brain injury which no helmet can prevent." Dr. Steven Miles of the University of Minnesota maintains that schools fail to adequately warn athletes of concussion risks and has recommended that the nation's schools eliminate football (Reed 2015, 50; Olson 2015).

School districts are facing an additional problem associated with football injuries. They may be held legally liable for continuing practices and procedures that knowingly lead to brain injuries of student-athletes. Both the NFL and NCAA have been sued for exposing players to conditions that likely cause CTE, and high school football programs are beginning to encounter similar litigation. In 2013, the NHFS faced a lawsuit on the grounds that the association had assumed a duty of care to student-athletes. The following year, lawyers for a former Illinois high school football player filed a class-action lawsuit against the Illinois High School Association over concussion protocols and management, reportedly the first-ever class action filed against a state high school association (Ganim 2014; Hannel, Gartman, and Karpel 2014, 44, 48). Other lawsuits have followed.

Nearly all the states have passed concussion laws, they are of varying strengths. In addition, the laws may encourage schools to assume that their liability is limited when athletes suffer the effects of concussions. In some instances, waivers may immunize schools against lawsuits. But the traditional defense of assumption of risk may not apply when a minor's brain is injured while participating in a school-sponsored sport. Schools generally have three legal duties imposed by statute: (1) to inform students about the risk of concussions; (2) to diagnose concussions at practices and games; and (3) to remove concussed players from competition and see that they don't return until cleared by medical authorities. Ignorance of these duties is unlikely to be accepted as an excuse by the courts. The schools' duties regarding subconcussive impacts are even less clear (Hannel, Gartman, and Karpel 2014, 45–47).

Parents are required to sign consent forms allowing minors to participate in certain activities. Schools continue to justify offering football on the grounds that everything involves some risk, but as chapter 7 discusses, there is a point at which the level of risk—to the school system and most importantly, to the student-athlete—becomes unacceptable.

In addition, interscholastic football has negative health and fitness consequences. To maintain aerobic fitness, adolescents should engage in sixty minutes of moderate to vigorous daily exercise, preferably in one continuous session or broken up into ten-minute sessions. High school football games feature twelve-minute quarters during which players engage in brief spurts of physical activity—typically about six seconds per play. With roughly two hundred plays during a high school game, an athlete who plays on both offense and defense (a shrinking minority) would engage in about twenty minutes of vigorous activity (Levy 2015, 9).

As coach Gray Levy (2015, 116) observes, "The positives of playing football are found in the *process* of preparation. The game itself is only special because of the work before kickoff." He explains, "A big part of any practice is repetition. Practices are designed to progressively drill aspects of a game plan through the week" (113). Organized practices are unquestionably beneficial in teaching game skills but may be less effective in developing aerobic fitness. Coaches talk for minutes at a time, and players stand in line awaiting their turn during drills. The vigorous calisthenics and running of laps are not actually football. While conditioning also includes weight training sessions supervised by coaches or trainers to develop muscle strength and endurance, it, too, is not actually football. In short, physical fitness among football athletes has little to do with the game itself. In addition, what football training and competition lack in sustained activity, they make up for in punctuated excess. The physical demands on and expectations of high school football players occasionally border on physical abuse, as when coaches employ exercise drills as punishment (Gerdy 2014, 184).

Moreover, participation in tackle football does little to promote healthy body weights among players and may promotes unhealthy weights, particularly among offensive and defensive linemen. During their high school careers football players may purposefully gain weight, often beyond healthy levels, in emulation of their college and NFL heroes, and to better their odds of earning a college athletic scholarship. Larger size becomes the norm and the goal for football players (Skinner 2013, 922).

Coaches often encourage weight gain as a means of improving the success of the team. If a player is going to use his body to physically intimidate opponents, the bigger the body the more effective the weapon. It is no secret that football players are larger than the average male, but never too large in the view of some coaches. The chair of the Kinesiology Department at a college in the South told the author that he routinely receives phone calls from high school coaches asking him for advice on how to put more weight on linemen. The professor soon realized that coaches were less interested in developing muscle tissue on their football players than increasing body weight per se.

In 1950, the average college interior offensive lineman weighed 189 pounds; in 2000, that number had risen to 307 pounds. In 2010, the offensive line at one Texas high school averaged 262 pounds, and high schools now have 300-pound offensive linemen (Easterbrook 2013, 179–82). Some of this gain comes from increased muscle mass from weight training, but some comes from use of human growth hormones and anabolic steroids (see chapter 8).

Chris Nowinski, director of the Sports Legacy Institute, went from 160 pounds as a 6'3" sophomore linebacker in high school to weighing 230 pounds as a senior. Four years later, when he was playing defensive tackle at Harvard, he stood 6'5" and weighed 295 pounds (Nowinski 2007, 12). Such dramatic weight increases cannot be all muscle. Weight training experts point out that only novice weightlifters can gain as much as 30 pounds in a year. Former Mr. Olympia Arnold Schwarzenegger notes that in his prime he never put on more than 25 pounds of muscle in any given year, and he admits to having used steroids to bulk up.

But even players who gain muscle weight without the use of dangerous drugs are too heavy to be healthy. A player who stands 6'4" and weighs 300 pounds would have a body mass index of 36.5, which is considered obese. To achieve a healthy body mass index (below 30), that player would need to lose nearly 60 pounds. Levy (2015, 118) describes a 6'6" football player who weighs 305 pounds as "lean." A normal, well-muscled adult male at this height would be rated obese at 285 pounds.

A study of high school football players in North Carolina found that fewer than half had healthy body weights, while about 35 percent were overweight, 15 percent were obese, and 7 percent were morbidly obese. Among linemen, only 8 percent had healthy weights, with 34 percent obese and 21 percent morbidly obese (Skinner 2013, 924, 927). Moreover, football players, especially linemen, increasingly have more than 30 percent body fat, far higher than the American College of Sports Medicine's recommendation that healthy males in their teens and twenties carry less than 20 percent fat. Athletes in other sports tend to have healthier body fat percentages (McMahon 2007, 86). NBA star Michael Jordan tested at less than 10 percent body fat during his playing career.

Carrying excess body weight can have serious health consequences, and many overweight athletes exhibit early indicators of diabetes and heart disease

(Easterbrook 2013, 184–85). In 2015, a thirteen-year-old Illinois football player who weighed more than 300 pounds collapsed during a June workout and died, with heart disease implicated in his death ("Granite City Teen" 2015).

Efforts to gain weight during adolescence may lead to the development of ongoing obesity that becomes even more severe when they no longer engage in regular physical activity. Overweight adolescents have an increased likelihood of remaining overweight as adults, which can lead to an increased risk of adverse health outcomes (Skinner 2013, 926; Yard and Comstock 2011, 189). Chris Mims, who played football at a Los Angeles High School, at the University of Tennessee, and in the NFL, weighed 465 pounds when he died of an enlarged heart at age thirty-eight (Easterbrook 2013, 184–86). According to one study, football players are twice as likely as athletes in most other sports to die before age fifty (Culverhouse 2012, 104–6).

Unsportsmanlike Conduct

Football coaches promote the importance of being tough and aggressive. Players are encouraged to make their opponents hurt, make them suffer. Coaches tell their athletes that they want them to be "animals." Football players are praised for being confrontational. One way athletes convey toughness is through ritual insults (Eder 1995, 61–63). What develops is a culture of verbal confrontation and provocative remarks—that is, trash talk. Bissinger (1990, 76) cites instances of trash talk employed by Texas high school football players during games: "Your mother's a whore" and "fuck you" were standard fare. Picture the high school golf coach putting up with such graphic insults on the links in the spirit of competition. The state of New Jersey actually banned trash talking in school sports; to what effect remains uncertain.

The accepted wisdom among football fans and sympathetic educators is that the sport helps students develop discipline and gives them a chance to channel their aggression. One hears this argument from former players who confound nostalgia for the game with an honest critique of its effects (Almond 2014b). The research paints a different picture. Tackle football normalizes physical violence. Studies indicate that football players are more violent than their male peers. It is plausible that aggressive boys are more likely to play heavy contact sports like football, but playing football doesn't appear to contain or channel violent behavior. The violent culture of football tends to carry over into school corridors and onto the streets (Kreager 2007, 716–19).

High school football players were found to be significantly more likely than male nonathletes to be involved in a serious fight, while playing basketball and baseball had no relationship to fighting. Moreover, males whose friends play football were a third more likely to engage in fighting than were other males, suggesting peer influence. Tackle football is a violent sport, but the evidence suggests that it's less the game then the culture of football that increases violent behavior. Violence, on the field and off, is interwoven with masculine status and identity. Physical aggression is the way that young males demonstrate their worthiness within a football-linked peer group (Kreager 2007, 716–18).

Given the culture of football, it is not surprising that coaches who attempt to limit aggressive behavior to the playing field haven't been particularly effective. Football players are introduced to the culture early on, and the violence becomes ingrained during their teen years if they continue to play in high school and college. In the view of critics, the culture is toxic. Steve Almond (2014a, 6), a former reporter and play-by-play announcer, concludes, "I happen to believe that our allegiance to football legitimizes and even fosters within us a tolerance for violence."

The violent inclinations of male football players extend to their behavior toward women. A study of student athletes at ten Division I universities revealed that while male athletes made up only 3.3 percent of the male university population, they represented 19 percent of the students reported for sexual assault. Of those reported for sexual assaults, two-thirds were football or basketball players (Crosset et al. 1995, 126–40) There have been some notorious incidents of high school football players involved in sexual assaults, as noted in chapter 8.

But most of the violence is directed at fellow football players during games. Coaches have been known to encourage players to injure opponents—for example, to "take out" the quarterback. Violent behavior is reinforced by watching televised football, where the player is portrayed as a battler and the body a weapon. Cameras focus on injured players as the commentators hype the violence. The NFL sets a poor example for young athletes. New Orleans Saints coaches were caught offering bounties to defensive players to injure opposing players during the 2011 season. Teenage football players are impressionable, and the normalization of injuring opponents carries down to school sports. Damaging the bodies of others and one's own body becomes the price one has to pay to play football. It is an unacceptable price, as the epidemic of football injuries makes clear.

◆ ◆ ◆

A few school districts are beginning to question football as a school-sponsored sport. No precise numbers are available on how many schools have eliminated their football programs because of safety concerns, but a number of high school teams have been disbanded. Schools have canceled football seasons due to excessive injuries or lack of players. A Michigan high school football coach went to the school administration to express his concerns about player safety. The team, decimated by injury and overmatched, voted to cancel the remainder of its season. The superintendent ratified the decision, commenting, "These kids have long lives ahead of them, and we need to keep the brains in their heads intact" (Almond 2014b).

In the fall of 2015, Camden Hills Regional High School in Maine canceled the final five games of its football season because player injuries had decimated the team. Ridgefield Memorial High School in New Jersey scrapped its varsity football program for the 2015–16 season because only thirteen students tried out. In 2010, Maplewood Heights, a Missouri high school with an enrollment of three hundred students, had thirty-eight players on the football team. Four years later, only twenty students were on the team roster, three fewer than the minimum recommended by the state athletics association. The team had to forfeit a game when injuries left the sideline depleted. The school board disbanded the high school football team in June 2015 amid growing concerns about player safety. The president of the school board reported that during the previous season, player injuries included a broken ankle, a torn ACL, and a significant head injury. A subsequent poll showed that only fifteen students were interested in trying out for the team, including only five returning players. Although a few alumni weren't happy with the board's proposal, no parents complained during board meetings (Belson 2015).

When schools are unable to field a squad to compete in eleven-man football, some states provide the option to play six- or eight-man football. Texas high schools with fewer than one hundred students can opt to play six-man football. The teams typically have no more than three coaches. Six-man football has proved popular in small-town schools in the Plains states. There are advantages to this version of the game. The playing field is eighty yards long, resulting in more scoring, and all offensive players are eligible to catch passes. The game requires a wider variety of both offensive and defensive skills, and it is more favorable to normal-sized kids. But there are also drawbacks: six-man football can be more violent than the eleven-man game because more space per player and more kickoffs (due to more scoring) means more open-field collisions (Levy 2015, 157–62, 166).

Schools could choose to pursue flag football rather than tackle football. Flag football is a relatively open game. With fewer players on a team, everyone is more involved in the action. And with minimal protective gear, the players enjoy greater freedom of movement and are less inclined to use their bodies as weapons. The American Academy of Pediatrics recommends increasing flag football and noncontact alternatives, particularly for younger students (Olson 2015). Some high schools already sponsor intramural flag or touch football leagues.

Some reformers suggest that rather than eliminating tackle football, the rules and mode of play could be modified to make the game safer. Gregg Easterbrook (2013, 317) advises reforming the sport to reduce vicious contact but preserve the game's excitement and aesthetic and athletic integrity. Student-athletes can be protected and afforded the benefits of team sport participation without unnecessary risks only if dramatic changes occur in how the game is played. A few such changes have previously been made. For example, in 1976, when the NFHS eliminated the head and face as the initial point of contact on blocking and tackling, football deaths dropped as a result (Brady 2014). The NFHS targeted helmet-to-helmet hits in 2007, and the head slap is no longer legal.

In 2012, the National Football League began promoting "Heads Up" blocking and tackling, but five years later, the initiative "showed no demonstrable effect on concussions" (Schmidle 2017, 44). Former NFL player Scott Peters's SafeFootball program teaches young players to initiate contact with their hands, but this technique is less relevant to tackling then to blocking and avoiding blocks (Hannel, Gartman, and Karpel 2014, 47). L. Syd Johnson (2012) suggests that changes should start "with a zero-tolerance policy regarding hits to the head, and then build on previous rule changes—such as outlawing spearing, butt-blocking, helmet-to-helmet hits, and horse-collar tackles." Johnson also endorses requiring linemen to start upright in a two-point stance rather than in the head-lowering three-point stance. Doing so would promote use of blocking with the body, shoulders, arms, and hands rather than the head.

Johnson (2012) also observes that substantive concussion prevention cannot be achieved without altering the modes of play as well as the rules. Eliminating tackling from football below age sixteen would be the most effective measure but would likely encounter considerable opposition. Other suggestions include shortening the football season, limiting on-field time during games, and adopting limits on the number of hits players are permitted to sustain. Football associations at various levels have restricted practices or contact during practice sessions, as noted. Some elements of reform have to be attitudinal, as the culture of football frames playing through pain as a badge of toughness, often deterring players from stepping aside to rest or recover from a hit because they don't want to be perceived as weak (Easterbrook 2013, 172–73, 177; Gehring 2001b, 5).

Critics of tackle football remain skeptical about the efficacy or feasibility of proposed rule changes in making the game safer. They point out that the concussion epidemic has persisted in the wake of previous rule changes. Observers note that the games' most appealing features are also the most risky for players. For example, fans would rebel against eliminating kickoffs, which are visually exciting. Attempts to institute such rule changes would likely provoke serious political blowback.

Roy Henderson, a former director of the Texas University Interscholastic League, asserted, "Football cannot be defended in the high school unless it is subordinated, controlled, and made to contribute something definite in the cause of education" (Ripley 2013a, 77). He made that statement in 1927. Nine decades later, a growing number of educators, journalists. former players, and private citizens continue to question the contribution that interscholastic football makes to schools' mission. Almond (2014b) bluntly asks, "What is a dangerous, insanely commercialized form of athletic combat doing in our public schools? In an era when parents lament rising class sizes, crumbling facilities and underpaid teachers, why are taxpayers underwriting a form of entertainment that quite literally causes students to suffer diminished brain function?"

A growing number of critics echo Almond. Bissinger, whose 1990 book about Texas high school football, *Friday Night Lights*, inspired a 2004 movie and an NBC television series that aired from 2006 to 2011, has become convinced that football should be banned in high school and college. Former president Barack Obama, an avid sports fan, has commented that if he had a son, he wouldn't let him play pro football, though he'd consider letting him play on the youth level (DeLessio 2014).

The former president is joined in his reservations about the game by several prominent professional athletes. NBA star LeBron James and former NFL players Larry Csonka, Terry Bradshaw, Kurt Warner, and Troy Aikman have all stated that they would not let their sons play football, as has current NFL quarterback Drew Brees. Warner characterized football as a "dangerous and violent sport." Green Bay Packers tight end Jermichael Finley, who suffered a spinal-cord injury in 2013, said he would not let his kids play football because of the things he'd been through and seen. And former NFL quarterback Brett Favre commented, "I'm almost glad I don't have a son because of the pressures he would face" (DeLessio 2014; Winograd and Hais 2012).

Dr. Bennet Omalu (2015) notes, "We have a legal age for drinking alcohol; for joining the military; for voting; for smoking; for driving; and for consenting to have sex. We must have the same when it comes to protecting the organ that defines who we are as human beings." So what is a safe age to play football, and what is a safe form of the game? Almond (2014a, 116) observes, "There are plenty who play football purely for kicks, who harbor no hope of competing in college or beyond. And it's pretty hard to argue with a kid who simply loves the game. If my son wants to head out to a park for a five-on-five, I'm not about to stop him." Like Almond, few people would object to touch football in the park. But the research offers compelling reasons why school-sponsored tackle football should be banned:

> Football, alone among high school sports, is inherently unsafe for the brain. Football is the one high school sport in which a primary objective is inflicting punishment on one's opponent.... Unlike other sports, you can't make football significantly safer for the brain without changing the fundamental nature of the game (e.g., banning blocking and tackling)....
>
> There simply aren't enough safety measures we can implement to overcome the fact that the brain isn't built to withstand the repetitive brain trauma inherent in a game built around violent collisions....
>
> Football proponents will argue that the game imparts lessons on the gridiron that can't be learned anywhere else. But life lessons like teamwork, leadership, perseverance, sacrifice, goal setting, discipline, etc., can be just as easily and effectively acquired by participating in sports other than football. (Reed 2015, 50)

In addition, the culture of interscholastic football appears to tolerate if not provoke misbehavior among male athletes, and football requires an inordinate amount of money. Even when gate receipts are factored in, the toll on the school's athletics budget is inequitable and indefensible.

Students can enjoy all the benefits of playing the game without incurring unreasonable risks of injury by competing in intramural flag football, which also offers less incentive to engage in hyperaggressive behavior or injure opponents.

11

THE TAIL THAT WAGS THE DOG

> Sport has become the 800-pound gorilla, eating up our resources, obscuring the real problems we need to deal with, and dominating our social traditions.
> —Robert McCabe

Almost from their conception, interscholastic sports have subverted schools' mission in various ways. They have distracted students, educators, and local citizens. As high school sports arenas became the cultural centers of communities across the nation, some parents seemed more interested in sports than academics, while a growing number of teachers became preoccupied with coaching. Commented Professor Neil Isaacs (1978, 16–17), "Our educational system often seems to use [sports] as its *raison d'être*."

Interscholastic sports are replete with the same excesses that plague college sports: elitism, ruthless competitiveness, commercialization and intrusive media, ever-longer seasons, overblown intersectional games and tournaments, and an obsession with rankings. As talented high school athletes focus on acquiring college athletic grants and harbor dreams of playing professionally, the number of single-sport athletes has proliferated and time devoted to sports has expanded. Student-athletes often neglect academics, and a growing number are enticed to use performance-enhancing drugs (Pruter 2013, 322–24).

Today's educators face serious issues surrounding interscholastic athletics. The most nettlesome problems include the loss of instructional time to the demands of sports; controversial no-pass, no-play rules; the lack of sportsmanship by players, coaches, and spectators; the task of retaining qualified coaches; an epidemic of injuries in contact sports; the burden of drug testing; mounting costs; an increasing reliance on private funding; and the aggressive, often unprincipled, recruitment of standout high school athletes by colleges and private schools.

The emphasis on highly competitive sports ignores practices that are in the best interests of the majority of students. Varsity sports programs that serve a small fraction of the student population and monopolize limited school facilities constitute a misappropriation of funds. Elitist sports programs drive school budgets and schedules and influence how personnel are utilized: the paradigm of misplaced priorities. School principals spend an inordinate amount of time dealing with sports issues; this time could be better spent on improving academics or addressing other administrative responsibilities. School districts struggle with teacher shortages. Secondary schools are having a particularly difficult time finding teachers in the sciences, math, and special education; meanwhile, high schools hire a dozen football coaches (Kralovic 2003, 68; Easterbrook 2013, 213).

Sports take administrators', teachers', and students' focus away from academics. The lives of student-athletes are defined by the amount of time and energy that must be devoted to sports. Between conditioning programs, team meetings, film sessions, daily practices, games, and travel, athletes may spend up to three dozen hours per week in sports activities and miss hours of class. Student-athletes increasingly receive the message that unless they're willing to devote all of their waking hours to a selected sport, their future opportunities will be limited (Roan 2006). Recalled the mother of one high school athlete, "On football game day, my son's day began at 6:45 am when he left for school; it ended between 9:30 and 10:30 at night, depending upon whether the game was home or away. He usually had about two hours after school to rest, eat, and start homework" (Winfrey 2010, xvi).

Sports-related activities—late-night band practices, elaborate pep rallies, frequent meetings with sports-obsessed parents—also require enormous time commitments from others in the school community. Interscholastic athletics even dictate when the school day starts—often before 8:00 a.m.

In Kentucky, high school basketball games take place even when school and church are canceled because of snow (O'Brien 2012, 189, 208). Like the US Postal Service, neither snow nor rain nor heat nor gloom of night stays sports fans from watching their games. The local crowds who follow high school sports aren't braving adverse weather conditions merely for the entertainment value of the spectacle, nor are the schools prioritizing the scheduling of athletic contests principally for the educational benefits of these activities. Spectator sports and their accommodation by local educators are driven by schools' and communities' need to identify with winning teams as well as an abiding—if misplaced—faith in the benefits of competition. A sign displayed in a Texas high school fieldhouse proclaims, "WE BELIEVE In God, In Family, In Our Community, In Our Ability to Win" (Levy 2015, 29).

High school administrators are sensitive to the expectations of local sports fans and have made the necessary accommodations. A growing number of high school programs have taken on the trappings of university-level sports. Frank Kovaleski, director of National Interscholastic Athletic Administrators Association, conceded that the college athletics arms race may be trickling down to the high school level. Charles Breithaupt, the former athletic director of the Texas University Interscholastic League, observed, "We're no different at the high school level than Florida State and Florida and Texas and Texas A&M" (Wieberg 2004). The major high school sports have been transformed into a miniature version of the collegiate game.

A Knight Foundation Report from the early 2000s concluded, "High school sports today can reflect the worst of their collegiate counterparts. In addition to commercial influences, recruitment and transfer of high school players are far too common, leading to disjointed academic experiences and absurdly dominant teams in some communities. Academic compromises are made for high school athletes as well, leaving them with a diploma but unprepared for college-level work" (Gehring 2001a, 16). And a 2004 Report of the Commission on High School Athletics released by the National Association of State Boards of Education warned that this trend threatens to undermine high schools' academic mission, calling on state boards and athletic associations to be more vigilant about questionable recruiting practices, corporate sponsorships, and other influences that could undermine schools' commitment to education. While the NCAA has taken steps to address similar issues at the college level over the past two decades, state education policymakers have engaged in little discussion or even acknowledgment of the increasingly troubling situation in interscholastic sports (Gehring 2004b, 18; Gehring 2005a).

The college model has influenced interscholastic sports budgets. Free spending by major college programs has spurred a high school arms race, bumping up coaches' salaries and promoting the construction of plush sports facilities and pushing competitors to keep pace. The fact that such a strategy isn't appropriate for high schools hasn't discouraged the practice. High schools resemble colleges in how they cover costs, and some of the excesses of interscholastic sports trickle down to the middle school level (Wieberg 2004; Edwards, Kanters, and Bocarro 2011, 603).

Even more troubling are the ways that the college model affects student-athletes. Many high school programs are too pressure-packed for physically and emotionally diverse adolescents. Major high school sports impose demands and create stressors that are inappropriate for this age group. Far too often, interscholastic sports are based on what is meaningful or convenient for adult promoters, not student-athletes. Schools increasingly base their prestige on winning sports teams rather academic achievement (Glover 1999).

If sports are so important, why don't schools allow everyone to compete? Rather than following a model that focuses on intramural competition and thus promotes the involvement of all students, schools prioritize participation for a few talented athletes. Public schools have a mandate to serve all students, and athletic budgets should be allocated fairly across sports and in ways that increase participation. The numbers could be increased significantly by implementing a no-cut policy—all interested students would be permitted to participate. The National Association for Sports and Physical Education suggests that all middle schools conduct interscholastic sports with a no-cut policy, and a few school districts have adopted such policies. Some private high schools require all freshmen to participate in the athletics program and allow them to play whatever sport interests them (Howard and Kennedy 2006, 350–51; Colabianchi, Johnston, and O'Malley 2012, 4).

The sort of cutting that is considered routine in the sports setting—a participant's removal as a consequence of a perceived lack of skill or potential—rarely occurs in other arenas of life. It results from the limited number of spots on the team and a focus on winning. Even when students freely acknowledge and accept the practice of cutting, it can affect their sense of innate worthiness during an important time in their physical, mental, and emotional maturation process. Students who have been cut describe being upset and occasionally mention how it affected them permanently when it was not handled appropriately (Seifried 2012, 80–81).

And making the team does not necessarily mean equal participation—or even any participation. Superior players receive the lion's share of the playing time, while the less skilled spend a disproportionate amount of time watching from the sidelines. Being a substitute appears to contradict the rationale behind involvement in sports. *Substitute* becomes a label of identity. Being a specialist in a team sport, such as a kicker in football, has a similar consequences when it comes to actual activity. Student-athletes suffer the emotional effects of riding the bench. During adolescence, a lack of playing time can hinder student-athletes' social lives. Students who play little or not at all may feel marginalized because they do not contribute on the field or court. Likewise, starters who are demoted can suffer emotional stress that can influence their future participation in sports (Ryall 2008, 56; Stanec and Lay 2008).

The primary aim of secondary school sports programs ought to be providing access to everyone. Yet many high schools continue to promote elitist varsity athletic teams while cutting back on physical education classes and neglecting intramural sports programs (Reed 2015, 92–93).

Former US Supreme Court justice Byron "Whizzer" White, an all-American college running back who played in the NFL in the late 1930s, observed that schools have consistent access to our youth, and if opportunities for recreation aren't available there, they may not be available at all. He advocated the creation of physical activity programs to produce strong and healthy youth without elaborate, overly competitive interscholastic athletics:

> The system of school against school... inevitably has unfortunate consequences for a truly comprehensive program: energy and effort are concentrated upon producing the school team; it is an exclusive system which leaves all but the chosen few sitting in the grandstands to cheer... the antithesis of a sound program. (Isaacs 1978, 165)

One area in which interscholastic athletics have made great progress is in the participation of women. More than three million American girls now participate in school sports—basketball, volleyball, track and field, cross country, fast-pitch softball, soccer, golf, tennis, and other sports. Nevertheless, as of 2012, girls' participation levels remained lower than the levels for boys in 1972, prior to the implementation of Title IX (National Women's Law Center 2012; Overman and Sagert 2012, 384). And in 2016, although 3.2 million girls played school sports, that number was 1.3 million less than the number of boys (NFHS.org). It may be, as critics of using participation rates as a metric argue, that teenaged girls are less interested than their male counterparts in competing in interscholastic sports, but the core issue is equal opportunity.

Gender segregation has remained the norm on playing fields, and in many cases, separate girls' and boys' teams are appropriate as consequence of physical differences. Nevertheless, competing together on gender-integrated teams can help boys and girls learn to work together toward common goals, encourage cross-gender friendships, diminish gender-based stereotypes (Edwards et al. 2011, 169).

The shortsighted emphasis on producing winning teams continues to distort the purpose of school sports. As professor of kinesiology Chad Seifried (2012, 80–84) observes, high school sports remain geared to high-level competition, and the programs focus on a few highly skilled athletes. Too much emphasis is placed on winning and not enough on participation. Local fans and the news/entertainment media promote this preference by focusing on popular spectator sports. The majority of students—disproportionately girls and underprivileged students—are left on the sidelines.

While elite competition may be appropriate for a select number of student-athletes, the Institute of Medicine and the National Association for Sport and Physical Education have recommended more inclusive intramural programs (Bocarro et al. 2014, S66). If we really believe that after-school sports activities benefit youngsters, we should focus on putting into place a comprehensive program serving every student who wants to participate. Intramural programs aimed at maximum participation would benefit far more students than elitist interscholastic athletics. Progressive educators are recommending an increased emphasis on intramural sports, which tend to include students of varying abilities and have lower administrative costs (Bocarro et al. 2014, S69).

Shifting to an intramural/sports club model would remove highly competitive, elitist sports from schools and place them under the purview of community-based groups. As John Gerdy (2006, 67) notes, the issue is one of balance and perspective. Athletics have a place within our educational institutions as a supplement to the other educational and extracurricular experiences. Elite athletics have a legitimate place in American culture, but whether schools are an appropriate setting for such elitism is debatable.

A few public school districts have discontinued interscholastic sports programs in favor of intramurals. In the 1990s, declining enrollment forced the Kansas's Shawnee Mission School District to close several junior high schools and establish middle schools. The new middle schools had no interscholastic sports but offered intramural programs in which any student could participate. The move initially generated resistance from some parents, but the system has worked well, and the intramural programs remain in place (Beem 2006; Blom 2014).

Some alternative schools have opted for a fresh approach to school sports. BASIS Charter Schools in Arizona, Texas, and Washington, D.C., don't offer tackle football, which was deemed too expensive and all-consuming. The schools offer basketball and soccer, with all students allowed to participate regardless of skill level. The BASIS school in Tucson competes in an alternative league that costs less and requires no long-distance travel, so students rarely miss class for games. Student-athletes who want to play at an elite level do so on their own, on private travel teams (Ripley 2013a, 77). The increasing number of private sports clubs has made this a viable option for young athletes in many urban and suburban areas.

Schools can design intramural sports programs to take into account factors such as the size of the student body and student needs and interests. For example, larger schools could organize intramural leagues based on level of competition and have teams play against each other in tournaments. Smaller schools might enter teams in extramural leagues with neighboring schools, coordinating competition among teams in selected sports, and with school districts providing buses to transport students. Under this model, extramural activities would constitute a natural outgrowth of the intramural program, unlike varsity programs, which reflect an agenda proposed by a state athletic association.

The private sports clubs, in contrast, would be formed based on participant interest, with students seeking out others who share those interests to serve both as teammates and as competition. Such clubs already exist for such activities as cycling and hiking

The transition from interscholastic sports to an intramural/sports club model would not necessarily be smooth and would no doubt spark significant opposition. But schools need to restore their focus on academics and provide extracurricular activities that are available to and beneficial for all students. It is time for secondary schools to implement a student sports revolution.

REFERENCES

Adams, Lorraine, and Dale Russakoff. "Dissecting Columbine's Cult of the Athlete." *Washington Post*, June 12, 1999, A1.
Adams, Natalie Guice, and Pamela Bettis. *Cheerleader! An American Icon*. New York: Palgrave Macmillan, 2003.
Adler, Jerry. "The Truth about High School." *Newsweek*, May 10, 1999, 56–58.
"After Prep Football Game Turns Violent, Parents Reportedly Attack Players." *FoxSports.com*, September 30, 2015. http://www.foxsports.com/buzzer/story/high-school-football-player-kicks-opponent-head-no-helmet-parents-attack-california-093015.
Allen, Dorothy, and Brian Fahey. *Being Human in Sport*. Philadelphia: Lea and Febiger, 1977.
Almond, Steve. *Against Football: One Fan's Reluctant Manifesto*. Brooklyn, NY: Melville House, 2014a.
Almond, Steve. "Sack those Quarterbacks! The Case for Banning High School Football." *WBUR.com*, October 15, 2014b. http://www.wbur.org/cognoscenti/2014/10/15/ban-high-school-football-steve-almond.
Almquist, Jon, Tamara C. Valovich McLeod, Angela Cavanna, Dave Jenkinson, Andrew E. Lincoln, Keith Loud, Bart C. Peterson, Craig Portwood, John Reynolds, and Thomas S. Woods. "Summary Statement: Appropriate Medical Care for the Secondary School-Aged Athlete." *Journal of Athletic Training* 43.4 (2008): 416–27.
Alsever, Jennifer "A New Competitive Sport: Grooming the Child Athlete." *New York Times*, June 25, 2006. http://www.nytimes.com/2006/06/25/business/yourmoney/25sport.html.
Atkin, Ross. "Strike Up the Band!" *Christian Science Monitor*, December 30, 1998. https://www.csmonitor.com/1998/1230/123098.feat.feat.2.html.
Austell, Andre. "Role Conflict in High School Teachers/Coaches." Master's thesis, Southern Illinois University, 2010.
Ayres, Karen. "Schools Get around 'No-Pass, No-Play' Law." *Dallas Morning News*, January 28, 2007, 3.
Badgeley, Marcus A., N. M. McIlvain, E. E. Yard, S. K. Fields, and R. D. Comstock. "Epidemiology of 10,000 High School Football Injuries: Patterns of Injury by Position Played." *Journal of Physical Activity and Health* 10.2 (2013): 160–69.
Bagnulo, Angela. "Cheerleading Injuries: A Narrative Review of the Literature." *Journal of the Canadian Chiropractic Association* 25.4 (2012): 292–99.
Baldwin, Peter. *The Narcissism of Minor Differences*. Oxford: Oxford University Press, 2011.

Baker, Matt. "Coaches Set to Go before OSSAA." *Tulsa World*, October 2, 2013. http://www.tulsaworld.com/sportsextra/highschools/coaches-set-to-go-before-ossaa/article_1abd35d1-89ac-5f4f-8dcc-143da7338c80.html.

"Bands of America Marching Championships." *Music for All*. N.d. http://www.musicforall.org/what-we-do/boa-marching-championships/grand-national-championships/grand-national-championships.

Barak, Tal. "Trophy Schools." *Education Week*, October 6, 2004. https://www.edweek.org/ew/articles/2004/10/06/06stjour.h24.html.

Bartsch, Adam, E. Benzel, V. Miele, and V. Prakash. "Impact Test Comparisons of 20th and 21st Century American Football Helmets." *Journal of Neurosurgery* 116.1(2012): 222–33.

Bean, Josh. "Public High School Coaching Salaries Survey: Some Near Six Figures but Job Has Many Duties." *Mobile Press-Register*, August 2, 2009. http://blog.al.com/press-register-sports/2009/08/public_high_school_coaching_sa.html.

Beem, Kate. "Righting the Balance in the Athletics-Academics Equation." *School Administrator* 63.6 (2006): 10–18.

Belson, Ken. "As Worries Rise and Players Flee, a Missouri School Board Cuts Football." *New York Times*, September 28, 2015. http://www.nytimes.com/2015/09/29/sports/football/As-Worries-Rise-and-Players-Flee-a-Missouri-School-Board-Cuts-Football.html.

Bennett, J. C. "The Secondary School Cheerleader and Ritualized Sexual Exploitation." *Clearing House* 64.1 (1990): 4–7.

Bercovici, Jeff. "Why an ESPN Columnist Didn't Blow the Whistle on High School Football Injury Bounties." *Forbes*, March 6, 2012. http://www.forbes.com/sites/jeffbercovici/2012/03/06/why-an-espn-columnist-didnt-blow-the-whistle-on-high-school-football-injury-bounties/.

Bettis, Pamela, and Natalie Guice Adams. "Short Skirts and Breast Juts: Cheerleading, Eroticism, and Schools." *Sex Education* 6.2 (2006): 121–33.

Bishop, Greg. "A $60 Million Palace for High School Football." *New York Times*, January 29, 2011. http://www.nytimes.com/2011/01/30/sports/30allen.html?_r=0andpagewanted=print.

Bissinger, H. G. *Friday Night Lights: A Town, a Team, and a Dream*. Cambridge, MA: Da Capo, 1990.

Blom, Dan. "Shawnee Mission Planning for the Return of Middle School Athletics; Keeping Intramurals." *Shawnee Mission Post*, January 28, 2014. https://shawneemissionpost.com/2014/01/28/shawnee-mission-planning-for-the-return-of-middle-school-athletics-keeping-intramurals-24550.

Bocarro, Jason, M. A. Kanters, M. B. Edwards, J. M. Casper, and T. L. McKenzie. "Prioritizing School Intramural and Interscholastic Programs Based on Observed Physical Activity." *American Journal of Health Promotion* 28.3 (2014): S65–S71.

Bogage, Jacob. "Girls' Soccer, Basketball Players Have Higher Concussion Rates Than Male Counterparts." *Washington Post*, March 27, 2017. https://www.washingtonpost.com/news/recruiting-insider/wp/2017/03/27/girls-soccer-has-highest-concussion-rate-of-high-school-sports-study-finds.

Bowean, Lolly. "State Law Requires Catastrophic Injury Insurance for High School Athletes." *Chicago Tribune*, October 13, 2013. http://articles.chicagotribune.com/2013-10-13/news/

ct-met-rockys-law-20131013_1_rocky-clark-high-school-athletes-catastrophic-injury-insurance.

Bowen, Daniel, and Collin Hitt. "High School Sports Aren't Killing Academics." *The Atlantic*, October 2013. http://www.theatlantic.com/education/archive/2013/10/high-school-sports-arent-killing-academics/280155/.

Bowen, William, and Sarah A. Levin. *Reclaiming the Game: College Sports and Educational Values*. Princeton: Princeton University Press, 2005.

Boyce, Rebecca. "Cheerleading in the Context of Title IX and Gendering in Sport." *Sport Journal* 11.3 (2008). http://www.thesportjournal.org/article/cheerleading-context-title-ix-and-gendering-sport.

Braddock, Jomills H., II, Jan Sokol-Katz, Anthony Greene, and Lorrine Basinger-Fleischman. "Uneven Playing Fields: State Variations in Boys' and Girls' Access to and Participation in High School Interscholastic Sports." *Sociological Spectrum* 25.2 (2005): 231–50.

Brady, Eric. "Why Are High School Football Players Dying?" *USA Today*, November 30, 2014. http://www.usatoday.com/story/sports/highschool/2014/11/30/high-school-football-deaths-damon-janes/19712169/.

Brady, Eric, and Mary Jo Sylwester. "Kentucky School Maintains Edge with Fund-Raising Booster Groups." *USA Today*, June 17, 2004. http://usatoday30.usatoday.com/sports/preps/2004-06-17-ky-highschool-boosters_x.htm.

Braig, Kevin P. "A Game Plan to Conserve the Interscholastic Athletic Environment after LeBron James." *Marquette Sports Law Review* 14.2 (2004): 343–429. http://scholarship.law.marquette.edu/sportslaw/vol14/iss2/5.

Brennan, Christine. "More Prep Football on TV? All about Networks, Not Kids." *USA Today*, October 22, 2013. http://www.usatoday.com/story/sports/columnist/brennan/2013/08/21/christine-brennan-high-school-tv/2683139/.

Brennan, Christine. "Would Football Stand a Chance If Invented Today?" *USA Today*, October 28, 2015. http://www.usatoday.com/story/sports/highschool/2015/10/28/high-school-football-deaths-head-injuries-concussions/74766208/.

Broh, Beckett. "Linking Extracurricular Programming to Academic Achievement: Who Benefits and Why?" *Sociology of Education* 75.1 (2002): 69–95.

Buchanan, Bruce. "Coaching for Life." *American School Board Journal* 193.8 (2006): 20–23.

Bukowski, Bruce. "A Comparison of Academic Athletic Eligibility in Interscholastic Sports in American High Schools." *Sport Journal* (2008). http://thesportjournal.org/article/a-comparison-of-academic-athletic-eligibility-in-interscholastic-sports-in-american-high-schools/.

Burstyn, Varda. *The Rites of Men: Manhood, Politics, and the Culture of Sport*. Toronto: University of Toronto Press, 1999.

Butterfield, Stephen, and Bruce R. Brown Jr. "Student-Athletes' Perceptions of High School Sports Participation." *Physical Educator* 48.3 (1991): 123–28.

Byl, John. "Organizing Effective Elementary and High School Intramural Programs." *Physical and Health Education Journal* 70.3 (2004): 22–24.

Campbell, Jim. "Why Intramurals?" In *Intramural Sports: Joining the Team*, 12–17. Austin, TX: Mason Crest, 2004.

Cantu, Robert, and Mark Hyman. *Concussions and Our Kids*. Boston: Houghton Mifflin Harcourt, 2012.

Carnovale, Antonio. *The Darkside of High School Sports*. Las Vegas: CreateSpace, 2012.
"The Case for High School Activities." *North Carolina High School Athletic Association Bulletin* 54.1 (2001): 1–2. https://www.nchsaa.org/sites/default/files/attachments/nfhs-case-for-hs-athletic.pdf.
Castile, Lianne, and Christy Collins. "The Epidemiology of New Versus Recurrent Sports Concussions among High School Athletes, 2005–2010." *British Journal of Sports Medicine* 46.8 (2012): 603–10.
Cavanagh, Sean. "Sour Economy Places Athletics in Jeopardy." *Education Week*, April 1, 2009, 6–7. https://www.edweek.org/ew/articles/2009/03/23/27sports.h28.html.
"Charter Schools and Interscholastic Sports." *National Charter School Resource Center Newsletter*, December 2012. http://www.charterschoolcenter.org/newsletter/december-2012-charter-schools-and-interscholastic-sports.
Clinchy, Evans. "The Educationally Challenged American School District." *Phi Delta Kappan*, December 1998, 272–77.
Cloos, Kassondra, and Julie Turkewitz. "Hundreds of Nude Photos Jolt Colorado School." *New York Times*, November 6, 2015. https://www.nytimes.com/2015/11/07/us/colorado-students-caught-trading-nude-photos-by-the-hundreds.html.
Cohen, Joyce. "Marching Band—A Threat to Hearing." *USA Today*, October 17, 2007. http://usatoday30.usatoday.com/news/health/2007-10-16-band-hearing_N.htm.
Colabianchi, Natalie, L. Johnston, and P. O'Malley. *Sports Participation in Secondary Schools: Resources Available and Inequalities in Participation—A BTG Research Brief*. Ann Arbor: Institute for Social Research, University of Michigan, 2012. http://docplayer.net/3416106-Sports-participation-in-secondary-schools-resources-available-and-inequalities-in-participation.html
Coleman, James S. *Equality of Educational Opportunity*. Washington, DC: US Department of Health, Education, and Welfare, 1966.
Conn, Steven. "In College Classrooms, the Problem Is High School Athletics." *Chronicle of Higher Education*, April 15, 2012. https://www.chronicle.com/article/In-College-Classrooms-the-/131550.
Cook, Bob. "Ex-College Coach Explains Why High School Sports Should Die." *Forbes*, May 8, 2012. http://www.forbes.com/sites/bobcook/2012/05/08/ex-college-coach-explains-why-high-school-sports-should-die/.
Cook, Bob. "States Strain for Creative Solutions to High School Sports Class Warfare." *Forbes*, March 25, 2013. http://www.forbes.com/sites/bobcook/2013/03/25/states-strain-for-creative-solutions-to-high-school-sports-class-warfare/.
Cook, Bob. "High School Sports, Transfers Are Creating Just Two Classes of Teams." *Forbes*, February 26, 2014. http://www.forbes.com/sites/bobcook/2014/02/26/in-high-school-sports-transfers-are-creating-just-two-classes-of-teams/.
Cook, Glenn. "Win at All Costs." *American School Board Journal*, August 2003, 12–16.
Cottingham, Marci D. "Interaction Ritual Theory and Sports Fans: Emotions, Symbols, and Solidarity." *Sociology of Sport Journal* 29.2 (2012): 168–85.
Cotton, Henry. "Athletics v. Academics." *Teacher Magazine*, February 1996, 42–43.

Cronin, Courtney, and Chris Whitaker. "3 Schools Pull Out of MHSAA." *Jackson Clarion-Ledger*, July 30, 2015, 1A, 4A.

Crosset, T. W., J. R. Benedict, and M. A. McDonald. "Male Student-Athletes Reported for Sexual Assault: A Survey of Campus Police Departments and Judicial Affairs Offices." *Journal of Sport and Social Issues* 19.2 (1995): 126–40.

Culbertson, Leon. "The Paradox of Bad Faith and Elite Competitive Sport." *Journal of the Philosophy of Sport* 32.1 (2005): 65–86.

Culverhouse, Gay. *Throwaway Players: The Concussion Crisis from Pee Wee Football to the NFL*. Lake Forest, CA: Behler, 2012.

Deford, Frank. "College Sports Excesses Seep into High Schools." *NPR Morning Edition*, September 27, 2006. https://www.npr.org/templates/story/story.php?storyId=6151334.

Deford, Frank. "School Bands Should Not Be Entertainment Adjunct for Sports." *NPR Morning Edition*, March 13, 2013. https://www.npr.org/2013/03/13/174138591/school-bands-should-not-be-entertainment-adjunct-for-sports.

Delaney, Tim. "Humanism and Sportsmanship in an Uncivil Society." *International Journal of the Humanities* 8.1 (2010): 23–31.

DeLessio, Joe. "9 NFL Players Who Wouldn't Let Their Sons Play Football." *New York Magazine*, November 14, 2014. http://nymag.com/daily/intelligencer/2014/11/9-nflers-who-wont-let-their-sons-play-football.html.

Denham, Bryan. "Alcohol and Marijuana Use among American High School Seniors: Empirical Associations with Competitive Sports Participation." *Sociology of Sport Journal* 28.3 (2011): 362–79.

DeNisco, Alison. "Bulking Up with Booster Clubs." *District Administration* 50.9 (2014): 73–76.

Dilley-Knoles, J., J. Burnett, and K. Peak. "Making the Grade: Academic Success in Today's Athlete." *Sport Journal* 13.1 (2010). http://thesportjournal.org/article/making-the-grade/.

Dodge, Tonya, and James Jaccard. "The Effect of High School Sports Participation on the Use of Performance-Enhancing Substances in Young Adulthood." *Journal of Adolescent Health* 39.3 (2006): 367–73.

Doleschal, Janis K. "Managing Risk in Interscholastic Athletic Programs: 14 Legal Duties of Care." *Marquette Sports Law Review* 17.1 (2006): 295–339.

Domb, Benjamin G., Chris Carter, Nathan A. Finch, Jon E. Harmmarstedt, Kevin F. Dunne, and Christine E. Stake. "Whole-Person Impairment in Younger Retired NFL Players: The Orthopaedic Toll of a Professional Football Career." *Orthopaedic Journal of Sports Medicine* 3.5 (2014). https://www.ncbi.nlm.nih.gov/pmc/articles/PMC4555538/.

Donaldson, Amy. "Game Assault Highlights Problems in High School Boys Soccer." *Deseret News*, March 30, 2014. http://www.deseretnews.com/article/865599845/Game-assault-highlights-problems-in-high-school-boys-soccer.html?pg=all.

Drape, Joe. "High School Football, under Prime-Time Lights." *New York Times*, September 17, 2006. http://www.nytimes.com/2006/09/17/sports/17highschool.html.

Dugan, Seymour, Leslie Seymour, Jon Roesler, Lori Glover, and Mark Kinde. "This Is Your Brain on Sports: Measuring Concussions in High School Athletes in the Twin Cities Metropolitan Area." *Minnesota Medicine* 97.9 (2014): 43–46.

Easterbrook, Gregg. *The King of Sports: Football's Impact on America.* New York: St. Martin's, 2013.

"Edelman Finds Meaning." *Stanford Daily*, December 1, 2011. https://www.stanforddaily.com/2011/12/01/edelman-finds-meaning/.

Eder, Donna. *School Talk: Gender and Adolescent Culture.* New Brunswick, NJ: Rutgers University Press, 1995.

Edwards, Michael, Jason N. Bocarro, Michael Kanters, and Jonathan Casper. "Participation in Interscholastic and Intramural Sport Programs in Middle Schools: An Exploratory Investigation of Race and Gender." *Recreational Sports Journal* 35.2 (2011): 157–73.

Edwards, Michael, Michael Kanters, and Jason Bocarro. "Opportunities for Extracurricular Physical Activity in North Carolina Middle Schools." *Journal of Physical Activity and Health* 8.5 (2011): 597–605.

Eitzen, Stanley. "Ethical Dilemmas in Sport." Speech delivered at Sport and American Values Symposium, San Angelo, TX, October 31, 1995. https://search.proquest.com/openview/42229e13cee262054c95740f0331d368/1.pdf?pq-origsite=gscholar&cbl=41532.

Eitzen, Stanley. *Fair and Foul: Beyond the Myths and Paradoxes of Sport.* Lanham, MD: Rowman and Littlefield, 2003.

Epstein, Timothy Liam. "Prep Plus: Evaluating the Motivations for and Effects of Enrollment Multipliers and Other Measures in High School Sports." *Texas Review of Entertainment and Sports Law* 10.2 (2009): 2–22.

Erwin, Heather. "Middle School Students' Leisure Activity Engagement: Implications for Park and Recreation Administrators." *Journal of Parks and Recreation Administration* 26.3 (2008): 59–74.

Fainaru-Wada, Mark, and Steve Fainaru. *League of Denial: The NFL, Concussions, and the Battle for Truth.* New York Three Rivers, 2013.

Farrey. Tom. *Game On: The All-American Race to Make Champions of Our Children.* New York: ESPN Books, 2008.

Fejgin, Naomi. "Participation in High School Competitive Sports: A Subversion of School Mission or a Contribution to Academic Goals?" *Sociology of Sport Journal* 1.3 (1994): 211–30.

Figone, Albert. "Teacher-Coach Role Conflict: Its Impact on Students and Student Athletes." *Physical Educator* 51.1 (1994): 29–34.

Finley, Peter, and Laura Finley. *The Sports Industry's War on Athletes.* Westport, CT: Praeger, 2006.

Finley, Peter, and Laura Finley. "They're Just as Sadistic as Any Group of Boys! A Content Analysis of News Coverage of Sport-Related Hazing Incidents in High Schools." *Journal of Criminal Justice and Popular Culture* 14.2 (2007): 197–219.

Foley, Douglas. "The Great American Football Ritual: Reproducing Race, Class, and Gender Inequality." *Sociology of Sport Journal* 7.2 (1990): 111–35.

Fortuna, Carolyn. "Paradise under the Field House Lights: A Teacher-Researcher Study around Gender Constructions in the Public High School." *Networks: An Online Journal for Teacher Research* 13.2 (2011): 1–8.

Fowler, Susan. "The Cost: Cheerleaders, Band Pay Big on, off the Field." *Jackson Clarion-Ledger*, August 21, 2016. http://www.clarionledger.com/story/news/2016/08/19/cost-cheerleaders-band-pay-big-field-off/88942768/.

Fowles, John. *Daniel Martin*. London: Cape, 1977.
Frantz, Bob. "High School Athletes No Longer Immune to Big-Time Pressure." *San Francisco Examiner*, February 11, 2008. http://www.sfexaminer.com/sanfrancisco/frantz-high-school-athletes-no-longer-immune-to-big-time-pressure/Content?oid=2146875.
Fuller, Dawn. "Can Sports Sponsorships Solve the High School Athletics Budget Crunch?" *University of Cincinnati News*, December 9, 2013. http://www.uc.edu/news/NR.aspx?id=18940.
Ganim, Sarah. "Class-Action Lawsuit Filed over High School Football, *CNN*, December 2, 2014. http://www.cnn.com/2014/12/01/us/concussion-lawsuit-high-school-football/.
Gantert, Tom. "Sports Spending at Bloomfield Hills Schools is $285 Per Pupil." *CAPCON: Michigan Capitol Confidential*, October 27, 2010. https://www.michigancapitolconfidential.com/13880.
Garcia, Angela. "Understanding High School Students' Sport Participation." *Sport Science Review* 4.3-4 (2015): 121-44.
Gardner, Margo, Jodie Roth, and Jeanne Brooks-Gunn. "Sports Participation and Juvenile Delinquency." *Sport, Exercise, and Performance Psychology* 1.S (2011): 19-37.
Garty, Judy. *Marching Band Competition*. Broomall, PA: Mason Crest, 2003.
Gatz, Margaret, Michael Messner, and Sandra Ball-Rokeach, eds. *Paradoxes of Youth and Sport*. Albany: SUNY Press, 2002.
Gavora, Jessica. *Tilting the Playing Field*. San Francisco: Encounter, 2002.
Gehring, John. "Panel Criticizes College, High School Sports." *Education Week*, July 11, 2001a, 16.
Gehring, John. "Summer Practices Bring Hot Weather Lessons." *Education Week*, September 5, 2001b, 5.
Gehring, John. "Drug Testing." *Education Week*, January 22, 2003, 10.
Gehring, John. "Educators Troubled by NFL-Draft Ruling." *Education Week*, February 18, 2004a, 3.
Gehring, John. "H. S. Out of Bounds, Report Warns." *Education Week*, October 27, 2004b, 1-19.
Gehring, John. "Off-Sides." *Teacher Magazine*, January–February 2004c, 13-14.
Gehring, John. "Maine Rallies behind Rules for Athletics: State Initiative Billed as National Model." *Education Week*, January 26, 2005a. https://www.edweek.org/ew/articles/2005/01/26/20sports.h24.html.
Gehring, John. "Pro Teams Bail Out Cleveland Athletics." *Education Week*, July 13, 2005b. https://www.edweek.org/ew/articles/2005/07/13/42sports.h24.html.
Gerdy, John R., ed. *Sports in School: The Future of an Institution*. New York: Teachers College Press, 2000.
Gerdy, John R. *Sports: The All-American Addiction*. Jackson: University Press of Mississippi, 2002.
Gerdy, John R. *Air Ball: American Education's Failed Experiment with Elite Athletics*. Jackson: University Press of Mississippi, 2006.
Gerdy, John R. *Ball or Bands: Football vs. Music as an Educational and Community Investment*. Bloomington, IN: Archway, 2014.
Gerdy, John R. Personal correspondence. 2015.

Gessel, Luke, Sarah Fields, and Christy Collins. "Concussions among United States High School and Collegiate Athletes." *Journal of Athletic Training* 42.4 (2007): 495–503.

Gioia, Dana. "Culture vs. Entertainment: Challenging Pleasures or Easy Comforts?" *Education Canada*, June 1, 2008, 54–57.

Glennie, Elizabeth, and Elizabeth Stearns. "Opportunities to Play the Game: The Effect of Individual and School Attributes on Participation in Sports." *Sociological Spectrum* 32.6 (2012): 532–57.

Glover, Chuck. "Intramural Sports." *Schools in the Middle*, October 1999, 30–33.

Goldberg, Alan. "Counseling the High School Student-Athlete." *School Counselor* 38.5 (1991): 332–40.

Goldenbach, Alan. "Physical Exams Required for Prep Athletes, but Questions Linger." *Washington Post*, November 2, 2006. http://www.washingtonpost.com/wp-dyncontent/article/2006/11/01/AR2006110103356.html.

Goldman, Jay P. "Balancing School Sports and Academics." *Education Digest* 56.8 (1991): 67–70.

Goldstein, Jeffrey. *Sports Violence*. New York: Springer, 1983.

Gordon, Ken. "Tailgates Boost Spirit, Revenue at High Schools." *Columbus Dispatch*, September 13, 2012. http://www.dispatch.com/content/stories/life_and_entertainment/2012/09/13/prep-pre-game.html.

Gorman, David. "The Effect of Athletic Participation on Academic Achievement for High School Seniors in Eastern Tennessee." EdD diss., Liberty University, 2010.

"Granite City Teen Dies Suddenly at Football Practice." *USA Today*, June 18, 2015. http://usatodayhss.com/2015/granite-city-teen-dies-suddenly-at-football-practice.

Grasmuck, Sherri. *Protecting Home: Class, Race, and Masculinity in Boys' Baseball*. New Brunswick, NJ: Rutgers University Press, 2005.

Green, Joseph P., Ashley Holtzapple, and Lauren McKinley. "Examining Gender Equity in Newspaper Coverage of West-Central Ohio High School Basketball Games." *Ohio Journal of Science* 116.2 (2016): 9–20.

Green, Lee. "Legal Perspectives, Recommendations on State Concussion Laws." *NFSH.org*, November 21, 2014. https://www.nfhs.org/articles/legal-perspectives-recommendations-on-state-concussion-laws/.

Gregory, Sean. "The Problem with Football." *Time*, January 28, 2010, 36–43.

Grenville-Cleave, Bridget. "Dare We Let Boys Be Boys? Positive Masculinity and Positive Psychology." *Positive Psychology News*, October 2010. http://positivepsychologynews.com/news/bridget-grenville-cleave/2010102714017.

Grey, Mark A. "Sports and Immigrant, Minority, and Anglo Relations in Garden City (Kansas) High School." *Sociology of Sport Journal* 9.3 (1992): 255–70.

Griffin, Robert. *Sports in the Lives of Children and Adolescents: Success on the Field and in Life*. Westport, CT: Praeger, 1998.

Grindstaff, Laura, and Emily West. "Not Just a Performance: Cheerleading and the Politics of Sport." Paper presented at the annual meeting of the American Sociological Association, Philadelphia, August 12, 2005. http://citation.allacademic.com/meta/p22067_index.html.

Gutowski, Thomas W. "Student Initiative and the Origins of the High School Extracurriculum: Chicago, 1880–1915." *History of Education Quarterly* 28.1 (1988): 49–72.

Haddix, Jason. "NFHS Network Begins Second Year of Covering High School Sporting Events." *NFHS.org*, November 21, 2014. https://www.nfhs.org/articles/nfhs-network-begins-second-year-of-covering-high-school-sporting-events/.

Hager, Jenna Bush, and Aliza Nadi. "Injuries Can Put Teen Athletes on Path to Addiction." *NBC News*, December 5, 2016. http://nbcnews.com/news/us-news/injuries-can-put-teen-athletes-path-addiction-N672741.

Halstead, Mark, and Kevin Walter. "Sport-Related Concussion in Children and Adolescents." *Pediatrics* 126:3 (2010): 597–615.

Hannel, G. Ivan, Andrew Gartman, and Jason Karpel. "CTE: The Developing Legal Case against High School Football." *Entertainment, Law, and Sports Law Journal* 25.1 (2014): 43–50.

Hartmann, Douglas, and Michael Massoglia. "Re-Assessing the Relationship between High School Sports Participation and Deviance: Bifurcated Effects." *Sociological Quarterly* 48.3 (2007): 485–505.

"Hazing Deaths on American College Campuses Remain Far Too Common." The Economist, October 13, 2017. https://www.economist.com/graphic-detail/2017/10/13/hazing-deaths-on-american-college-campuses-remain-far-too-common.

Heffron, Jack. "Purple Hearts." *Cincinnati*, November 2009, 80–83, 128–34.

Heinemann, Klaus, ed. *Sport Clubs in Various European Countries*. Stuttgart: Hoffman, 1999.

Heitin, Liana. "U.S. Achievement Stalls as Other Nations Make Gains." *Education Week*, December 26, 2014, 1–5.

Hemphill, Dennis A. "Revisioning Sport Spectatorism." *Journal of the Philosophy of Sport* 22.1 (1995): 48–60.

Hickey, Chris. "Physical Education, Sport, and Hyper-Masculinity in Schools." *Sport, Education, and Society* 13.2 (2008): 147–61.

Higgs, Robert J. "Muscular Christianity, Holy Play, and Spiritual Exercises: Confusion about Christ in Sports and Religion." *Arete* 1.1 (1983): 59–85.

"High School Athletes Choosing to Be Overweight?" *IU Newsroom*, September 8, 2015. http://newsinfo.iu.edu/news-archive/3945.html.

Hoch, David. "Academic Standards for the Student-Athlete." *Coach and Athletic Director* 76.3 (2006): 17.

Hoff, David. "Role of H.S. Sports Subject of Study." *Education Week*, January 17, 2006, 9. https://www.edweek.org/ew/articles/2006/01/18/19sports.h25.html.

Hoffman, Lynn M. "Why High Schools Don't Change: What Students and Their Yearbooks Tell Us." *High School Journal*, December 2002–January 2003, 22–37.

Honea, Joy Crissey. "Youth Cultures and Consumerism: Alternative Sport and Possibilities for Resistance." Paper presented at the annual meeting of the American Sociological Association, San Francisco, August 14, 2004.

Howard, Adam, and Elizabeth England Kennedy. "Breaking the Silence: Power, Conflict, and Contested Frames within an Affluent High School." *Anthropology and Education Quarterly* 37.4 (2006): 347–65.

HSLDA. "Sports and Public School Classes." 2017. *HSLDA.org*. http://www.hslda.org/docs/nche/issues/s/state_sports.asp.

Hudson, Al. "How Will the Economy Affect Sports?" *Diamond Prospects*, November 12, 2008. http://thediamondprospects.com/component/content/article?id=1525:nov08-sp-424413107.

Hughson, John, Davis Inglis, and Marcus Free. *The Uses of Sport: A Critical Study*. New York: Routledge, 2005.

Huizinga, Rob. *"You're Okay, It's Just a Bruise": A Doctor's Sideline Secrets about Pro Football's Most Outrageous Team*. New York: St. Martin's Griffin, 1994.

Humphrey, James H. *Principles and Practices in Interscholastic Athletics: Guidelines for Administrators*. New York: Nova Science, 2002.

Hursh, David. "Exacerbating Inequality: The Failed Promise of the No Child Left Behind Act." *Race Ethnicity and Education* 10.3 (2007): 295–308.

Hyland, Drew A. *Philosophy of Sport*. St. Paul, MN: Paragon, 1990.

Isaacs, Neil. *Jock Culture, U.S.A.* New York: Norton, 1978.

Jaczynowski, Lech, A. Smolen, and Lukasz Wiater. "Sports Clubs in School Environment in Poland." *Journal of Martial Arts Anthropology* 12.4 (2012): 26–35.

Jenkins, Simon. "John R. Wooden, Steven R. Covey, and Servant Leadership." *International Journal of Sports Science and Coaching* 9.1 (2014): https://doi.org/10.1260/1747-9541.9.1.1.

Jensen, Clayne, and Steven J. Overman. *Administration and Management of Physical Education and Athletic Programs*. Prospect Heights, IL: Waveland, 2003.

Joffe, Alain. "Overdoing It in Youth Sports." *Pediatrics Digest*, January 2008, 1–2.

Johnson, L. Syd. "Return to Play Guidelines Cannot Solve the Football-Related Concussion Problem." *Journal of School Health* 82.4 (2012): 180–85.

Jordan, Jessica. "High School Sports Budgets: A Level Playing Field?" *Gainesville Times*, March 21, 2009. https://www.gainesvilletimes.com/opinion/high-school-sports-budgets-a-level-playing-field/.

Jordon, Steve. "Playing It Safe: Insurance for Sports Injuries Is More Than Just a Business for Mutual of Omaha Team." *Omaha World-Herald*, September 20, 2006, 1D.

"Jury Is Out on Effectiveness of Drug Testing in Schools." *Minneapolis Star Tribune*, January 20, 2014. http://www.startribune.com/jury-is-out-on-effectiveness-of-drug-testing-in-schools/241208771/.

Kahn, Susan K. *Coming on Strong: Gender and Sexuality in Twentieth-Century Women's Sport*. New York: Macmillan, 1991.

Kalahar, Gary. "Job of High School Athletic Director Evolving into Multiple Duties, Resulting in Increased Burnout and Turnover." *Jackson Citizen Patriot*, February 20, 2011. http://www.mlive.com/sports/jackson/index.ssf/2011/02/job_of_high_school_athletic_di.html.

Kanters, Michael, Jason N. Bocarro, Michael B. Edwards, Jonathan M. Casper, and Myron F. Floyd. "School Sport Participation under Two School Sport Policies: Comparisons by Race/Ethnicity, Gender, and Socioeconomic Status." *Annals of Behavioral Medicine* 45.S (2013): 113–21.

Kleps, Kelvin. "It Can Be a 'Dirty' Game When Shoe Companies Get Involved in High School Sports." *Crain's Cleveland Business*, November 30, 2014. http://www.crainscleveland.com/article/20141130/sub1/311309977.

Klungseth, Scott. "The Five NCAA Recruiting Rules That High School Coaches Should Know." *Coach and Athletic Director* 74.9 (2005). https://www.highbeam.com/doc/1G1-132153809.html.

Knowles, S. B., S. W. Marshall, T. Miller, R. Spicer, J. M. Bowling, D. Loomis, R. W. Millikan, J. Yang, and F. O. Mueller. "Cost of Injuries from a Prospective Cohort Study of North Carolina High School Athletes." *Injury Prevention* 13.6 (2007): 416–21.

Kohn, Alfie. *No Contest: The Case against Competition.* New York: Houghton Mifflin, 1992.

Kolker, Ken. "High School Football: Allegations of Recruiting." *WoodTV.com*, November 9, 2015. http://woodtv.com/investigative-story/target-8-high-school-football-allegations-of-recruiting/.

Kralovec, Etta. *Schools That Do Too Much: Wasting Time and Money in Schools, and What We Can All Do about It.* Boston: Beacon, 2003.

Kramer, Jerry. *Instant Replay: The Green Bay Diary of Jerry Kramer.* New York: New American Library, 1968.

Kreager, Derek. "Unnecessary Roughness? School Sports, Peer Networks, and Male Adolescent Violence." *American Sociological Review* 72.5 (2007): 705–24.

Lake, Thomas. "The Boy Who Died of Football." *Sports Illustrated*, December 6, 2010. https://www.si.com/vault/2010/12/06/106012866/the-boy-who-died-of-football.

Lane, Kristen. "Forward, March." *Indianapolis Monthly*, August 2001, 104–7, 155–59.

Langbein, Laura, and Roseana Bess. "Sports in School: Source of Amity or Antipathy?" *Social Science Quarterly* 83.2 (2002): 436–54.

Lasch, Christopher. "Corrupt Sports: An Exchange." *New York Review of Books*, September 29, 1977. http://www.nybooks.com/articles/archives/1977/sep/29/corrupt-sports-an-exchange/.

Lasch, Christopher. "The Corruption of Sports." In *American Sport Culture: The Humanistic Dimensions*, ed. Wiley Umphlett, 50–67. Lewisburg, PA: Bucknell University Press, 1985.

Lee, Jason, and Jeffrey Lee, eds. *Sport and Criminal Behavior.* Durham, NC: Carolina Academic, 2009.

Lee, Martin J. "From Rivalry to Hostility among Sports Fans." *Quest* 37.1 (1985): 38–49.

Lee, Valerie. "Does the Size of a School Matter?" *New York Times*, March 11, 2010. http://roomfordebate.blogs.nytimes.com/2010/03/11/does-the-size-of-a-school-matter/.

Leek, Desiree, Jordan A. Carlson, Kelli L. Cain, Sara Henrichon, Dori Rosenberg, Kevin Patrick, and James F. Sallis. "Physical Activity during Youth Sport Practices." *Archives of Pediatrics and Adolescent Medicine* 165.4 (2011): 294–99.

Lefkowitz, Bernard. *Our Guys: The Glen Ridge Rape and the Secret Life of the Perfect Suburb.* New York: Vintage, 1998.

Lehrer, Jonah. "The Fragile Teenage Brain." *Grantland.com*, January 10, 2012. http://www.grantland.com/print?id=7443714.

Levy, Gray. *Big and Bright: Deep in the Heart of Texas High School Football.* Lanham, MD: Taylor, 2015.

Lewis, Anders, Jennifer Butler, Melanie Winklosky, and Sandra Stotsky. "The Anti-Civic Effects of Popular Culture on American Teenagers." *Estudios sobre Educación* 2 (2002): 53–66.

Lipsyte, Robert. *SportsWorld: An American Dreamland.* New York: Quadrangle, 1977.

Loh, Stefanie. "Club Sports Is King in Europe, but There Are Downsides to That System Too." *Mechanicsburg Patriot News*, May 19, 2011. http://blog.pennlive.com/patriotnewssports/2011/04/club_sports_is_king_in_europe.html.

Longman, Jeré. "High School Football, Inc." *New York Times*, September 18, 2015. https://www.nytimes.com/2015/09/19/sports/football/high-school-football-inc.html.

Lopez, Mark Hugo. "Participation in Sports and Civic Engagement." *Center for Information and Research on Civic Learning and Engagement*, February 2006. http://www.civicyouth.org/PopUps/FactSheets/FS_06_Sports_and_Civic_Engagement.pdf.

Lowry, Richard, Sarah M. Lee, Janet E. Fulton, Zewditu Demissie, and Laura Kann. "Obesity and Other Correlates of Physical Activity and Sedentary Behaviors among U.S. High School Students." *Journal of Obesity* (2013): 1–10. http://dx.doi.org/10.1155/2013/276318.

Lueschen, Guenther. "Cheating in Sports." In *Social Problems in Athletics: Essays in the Sociology of Sport*, ed. Daniel Landers, 67–72. Urbana: University of Illinois Press, 1976.

Lurie, Julia. "A Not-So-Brief and Extremely Sordid History of Cheerleading." *Mother Jones*, December 15, 2014. http://www.motherjones.com/media/2014/12/cheerleader-history-timeline.

Macur, Juliet. "In Steubenville Rape Case, a Lesson for Adults." *New York Times*, November 26, 2013. http://www.nytimes.com/2013/11/27/sports/in-steubenville-rape-case-a-lesson-for-adults.html?_r=0.

Malina, Robert. "Early Sport Specialization: Roots, Effectiveness, Risk." *Sports Medicine Report* 9.6 (2010): 364–71.

Malina, Robert, and Gaston Beunen. "The Child and Adolescent Athlete." In *Encyclopaedia of Sports Medicine*, ed. Oded Bar Or, 6:203–11. Oxford: Blackwell Science, 1996.

Malina, Robert, and Michael Clark, eds. *Youth Sports: Perspectives for a New Century*. Monterey, CA: Coaches Choice, 2003.

Malina, Robert, Sharon Shields, and Elizabeth Gilbert. "School Sports—Overview, Role in Student's Social and Emotional Development." *Education Encyclopedia*. 2015. http://education.stateuniversity.com/pages/2443/Sports-School.html.

McKeon, Jennifer Medina, S. C. Livingston, A. Reed, R. G. Hosey, W. S. Black, and H. M. Bush. "Trends in Concussion Return-to-Play Timelines among High School Athletes from 2007 through 2009." *Journal of Athletic Training* 48.6 (2013): 836–45.

McMahon, Regan. *Revolution in the Bleachers: How Parents Can Take Back Family Life in a World Gone Crazy over Youth Sports*. New York: Gotham, 2007.

McMillen, Tom, with Paul Coggins. *Out of Bounds*. New York: Simon and Schuster, 1992.

McNeal, Ralph, Jr. "High School Extracurricular Activities: Closed Structures and Stratifying Patterns of Participation." *Journal of Educational Research* 91.3 (1998): 183–91.

Meir, Rudi. "Tribalism: Definition, Identification, and Relevance to the Marketing of Professional Sports Franchises." *International Journal of Sports Marketing and Sponsorship* 8.4 (2007): 330–46.

Michener, James A. *Sports in America*. New York: Dial, 1987.

Miller, Kathleen, Merrill J. Melnick, Grace M. Barnes, Michael P. Farrell, and Don Sabo. "Untangling the Links among Athletic Involvement, Gender, Race, and Adolescent Academic Outcomes." *Sociology of Sport Journal* 22.2 (2005): 178–92.

Miller, Kathleen, Merrill J. Melnick, Grace M. Barnes, Don Sabo, and Michael P. Farrell. "Athletic Involvement and Adolescent Delinquency." *Journal of Youth and Adolescence* 36.5 (2007): 711–23.

Miller, Kathleen, Don Sabo, Merrill J. Melnick, Michael P. Farrell, and Grace M. Barnes. "Jocks and Athletes: College Students' Reflections on Identity, Gender, and High School Sports." Paper presented at the American Sociological Association Annual Meeting, Montreal, 2006.

Miller, Richard, and Kelli Washington. *Sports Marketing*. Atlanta: Miller and Associates, 2014.

Miracle, Andrew, and C. Roger Rees. *Lessons of the Locker Room: The Myth of School Sports*. New York: Prometheus, 1994.

Morgan, William. *Leftist Theories of Sport: A Critical Reconstruction*. Urbana: University of Illinois Press, 1994.

Mosher, Donald L., and Silvan S. Tompkins. "Scripting the Macho Man: Hypermasculine Socialization and Enculturation." *Journal of Sex Research* 25.1 (1988): 60–84.

Munro, Allison Wright. "Yee-Haws and Yells: Cheerleading in the Lone Star State." *Journal of the American Studies Association of Texas* 37 (November 2006): 21–32.

Murphy, C. S. "Pay for Coaches Seen as out of Line." *Arkansas Democrat-Gazette*, March 2, 2008. http://www.arkansasonline.com/news/2008/mar/02/pay-coaches-seen-out-line/.

NASBE. *Athletics and Achievement*. Alexandria, VA: National Association of State Boards of Education, 2004. http://www.nga.org/files/live/sites/NGA/files/pdf/AthleticsCommissionreport2.pdf.

National Women's Law Center. *Title IX: 40 Years and Counting*. June 2012. https://nwlc.org/wp-content/uploads/2015/08/nwlcstem_titleixfactsheet.pdf.

NCAA Eligibility Center. *Guide for the College Bound Student-Athlete*. 2017–18. https://www.ncaapublications.com/productdownloads/CBSA18.pdf.

NCAA Research. "Estimated Probability of Competing in Athletics beyond the High School Interscholastic Level." *NCAA.org*, 2013. https://www.ncaa.org/sites/default/files/probability-of-going-pro-methodology_Update2013.pdf.

Neddenriep, Kyle. "Strapped for Cash, High Schools Sell Football Stadium Names." *Indianapolis Star*, September 10, 2016. http://www.indystar.com/story/sports/high-school/2016/09/09/strapped-cash-high-schools-sell-football-stadium-names/89954788/.

Nowinski, Christopher. *Head Games: Football's Concussion Crisis*. East Bridgewater, MA: Drummond, 2007.

Nuwer, Hank, ed. *The Hazing Reader*. Bloomington: Indiana University Press, 2004.

O'Brien, Keith. *Outside Shot: Big Dreams, Hard Times, and One County's Quest for Basketball Greatness*. New York: St. Martin's, 2012.

OECD. *Programme for International Student Assessment (PISA) Results from PISA 2012: United States*. https://www.oecd.org/unitedstates/PISA-2012-results-US.pdf.

Olson, Jeremy. "Minnesota Doctors Call for Removal of Football from Public Schools." *Minneapolis Star Tribune*, November 21, 2015.http://www.startribune.com/minnesota-doctors-call-for-removal-of-football-from-public-schools/352464821/.

Omalu, Bennet. "Don't Let Kids Play Football." *New York Times*, December, 7, 2015. http://www.nytimes.com/2015/12/07/opinion/dont-let-kids-play-football.html?_r=3.

Osterhoudt, Robert G. *Sport as a Form of Human Fulfillment*. Vol. 2. Victoria, BC: Trafford, 2006.

Overman, Steven J., and Kelly Boyer Sagert. *Icons of Women's Sport*. Santa Barbara, CA: Greenwood, 2012.

Palka, Mary Kelli. "High School Football Makes Money, but Not Enough: Even the Most Popular Sport, Football, Often Comes Up Budget Short." *Florida Times-Union*, July 13, 2009. http://www.jacksonville.com/article/20090713/NEWS/801231438.

Pandina, Robert, Valerie L. Johnson, Leah M. Lagos, and Helene R. White. "Substance Use among High School Athletes: Implications for Prevention Interventions." *Journal of Applied School Psychology* 21.2 (2005): 115–43.

Pannoni, Alexandra. "Doping Rises among High Schoolers, but Few Districts Test." *U.S. News and World Report*, August 11, 2014. http://www.usnews.com/education/blogs/high-school-notes/2014/08/11/testing-high-school-athletes-for-doping-uncommon.

Pascoe, C. J. *Dude, You're a Fag: Masculinity and Sexuality in High School*. Berkeley: University of California Press, 2007.

Patoski, Joe N., and Suzy Banks. "Three Cheers for High School Football." *Texas Monthly*, October 1999, 110–15.

Patsko, Scott. "Compilation of How All 50 States Handle Competitive Balance." *Cleveland.com*, May 14, 2014. http://highschoolsports.cleveland.com/news/article/-4000324031846785879/ohsaas-competitive-balance-referendum-the-latest-round-in-a-national-fight-between-public-and-private-schools/.

Peterson, Jeffrey, and David Pierce. "On-Site Sponsorship Activation in Texas High School Football." *TAHPERD Journal* 82.2 (2014): 8–11.

Peterson, Paul. "A Courageous Look at the American High School." *Education Next*, Spring 2010, 24–33.

Physical Activity Facts: Adolescent and School Health. Atlanta: Centers for Disease Control, 2013. http://www.cdc.gov/healthyyouth/physicalactivity/facts.htm.

Pierce, David, and Leigh Ann Bussell. "National Survey of Interscholastic Sport Sponsorship in the United States." *Sport Management International Journal* 7.1 (2011): 43–62.

Pollack, William. *Real Boys: Rescuing Our Sons from the Myths of Boyhood*. New York: Holt, 1998.

Popke, Michael. "High School Administrators Encourage Tailgating with Boundaries." *Athletic Business*, July 2006. http://www.athleticbusiness.com/high-school-administrators-encourage-tailgating-with-boundaries.html.

Pound, Richard. "NCAA's Clearinghouse Rules—Who's Looking Out for the Student-Athlete?" *Fastweb*, April 21, 2009. http://www.fastweb.com/student-life/articles/ncaa-s-clearinghouse-rules-who-s-looking-out-for-the-student-athlete.

Powell, Shaun, *Souled Out? How Blacks Are Winning and Losing in Sports*. Champaign, IL: Human Kinetics, 2008.

Pringle, Richard G., and Christopher Hickey. "Negotiating Masculinities via the Moral Problematization of Sport." *Sociology of Sport Journal* 27.2 (2010): 115–38.

Pruter, Robert. *The Rise of American High School Sports and the Search for Control, 1880–1930*. Syracuse: Syracuse University Press, 2013.

Pusch, Jennifer. "Urban Struggles: An Analysis of Title IX and Urban High School Athletic Opportunities for Girls." *Wisconsin Journal of Law, Gender, and Society* 29.2 (2014): 317–40.

Putnam, Douglas. *Controversies of the Sports World.* Westport, CT: Greenwood, 1999.

Putnam, Robert D. *Bowling Alone: The Collapse and Revival of American Community.* New York: Simon and Schuster, 2000.

Quirk, Kevin. *Not Now Honey, I'm Watching the Game: What to Do When Sports Come between You and Your Mate.* New York: Fireside, 1997.

Quiroz, Pamela, Nilda Flores González, and Kenneth A. Frank. "Carving a Niche in the High School Social Structure: Formal and Informal Constraints on Participation in the Extra Curriculum." *Research in Sociology of Education and Socialization* 11 (1996): 93–120.

Reed, Ken. *How We Can Save Sports: A Game Plan.* Lanham, MD: Rowman and Littlefield, 2015.

Rees, C. Roger, and Frank Howell. "Do High School Sports Build Character? A Quasi-Experiment on a National Sample." *Social Science Journal* 27.3 (1990): 303–15.

Reifman, Alan. "Measuring School Spirit: A National Teaching Exercise." *Teaching of Psychology* 31.1 (2004): 18–21.

Reilley, Mike. "Good Coaches Are Hard to Find and Just as Hard to Keep." *Los Angeles Times*, January 2, 1991. http://articles.latimes.com/1991-01-02/sports/sp-6985_1_high-school-teams.

Ringwalt, Chris, Amy A. Vincus, Susan T. Ennett, Sean Hanley, J. Michael Bowling, George S. Yacoubian Jr, and Louise A. Rohrbach. "Random Drug Testing in US Public School Districts." *American Journal of Public Health* 98.5 (2008): 826–28.

Rios, Edwin. "We Had No Idea This Many Kids Have Died Playing High School Football This Year." *Mother Jones*, October 21, 2015. http://www.motherjones.com/media/2015/10/high-school-football-death-camron-matthews.

Ripley, Amanda. "The Case against High-School Sports." *The Atlantic*, October 2013a, 72–78.

Ripley, Amanda. *The Smartest Kids in the World: And How They Got That Way.* New York: Simon and Schuster, 2013b.

Roan, Shari. "Narrowing the Field." *Los Angeles Times*, October 2, 2006. http://articles.latimes.com/print/2006/oct/02/health/he-sports2.

Robbins, Alexandra. *The Overachievers: The Secret Lives of Driven Kids.* New York: Hyperion, 2006.

Roberts, Jack. "A Sane Island Surrounded." *Phi Delta Kappan*, December 2007, 278–82.

Roberts, Joshua. "Dispelling the Rational Basis for Homeschooler Exclusion from High School Interscholastic Athletics." *Journal of Law and Education* 38.1 (2009): 195–203.

Roberts, Randy, and James Olson. *Winning Is The Only Thing: Sports in America since 1945.* Baltimore: Johns Hopkins University Press, 1989.

Rodriguez, Ken. "Hearing Raises More Questions in Football Referee Attack Investigation." *Sports Illustrated*, October 15, 2015. http://www.si.com/high-school/2015/10/15/referee-attack-investigation-hearing-texas-high-school-football-robert-watts.

Rosenau, Pauline V. *The Competition Paradigm: America's Romance with Conflict, Contest, and Commerce.* Lanham, MD: Rowman and Littlefield, 2003.

Roslow Research Group. "Physical Education Trends in Our Nation's Schools: A Survey of Practicing K–12 Physical Education Teachers." Port Washington, NY: Polar Electro, 2009.

Royals, Kate. "Feds Investigating Possible Title IX Violations at JPS." *Jackson Clarion-Ledger*, August 31, 2015, A4.

Ryall, Emily. "Being-on-the-Bench: An Existential Analysis of the Substitute in Sport." *Sport, Ethics, and Philosophy* 2.1 (2008): 56–70.

Ryan, Joan. *Little Girls in Pretty Boxes*. New York: Doubleday, 1995.

Ryan, Molly. "Title IX and the Drive for Gender Equality in Sports." *Minority Trial Lawyer* 11.1 (2012–13): 2–6.

Ryan, Rick. "The High Cost of Getting in Gear." *Charleston Gazette*, October 29, 2010. http://www.nitrowildcatfootball.com/files/2010/2010newspaper/2010-10-29GAZ-TheHighCostOfGettingInGear.pdf.

Sabedra, Darren. "New Transfer Rule: CIT to Allow Athletically Motivated Moves." *San Jose Mercury News*, April 11, 2017. http://www.mercurynews.com/2017/04/11/new-transfer-rule-cif-to-allow-athletically-motivated-moves/.

Sabo, Don. *Progress without Equity: The Provision of High School Athletic Opportunity in the United States by Gender, 1993–94 through 2005–06*. East Meadow, NY: Women's Sports Foundation, 2011. https://www.womenssports foundation.org/research/article.

Sacks, Hannah Ross. " Debate Surfaces on Place of High School Athletics." *Education Week*, May 25, 2012. http://blogs.edweek.org/edweek/schooled_in_sports/2012/05/a_debate_surfaces_on_the_place_of_high_school_athletics.html.

Sage, George H. *Power and Ideology in American Sport: A Critical Perspective*. 2nd ed. Champaign: University of Illinois Press, 1998.

Sailer, Steve. "Smells Like Team Spirit." *American Conservative*, December 3, 2007, 25–27.

Samuelson, Anne, Leslie Lytle, Keryn Pasch, Kian Farbakhsh, Stacey Moe, and John Ronald Sirard. "The Physical Activity Climate in Minnesota Middle and High Schools." *Journal of Physical Activity and Health* 7.6 (2010): 811–17.

Santayana, George. *The Last Puritan*. 1936. Cambridge: MIT Press, 1994.

Scelfo, Julie, and Dirk Johnson. "Texas, Football, and Juice." *Newsweek*, March 7, 2005, 46–47.

Schafer, Walter. "Sport and Youth Countercultures: Contrasting Socialization Themes." In *Social Problems in Athletics: Essay in the Sociology of Sport*, ed. Daniel Landers, 183–200. Urbana: University of Illinois Press, 1976.

Schmidle, Nicholas. "Can Football Be Saved?" *New Yorker*, January 8, 2017, 38–51.

"Schools and Hard Knocks." *The Economist*, March 5–11, 2016, 14.

Seifried, Chad. "Managing the Selection of Highly Competitive Interscholastic Sport Teams: Recommendations from Coaches on Cutting Players." *Journal of Sport Administration and Supervision* 4.1 (2012): 79–91.

Sell, Samantha. "Running an Effective School District: School Boards in the 21st Century." *Journal of Education* 186.3 (2006): 71–97.

Sentell, Jeff. "The Future of High School Football: Concussions and Safety Issues Have Parents Making Tough Choices." *Alabama Media Group*, December 2, 2014. www.al.com/sports/index.ssf/2014/12/the_future_of_high_school_foot_1.html.

Sherman, Mark. "High School Sports Recruiting Limited." *USA Today*, June 21, 2007. http://usatoday30.usatoday.com/news/washington/2007-06-21-2640043768x.htm.

Shields, David, and Brenda Bredemeier. "Coaching for Civic Character." *Journal of Research in Character Education* 9.1 (2011): 25–33.

Shields, Edgar, Jr. "Intimidation and Violence by Males in High School Athletics." *Adolescence* 34.135 (1999): 503–22.

Shirley, Brent. "As High School Football Popularity Soars, So Do Coaches' Salaries." *Fort Worth Star-Telegram*, August 18, 2011. http://www.star-telegram.com/sports/article3828640.html.
Sieck, Ben. "A House Divided: Homeschool Students on School Sports Teams." *NFHS News*, April 20, 2015. https://www.nfhs.org/articles/a-house-divided-homeschool-students-on-school-sports-teams/#.
Simon, Robert L. *Fair Play: Sports, Values, and Society*. Boulder, CO: Westview, 1991.
Sitkowski, Lee. "The Effects of Participation in Athletics on Academic Performance among High School Sophomores and Juniors." PhD diss., Liberty University, 2008.
Skinner, Asheley Cockrell. "Is Bigger Really Better? Obesity among High School Football Players, Player Position, and Team Success." *Clinical Pediatrics* 52.10 (2013): 922–28.
Smith, Cam. "Picking All-Stars Not Easy." *USA Today*, January 3, 2015. http://www.usatoday.com/2015/u-s-army-all-american-bowl.
Smith, Corbett. "Special Report: Some Texas schools Fail to Provide Catastrophic Care for Injuries (Part 1)." *Dallas Morning News*, November 9, 2013. https://www.dallasnews.com/news/education/2013/11/09/special-report-some-texas-schools-fail-to-provide-catastrophic-care-for-injuries.
Smith, Nicole, Monica Lounsbery, and Thomas McKenzie. "Physical Activity in High School Physical Education." *Journal of Physical Activity and Health* 11.2 (2014): 127–35.
Sokol-Katz, Jan, Margaret S. Kelley, Lorrie Basinger Fleischman, and Jomills Henry Braddock II. "Re-Examining the Relationship between Interscholastic Sport Participation and Delinquency: Type of Sport Matters." *Sociological Focus* 39.3 (2006):, 173–92.
Sokolove, Michael. *Warrior Girls: Protecting Our Daughters against the Injury Epidemic in Women's Sport*. New York: Simon and Schuster, 2008.
"Sports Marketing Experts Acquires TexasHSFootball.com, the Leading Texas High School Sports Network." *PR Newswire US*, August 21, 2014. https://www.prnewswire.com/news-releases/sports-marketing-experts-acquires-texashsfootballcom-the-leading-texas-high-school-sports-network-272134471.html.
Stanec, Amanda, and Eric Lay. "Quality Physical Education: Why the Sport Requirement Can't Do It Alone." *Independent School* 68.1 (2008): 112–22.
Steidinger, Joan. *Sisterhood in Sports: How Female Athletes Collaborate and Compete*. Lanham, MD: Rowman and Littlefield, 2014.
Stein, Julian. "Should State High School Associations Allow Out-of-Season Practice Sessions for Interscholastic Sports?" *Journal of Physical Education, Recreation, and Dance* 84.1 (2013): 52–54.
Stillwell, Jim, and Carl Willgoose. *The Physical Education Curriculum*. Needham Heights, MA: Allyn and Bacon, 1997.
Streich, Michael. "The Downside of Athletic Programs Destroys Academic Balance." *Wrestling Talk Forums*, May 1, 2009. http://www.usawks.com/forums/ubbthreads.php?ubb=showflatandNumber=149755.
Stromberg, Peter G. *Caught in Play: How Entertainment Works on You*. Stanford: Stanford University Press, 2009.
Stromberg, Peter G. "Person and Community in the Culture of Entertainment." *Pastoral Psychology* 60.5 (2011): 737–44.

Sussman, Eliahu. "Inside the Biggest Band in Texas." *School Band and Orchestra* 14.5 (2011): 18–32.

Svare, Bruce B. *Reforming Sports before the Clock Runs Out*. Delmar, NY: Sports Reform, 2004.

Svokos, Alexandra. "A Majority of High Schools Lack Full-Time Trainers to Keep Kids Safe." *Huffington Post*, November 18, 2014. http://www.huffingtonpost.com/2014/11/18/high-school-athletic-trainers_n_6146672.html.

Szabo, Liz. "Study: Most Teens Start School Too Early in Morning to Get Enough Sleep." *USA Today*, August 6, 2015. http://www.usatoday.com/story/news/2015/08/06/teen-sleep-school-start/31212457.

Taylor, Robert. "Compensating Behavior and the Drug Testing of High School Athletes." *CATO Journal* 16.3 (1997): 351–64.

Teitelbaum, Stanley. *Sports Heroes, Fallen Idols*. Lincoln: University of Nebraska Press, 2005.

Terzian, Sevan. "The Elusive Goal of School Spirit in the Comprehensive High School: A Case History, 1916–1941." *High School Journal* 88.1 (2004): 42–51.

"Texas Steroid Testing Finds Use by Just Two High School Athletes." *Education Week*, July 30, 2008, 1–9.

Thompson, Derek. "The Shameful Triumph of Football." *The Atlantic*, January 6, 2015. http://www.theatlantic.com/business/archive/2015/01/the-shameful-triumph-of-college-football/384234/.

"To March or Not to March, That Is the Question!" *Indiana Wind Symphony Blog*, November 16, 2010. https://inwindsymphony.wordpress.com/tag/band/.

Tonso, Karen. "Reflecting on Columbine High: Ideologies of Privilege in 'Standardized' Schools." *Educational Studies* 33.4 (2002): 389–403.

Toporek, Bryan. "2010–11 High School Athletics Participation Survey." *Education Week*, August 31, 2011a. https://www.edweek.org/ew/articles/2011/08/31/02 report-b1.h31.html.

Toporek, Bryan. "Circumventing Pay-to-Play." *Education Week*, August, 31, 2011b. https://www.edweek.org/ew/articles/2011/08/31/02blogs.h31.html.

Toporek, Bryan. "Gender Gap Grows in High School Sports." *Education Week*, October 17, 2012a. http://blogs.edweek.org/edweek/schooled_in_sports/? page=73.

Toporek, Bryan. "High School Football Can Lead to Long-Term Brain Damage, Study Says." *Education Week*, December 8, 2012b. http://blogs.edweek.org/edweek/schooled_in_sports/2012/12/long-term_brain_damage_found_in_six_former_hs_football_players.html.

Toporek, Bryan. "Survey Finds Drop in P.E. Classes, but Rise in Sports." *Education Week*, March 28, 2012c. https://www.edweek.org/ew/articles/2012/03/28/26gao.h31.html.

Toporek, Bryan. "CDC Reveals Positive Physical Education Trends over Past Decade." *Education Week*, August 30, 2013. http://blogs.edweek.org/edweek/schooled_in_sports/2013/08/cdc_reveals_positive_physical_education_trends_over_past_decade.html.

Trotter, Andrew. "NCAA Boosts Scrutiny of 'Nontraditional' High Schools." *Education Week*, May 9, 2006. https://www.edweek.org/ew/articles/2006/05/10/36ncaa.h25.html.

Tucker, Marc. *Governing American Education*. May 2013. https://www.americanprogress.org/wp-content/uploads/2013/05/TuckerGoverningReport.pdf.

References

Tufte, John E. *Crazy-Proofing High School Sports*. Lanham, MD: Rowman and Littlefield, 2012.

Umphlett, Wiley. *American Sport Culture: The Humanistic Dimensions*. Lewisburg, PA: Bucknell University Press, 1985.

US Department of Education, National Center for Education Statistics. *Public High School Graduation Rates*. 2017. https://nces.ed.gov/fastfacts/display.asp?id=805.

Van Milligan, Dennis. "Numbers Crunch." *Athletic Business*, December 2014, 40–43.

Vasco, Bill. "Why the Trend for Non-Teachers Filling High School Coaching Jobs?" *Linkedin.com*, June 17, 2014. https://www.linkedin.com/pulse/20140617172312-33469656-why-the-trend-for-non-teachers-filling-high-school-coaching-jobs.

Venosa, Ali. "Cheerleading Stunts, Tumbling Responsible for More Catastrophic Injuries Than Most Other High School Sports." *Medical Daily*, December 11, 2015. http://www.medicaldaily.com/cheerleading-stunts-tumbling-responsible-more-catastrophic-injuries-most-other-high-364952.

Walsh, Mark. "Texas District Eyes Extra Fee for Football Tickets." *Education Week*, December 4, 2002. https://www.edweek.org/ew/articles/2002/12/04/14seats.h22.html.

Wann, Daniel, Merrill Melnick, Gordon Russell, and Dale Pease. *Sport Fans: The Psychology and Social Impact of Spectators*. New York: Routledge, 2001.

Warbelow, Kathy. "High School Stadiums, Packed with Loopholes." *Bloomberg Businessweek*, October 1, 2012, 39–40.

Ward, Joe, Josh Williams, and Sam Manchester. "111 N.F.L. Brains. All but One Had C.T.E." *New York Times*, July 25, 2017. https://www.nytimes.com/interactive/2017/07/25/sports/football/nfl-cte.html.

Ward, Russell E., Jr. "Athletic Expenditures and the Academic Mission of American Schools: A Group-Level Analysis." *Sociology of Sport Journal* 25.4 (2008): 560–78.

Washington, Sharon. "Let's Celebrate Academics, as Well as Athletics." *Education Week*, February 23, 2011. https://www.edweek.org/ew/articles/2011/02/23/21letter-3.h30.html.

Wieberg, Steve. "Millions of Dollars Pour into High School Football." *USA Today*, October 6, 2004. http://usatoday30.usatoday.com/sports/preps/football/2004-10-05-spending-cover_x.htm#.

Whannel, Garry. "Sport and Popular Culture: The Temporary Triumph of Process over Product." *Innovation: The European Journal of Social Science Research* 6.3 (1993): 341–49.

"What Effect Do AAU/Travel Ball Teams Have on Sport Participation at the High School and Middle School Level?" *JOHPERD* 85.7 (2014): 46–47.

White, Mike. "Not Easy Being a Three-Sport Athlete at a Large High School." *Pittsburgh Post-Gazette*, May 9, 2010. http://www.post-gazette.com/sports/hsother/2010/05/09/Not-easy-being-a-three-sport-athlete-at-a-large-high-school/stories/201005090177.

Wicker, Pamela, Steven Vos, Jeroen Scheerder, and Christoph Breuer. "The Link between Resource Problems and Interorganisational Relationships: A Quantitative Study of Western European Sport Clubs." *Managing Leisure* 18.1 (2013): 31–45.

Willett, Jennifer B., Bernie Goldfine, Todd Seidler, Andy Gillentine, and Scott Marley. "Deciphering the Law—What Every Coach and Administrator Should Know." *JOHPERD* 85.9 (2014): 15–19.

Williams, Grace M. "How the Jock Culture and the Boys Will Be Boys Mentality Encourages Rape." *HubPages*, 2015. http://gmwilliams.hubpages.com/hub/How-The-Jock-Culture-And-The-Boys-Will-Be-Boys-Mentality-Encourages-Rape.

Winfrey, Michelle W. *A Mom's Guide to Surviving High School Athletics*. Jackson, NJ: Hobby House, 2010.

Winograd, Morley, and Michael Hais. "Millennial Generation Could Kill the NFL." *Christian Science Monitor*, October 19, 2012. http://www.csmonitor.com/Commentary/Opinion/2012/1019/Millennial-generation-could-kill-the-NFL.

Winzelberg, David. "Calling All Coaches (Nonteachers Welcome)." *New York Times*, March 4, 2001. http://www.nytimes.com/2001/03/04/nyregion/calling-all-coaches-nonteachers-welcome.html.

Wunsch, Travis, and Boyd Jones. "Pros and Cons of Interscholastic Sport." *21st Century American Sport Blog*, October 2012. http://21stcenturyamericansport.blogspot.com/2012/10/pros-cons-of-interscholastic-sport.html.

Yanity, Molly, and Aimee Edmondson. "The Ethics of Online Coverage of Recruiting High School Athletes." *International Journal of Sport Communication* 4.4 (2011): 403–21.

Yard, Ellen, Christy L. Collins, and R. Dawn Comstock. "A Comparison of High School Sports Injury Surveillance Data Reporting by Certified Athletic Trainers and Coaches." *Journal of Athletic Training* 44.6 (2009): 645–52.

Yard, Ellen, and Dawn Comstock. "Injury Patterns by Body Mass Index in US High School Athletes." *Journal of Physical Activity and Health* 8.2 (2011): 182–91.

Yen, Alfred. "Early Scholarship Offers and the NCAA." *Boston College Law Review* 52.2 (2011): 585–616.

Young, Deborah, Gwen M. Felton, Mira Grieser, John P. Elder, Carolyn Johnson, Jung-Sun Lee, and Martha Y. Kubik. "Policies and Opportunities for Physical Activity in Middle School Environments." *Journal of School Health* 77.1 (2007): 41–47.

Zimmerman, Jonathan. "Columbine and the Cult of High School Sports." *Education Week*, June 2, 1999. https://www.edweek.org/ew/articles/1999/06/02/38zimm.h18.html.

INDEX

academics. *See* student-athlete
African American athletes, 15, 29, 96, 126–27, 136
Alabama, 15, 48, 79, 81, 119, 122, 200
Alabama, University of, 122
all-star games, 67, 129, 179–80, 184, 188
Almond, Steve, 72–73, 96, 211, 214–15
alumni, 20, 25, 27, 66, 68–69, 74, 80, 91, 97–98, 180, 212
Amateur Athletic Union (AAU), 26, 85
American Academy of Pediatrics, 127, 144, 213
American Association of School Administrators, 43, 186
American College of Sports Medicine, 209
American Heart Association, 5
American Legislative Exchange Council, 52
American Medical Association, 202
American Recovery and Reinvestment Act (2009), 161
Arizona, 222
Arizona Charter Athletic Association, 196
Arizona Interscholastic Association, 196
Arkansas, 46–48, 52, 56, 144
Arkansas Activities Association, 143
athlete. *See* student-athlete
athletic director, 37–40, 43, 45, 51, 57–59, 63, 69, 131–32, 181, 183, 187, 219
Australia, 35

Baldwin, Peter, 36
Banks, Suzy, 79

baseball, 14, 17, 24–27, 29, 42, 44–46, 48, 50, 53–54, 71, 80, 85, 137–40, 145, 167, 172, 189–90, 196, 202, 204, 211
basketball, 5, 13–16, 18, 26–34 passim, 40–56 passim, 61–75 passim, 79–86 passim, 91, 95–100, 104, 112, 121–50 passim, 158, 161, 163, 167, 171–96 passim, 202, 210–11, 218, 221–22
Belgium, 32–33, 35
Bissinger, H. G., 18, 56, 95, 202, 210, 214
boosterism, 67–68, 100; booster clubs, 38, 44–45, 59, 80–82, 113–14, 142, 181
Bowen, Daniel, 119–21, 123
Bowen, William, 190
Brain Injury Research Institute, 204
Breithaupt, Charles, 219
Brennan, Christine, 199
British sports, 24, 32, 34–36
Broh, Beckett, 9, 124
Bryant, Paul, 70

California, 5, 14, 30, 43, 47, 52, 83–84, 86, 104, 132, 180–81, 192–93
California Interscholastic Federation, 86, 181, 192
Canada, 32
Cardinal Principles of Secondary Education, 4, 74
Carnegie Foundation Report on American College Athletics, 29
Carnovale, Antonio, 40
celebrity culture, 23, 66, 73, 77, 94–97, 100, 115, 156, 183–86, 208

Centers for Disease Control and Prevention, 6, 127
character-building benefits of sports, 151–56
cheerleading, 6, 9–10, 16, 18–19, 22, 32, 43, 51, 53, 59, 72, 79, 91, 99–115, 119, 122–23, 142, 160–61, 164, 189; competitive, 102–4, 108; injuries, 108; sexualizing of, 105–7; Title IX issues, 102–4; Universal Cheerleaders Association, 103–4
Chicago schools, 24–29, 46
Cicero (Roman philosopher), 18
civic education, 71–73
civic engagement, 68, 153
club sports, 33–36, 84–87, 136, 222–23; travel teams, 85, 222
coaches: coaching style, 60–62, 86, 123, 154; nonteaching coaches, 48, 50, 55, 59–60; pressure to win, 29, 55, 57, 59, 63, 69; salary/stipend, 8, 35, 48–55 passim, 63, 81; schedule, 7, 48, 56, 63–64, 127; staffing, 7–8, 53–55, 58–60; teacher-coach, 7, 47, 51, 55, 57, 59, 63; unethical behavior, 56, 58, 60–62, 122, 129–31, 159, 166, 172–73, 175, 192, 202, 205, 208, 211; women coaches, 54–56
Coleman, James, 91
college athletic scholarships, 33, 59, 68, 85–86, 123, 126, 167, 187–88, 195, 205, 208, 214, 217
college sports, 19, 24, 28–31, 37, 41–42, 47, 49, 72, 80, 94–95, 99–100, 126, 131, 133, 154, 179, 184, 186–87, 189–91, 195, 199, 208–9, 217, 219
Colorado, 176
Columbine High School, 93, 95
commercialism, 179–83; corporate sponsorship, 181–83
community, 66–72, 77, 79–90 passim
competition: hypercompetitiveness, 62, 86, 134, 161–64, 217; positive elements, 162–63

consumerism, 68, 72, 75–76, 81, 180–82
contact sports, 19, 61–62, 96, 147, 156, 158–59, 170–72, 206, 210, 217
corporate sponsorship/funding, 45, 180–83, 185, 219

Denmark, 33
District of Columbia, 38, 149
drug testing, 168–69, 217
drug use. *See* student-athlete
Duncan, Arne, 161

Easterbrook, Greg, 188, 213
Edelman, Marian Wright, 72
elementary school, 14, 49, 52–53, 110, 120, 152
elitism, 16, 29, 33, 156, 217, 220–22; bench warmer/substitute, 138, 220; participation rate (varsity sports), 74, 85, 97, 102, 108, 126
entertainment culture, 15, 18, 50, 60, 66, 71–79, 87, 93–94, 96, 110–11, 115, 183, 186, 214, 218, 221
extracurriculum, 7–10, 12–18 passim, 24–39 passim, 43, 51, 90, 97–102, 109–43 passim, 156, 169, 174, 197, 222–23; co-curriculum, 8–9, 98, 156

fandom, 7, 19, 23, 28, 40–41, 44–45, 50, 56–57, 67–68, 72–84, 86–87, 94, 99–100, 112, 115, 126, 179–191 passim, 214, 218, 221; fan rivalry, 41, 67, 82–84, 88, 163
feminism, 31, 102–3
Florida, 8, 43–48 passim, 51, 102, 121, 137, 143, 159, 168, 180, 192–96 passim, 219
Florida High School Athletic Association, 43, 196
football (tackle), 3, 14–20 passim, 24–28, 30–32, 38, 40–63 passim, 66–84 passim, 90, 97, 139–49 passim, 153–98 passim, 199–215, 218, 220, 222; six/eight-man, 16, 212; flag football, 63, 137, 196, 212–13, 215

football helmets, 50, 63, 173, 201, 205–7
Fowles, John, 73
fund raising, 12, 44–45, 59, 81–82, 90, 102

Georgia, 15, 49, 52, 97, 161; Governor's Cup Program, 161
Georgia High School Association, 181, 195
Gerdy, John, 3, 4, 7, 20–21, 71, 73, 83, 87, 111–12, 121, 134, 156, 222
German sports, 24, 33, 35
Gioia, Dana, 76
girls'/women's sports, 12–13, 29–31, 43, 138, 153, 158, 189, 221
Goldberg, Alan, 134
golf, 15–16, 28–29, 44, 84, 123, 137–38, 162, 171, 210
Gorman, David, 125
Government Accountability Office, 6
gymnastics, 4, 14–15, 25, 28, 60, 84, 102–3, 108, 115, 138, 158

Harvard University, 100, 110, 209
Hawaii, 22, 144
hazing, 164–66; initiation ritual, 164–66
health. *See* student health
health care teams (athletics), 141, 150; athletic trainers, 139, 143–46, 150; team physicians, 27, 51, 63, 80, 140–45
health education, 6, 170
Henderson, Roy, 214
history of school sports, 23–32, 151, 158
Hitt, Colin, 119–21, 123
Holmes, Oliver Wendell, 24
homophobia, 156, 160, 165
Horney, Karen, 62

ice hockey, 15, 31, 62, 80, 83–84, 146–47, 153, 158, 172, 186, 189–90, 206
Illinois, 16, 25–27, 42, 142, 207
Illinois, University of, 110, 146
Illinois High School Association, 143, 207
Indiana, 18, 41, 74, 114, 182, 184

Indiana High School Athletic Association, 28
injuries. *See* student-athlete
Institute of Medicine, 143, 221
insurance: accident protection, 38, 51, 141–43, 150; assault, 173; liability, 69
international sports, 32–36
intramural sports, 10–14, 16, 20–36 passim, 43, 51, 62–64, 74, 86–87, 134, 137, 150, 186, 198, 213, 215, 220–22
intramural/sports club model (schools), 22, 33–36, 62–64, 86, 134, 150, 198, 222–23
Isaacs, Neil, 217

James, LeBron, 183
Japan, 32
Jerome, Jerome K., 73
jock culture, 92–97, 106, 115, 175
Johnson, L. Syd, 213
Jordan, Michael, 209
junior varsity teams, 16, 47, 90
juvenile delinquency, 32, 96, 120, 172–77

Kansas, 222
Kentucky, 41, 44–45, 47, 61, 67–69, 75, 95, 99, 113–14, 121, 126, 128–29, 133, 167, 184, 191, 193, 218
Kentucky, University of, 191
Knight Foundation Report, 219
Kovaleski, Frank, 219
Kralovec, Etta, 10, 87, 90
Kreager, Derek, 156

lacrosse, 14–15, 26, 147
Lasch, Christopher, 75
League of Women Voters, 71
Lee, Valeria, 71
Levy, Grey, 58, 66, 68, 99, 129, 155, 203, 208, 209
litigation, 43, 101, 108, 194, 207
Louisiana, 15, 194
Lowell, A. Lawrence, 100

Lynd, Helen Merrell, 94
Lynd, Robert, 94

Maine, 21, 212
Maine, University of, Center for Coaching and Sport, 21
marching bands, 109–15; competition, 114; history, 109; military model, 109
Maryland, 61, 82, 166, 193
masculinity: affirmative, 24, 156–57; "boy code," 157; hypermasculinity, 96, 156–61, 176–77, 211
Massachusetts, 120
McMillan, Tom, 73
McNeal, Ralph, 122
media (news/entertainment), 80, 179, 183–86; Internet, 179, 185, 188–89, 193; print, 93, 179, 185–86, 188; radio, 184; television, 184–85, 188, 191
Michener, James, 71
Michigan, 42, 53, 110, 192, 200, 212
Michigan High School Athletic Association, 38, 141
middle school, 3, 5, 7, 12–14, 21, 23, 40, 42–43, 48, 52–53, 59, 63, 81, 85, 88, 92, 124, 127, 133, 137, 145, 164, 167, 176, 192, 194, 201, 219–20, 222
Miles, Steven, 207
Mims, Chris, 210
Minnesota, 6, 13, 41, 100, 146, 163, 182, 207
Minnesota, University of, 100, 207
Mississippi, 120
Mississippi High School Activities Association, 194
Missouri, 22, 212
Missouri State High School Activities Association, 22
muscular Christianity, 24, 151

National Assessment of Educational Progress, 52
National Association for Sport and Physical Education, 11, 220–21
National Association of Secondary School Principals, 29
National Association of Sports Officials, 173
National Association of State Boards of Education, 118, 131, 219; Report of the Commission on High School Athletics, 219
National Center for Catastrophic Sports Injury Research, 142, 200, 202–3
National Center for Education Evaluation, 169
National Center for Education Statistics, 10
National Collegiate Athletic Association (NCAA), 16, 28, 103, 118, 131, 187, 189–91, 194, 207, 225
National Collegiate Scouting Association, 188
National Education Association, 4
National Federation of State High School Associations (NFHS), 14, 17, 28–29, 37–38, 45–47, 54, 59, 62, 118, 131, 184–85, 187, 189, 194, 200, 213, 221
National Governors Association, 118
National Institute for Sports Reform, 32
National Interscholastic Athletic Administrators Association, 40–41, 219
National Research Council, 143
National School Boards Association, 186
National Spinal Cord Injury Statistical Center, 142
National Women's Law Center, 15, 140
New Jersey, 8, 10, 17, 91, 107, 119, 132, 169, 176, 203, 210, 212
New York, 15, 22, 60, 69, 96, 128
New York Board of Regents, 60
New York State Athletic Association, 45, 194
New Zealand, 35
nonrevenue sports, 44, 125
North Carolina, 13, 47, 130, 142, 209
North Carolina High School Athletic Association, 9, 130

Notre Dame University, 191
Nowinski, Chris, 209

Obama, Barack, 214
O'Brien, Keith, 61, 121, 133, 193, 212
Ohio, 80, 82, 113–14, 123, 129, 175, 184, 193
Oklahoma, 130, 144, 186, 204, 58
Olympic Games, 23, 85, 162
Omalu, Bennett, 205–6, 214
O'Neil, Terry, 201
Oregon, 169, 181
Organization for Economic Coordination and Development, 118
Otto, Kadence, 156
overemphasis (varsity sports), 217–19

Paige, Satchel, 23
Parent Teachers Association, 3, 4
Partnership for Drug-Free Kids, 167
Pascoe, C. J., 176
Patoski, Joe, 79
pay-to-play/participation fees, 22, 45–46, 125, 181
peer culture, 9, 88, 92, 94–96, 106, 108, 124, 126, 153–54, 159–60, 165–75 passim, 210–11
Pennsylvania, 49, 59, 113, 129
pep rally, 54, 74, 90–91, 97–99, 103–5, 110–11, 123, 128, 218
pep squad, 8, 16, 105
Perdue, Sonny, 161
Peters, Scott, 213
physical education, 4–7, 20, 25, 34, 51, 55–56, 110, 136–37, 220; teachers, 55–56
physical fitness. *See* student-athlete
Poland, 32, 34
popular culture, 24, 71, 93
Powell, Shaun, 96, 126
President's Council on Physical Fitness and Sport, 16
Princeton University, 110
private schools, 5, 16, 38, 143, 187, 192–97, 217; Catholic schools, 29, 47, 61, 159, 163, 193–94; charter schools, 120, 193, 195–96, 222; home schooling, 196–97; Paideia School, 97; sports academies, 190, 195
professional sports/athletes, 33–34, 87, 126, 154, 186, 189–90, 211, 213–14; Major League Baseball (MLB), 190; National Basketball Association (NBA), 76, 95, 189–90, 209, 214; National Football League (NFL), 213–14, 189–90, 195, 205, 207–8, 210–11, 213–14, 220; National Hockey League (NHL), 190
Program for International Student Assessment, 118
Progressive Era, 173
Pruter, Robert, 18
Purdue University, 110

Quirk, Kevin, 77

recruiting (by colleges, private schools), 29, 58, 84–85, 180, 185–93, 196–98, 217, 219; recruiting camps, 187–88; signing ceremonies, 95, 123, 191
reform efforts, 21–22, 28–30, 32, 36, 84, 87–88, 117–18, 127, 129–30, 134, 149, 161, 187, 191, 213; education reform, 117–18
Rice, Grantland, 177
Ripley, Amanda, 4, 53, 118–20, 122
risk, sport-related, 28, 50, 139–40, 143–44, 146, 150, 157–58, 213; tackle football, 147, 199–200, 202–8, 210, 214–5
Roberts, Joshua, 197
Romanowski, Bill, 205
Roosevelt, Theodore, 28

Santayana, George, 161
school board, 8, 36–40, 43, 52, 57, 62, 65–66, 69, 119, 130–33, 166, 186, 192, 194, 198, 212
school budget, 6, 16, 40–47, 53–60, 63, 81, 87, 97, 115, 119, 168, 180–82, 200, 215, 218–19, 222; athletics budget, 6, 42–47, 50–53, 70, 181, 219–20; capital expenditures, 42, 46, 49–50, 82, 87; revenue bond, 42, 49, 52,

67–68; salaries/stipends (coaching), 43, 46, 48–50, 52–53, 55, 63, 81, 219; tax base, 30, 39–43, 49, 51–53, 66–67, 182; teachers' salaries, 48, 49, 55
school consolidation, 70, 193
school culture, 89–93; cliques, 92–94, 101, 115; hall of fame, 90–91, 191; homecoming, 90–91, 98, 110, 128, 140; nerd culture, 92, 160; powder puff games, 160–61; rites of passage, 90; trophy case, 91; yearbook, 8–10, 89–90, 132
school district, 5, 6–9, 14–15, 22–31 passim, 39–54 passim, 79, 81–82, 84, 86, 101, 119, 129–33, 141–43, 150, 161, 166, 168, 181–82, 190, 196–97, 207, 217; local control, 65–66
School Health Policies and Programs Study, 5–6
school principal, 8, 18, 29, 38–40, 53–59 passim, 63, 69–70, 84, 91, 97, 99, 112, 123–24, 130–33, 152, 167, 175, 181, 197, 218–22 passim
school schedule, 7, 10, 13, 17, 55, 113, 123, 127–28, 174, 218
school spirit, 8, 18–19, 32, 97–100, 106, 110, 120, 197
schools without interscholastic athletics, 97, 100, 222; canceling teams/seasons, 166, 212
Schwarzenegger, Arnold, 209
Scotland, 32
Seifried, Chad, 221
sexism/misogyny, 95, 101, 107, 156, 160, 165–66
Sitkowski, Lee, 125
socioeconomic factors, 15–16, 36, 49, 82, 120, 125, 136; lower class, 16, 49, 136; middle class, 72, 93, 151, 156; upper-middle class, 122
softball, 14–15, 45, 137–140, 196, 221
Sousa, John Philip, 109–10
South Carolina, 15, 40, 47, 169, 196

South Korea, 119
spectatorism, 73–77
spectator sports, 18–19, 67–68, 72, 74–82, 115, 127, 218, 221; ticket sales, 25, 30, 42, 44, 51, 63, 79–80
sport facilities, 12, 26–27, 30, 35, 41–45, 49–50, 52, 87, 101, 136–37, 181–83, 219; electronic scoreboards, 41, 49–50, 72, 82, 87, 99, 182
sport fatalities, 28, 108, 199, 202–3, 138, 141, 199, 202–5, 210, 213
sport officials/referees, 11, 26, 37–38, 51, 53, 63, 83, 141, 173, 176
sport season: length, 17, 28, 30, 128–29, 155, 213, 217; off-season training, 129, 203; sports camps, 34, 48, 183, 187–88
Sports Journal, 74
Sports Legacy Institute, 209
sportsmanship, 59, 63, 151, 153–54, 177; gamesmanship, 154; lack of/cheating, 27, 29, 58, 63, 163, 210–11, 217
sports medicine, 144, 209
state athletic associations, 11, 30, 37–38, 47, 62, 129, 131–33, 141, 169, 181, 192–96, 212, 222
Stevens, Len, 86
Stowe, Harriet Beecher, 37
street parades, 22, 66, 98, 109–11, 114–15
Stromberg, Peter G., 71
student-athlete, 21–22, 27, 29, 35, 40, 47, 53–54, 57–63 passim, 86–88, 93, 119–55 passim, 161, 167, 169, 177, 180, 186–93 passim, 198, 207–8, 217–20, 222; academic eligibility, 40, 129–33, 197; academic performance, 18, 21, 29, 70, 118–34, 147, 190, 197–98, 217–19; academic shortcuts/cheating, 57–58, 69–70, 118, 121–22, 124, 128, 130; academic suspension, 132; ACL injuries, 142, 145, 212; aggression, 154, 157–60, 163, 168, 170–73, 176, 210–11, 215; aptitude tests (ACT/SAT), 122, 125; bullying, 93–96, 165; chronic traumatic

encephalopathy (CTE), 148, 205; concussion/brain injury, 28, 50, 61, 108, 142–50, 168, 172–73, 200, 202–7, 213–15; criminal acts, 82, 132, 165–67, 172–73, 175; drug/alcohol use, 9, 93, 96, 165–70, 175; eating disorders, 138–39; female athletes, 14–15, 29–31, 96–97, 102–4, 108, 126, 153, 163, 171, 176–77, 189, 200, 221; fighting, 27, 159, 171–72, 210–11; graduation rate, 24, 119, 125–26; Hispanic athletes, 126, 136; injuries (general), 20, 27–28, 50, 61–62, 108, 128, 139–50, 166, 199–207, 211–15, 217; misbehavior, 170–77; nonathletes, in comparison, 92–93, 120–26, 153–54, 160, 167–75 passim, 210; no pass, no play, 21, 129–30, 134, 193, 217; obesity, 139–40, 200, 209–10; overuse injuries, 86, 139, 144–45; parents of, 3, 9–22, 33–36, 40, 43–64 passim, 69–70, 73, 81–87, 95, 101–4, 112–13, 133–222 passim; performance enhancing drugs, 155, 167–70, 177, 217; physical exam, 141; physical fitness, 5, 7, 17, 19, 34, 135–51, 208; post-concussion syndrome, 149; Proposition 48 (NCAA), 190; redshirting, 133; return-to-play procedure (RTP), 149; second impact syndrome, 147–48, 204; sexual misbehavior, 161, 165, 172, 175–76, 211; subconcussive blows, 148–49, 203, 205, 207; verbal aggression/trash talk, 61, 210

student health, 7, 18–19, 74–76, 107, 135–40, 183, 207, 209–10, 221; body weight, 74, 107, 135–40, 144, 150, 208–10; physical fitness, 5, 7, 135–37, 150, 208; sedentary lifestyle, 20, 135–36

Sussman, Eliahu, 71

Svare, Bruce, 32

swimming, 15–16, 28, 50, 85, 123, 136, 162

tailgate parties, 80–81

team travel, 22, 29, 32, 34, 38, 43, 47, 51, 54, 79, 127, 134, 155, 222

televised sports, 18, 48, 50, 73–74, 77, 79–80, 93, 180, 183–85, 191, 195, 211, 214

Tennessee, 15, 152, 194, 210

Tennessee Secondary School Athletic Association, 194

tennis, 13–15, 18, 29, 53–54, 63, 81, 84, 138, 141, 162, 171, 195

Texas, 14–15, 18, 25, 38, 41–71 passim, 79–83 passim, 95–133 passim, 140, 143, 155, 163, 169, 173, 180–86 passim, 193–96, 201, 203, 209–22 passim

Texas Association of Private and Parochial Schools, 194

Title IX (Education Amendments Act of 1972), 12, 14, 31, 43, 55, 60, 102–4, 221

track and field, 14–15, 24–26, 34, 44, 54, 137, 202, 221

Tufte, John, 19, 69–70

University Interscholastic League (Texas) (UIL), 38, 143, 193, 196, 214, 219

urban/suburban/rural factors, 5, 12, 15, 24, 42, 46, 67, 70, 80, 173, 182, 222

US Department of Health and Human Services, 136

US Supreme Court, 168–69, 194, 220

Utah, 173, 181

Utah High School Athletics Association, 173

Vasco, Bill, 59

Victorian era, 24, 151, 156

Virginia, 46, 81

virtual sports, 76

volleyball, 5, 13–15, 26, 29, 53–54, 99, 103, 138, 140, 145, 179, 196, 221

Washington State, 196

Washington State University, 192

Whannel, Gary, 87

White, Byron "Whizzer," 220–21

Wieberg, Steve, 48

Wisconsin, 28
Wisconsin, University of, 110
Wooden, John, 62
wrestling, 14–16, 28, 31, 44, 90, 139–41, 147, 158–59, 162, 165, 169, 172

yearbook, 8–10, 89–90, 132
YMCA, 26, 36
youth sports, 85, 87, 145, 180

www.ingramcontent.com/pod-product-compliance
Lightning Source LLC
Chambersburg PA
CBHW030618230426
43661CB00053B/2039